The Canadian Balance of Payments

of Payments

Perspectives and Policy Issues

The Canadian Balance of Payments

Perspectives and Policy Issues

The First John Deutsch Round Table
on Economic Policy

Edited by
Douglas D. Purvis
Assisted by
Frances Chambers

Proceedings of a Conference Sponsored by
The Institute for Research on Public Policy
and
The John Deutsch Memorial for the Study of
Economic Policy
31 October 2 – November 1980

The Institute for Research on Public Policy
L'Institut de recherches politiques
Montreal

593239

Legal Deposit Second Quarter
Bibliothèque nationale du Québec

Canadian Cataloguing in Publication Data
Main entry under title:
 The Canadian balance of payments

(The John Deutsch round tables on economic policy)
ISBN 0-920380-83-2

1. Balance of payments — Canada — Congresses. 2. Canada —
Economic policy — 1971- — Congresses.* I. Purvis,
Douglas D. II. Chambers, Frances, 1931- III. Institute
for Research on Public Policy. IV. John Deutsch Memorial
for the Study of Economic Policy. V. Series.

HG3883.C3C36   332.1'52'0971   C83-090009-8

The Institute for Research on Public Policy/L'Institut de recherches politiques
2149 Mackay Street, Montreal, Quebec H3G 2J2

HG
3883
.C3
C 36
1983

The Canadian Balance of Payments
Perspectives and Policy Issues

The First John Deutsch Round Table
on Economic Policy

Edited by
Douglas D. Purvis
Assisted by
Frances Chambers

Proceedings of a Conference Sponsored by
The Institute for Research on Public Policy
and
The John Deutsch Memorial for the Study of
Economic Policy
31 October 2 – November 1980

The Institute for Research on Public Policy
L'Institut de recherches politiques
Montreal

593239

Printed in Canada

Legal Deposit Second Quarter
Bibliothèque nationale du Québec

Canadian Cataloguing in Publication Data
Main entry under title:
  The Canadian balance of payments

(The John Deutsch round tables on economic policy)
ISBN 0-920380-83-2

1. Balance of payments — Canada — Congresses. 2. Canada —
Economic policy — 1971-   — Congresses.* I. Purvis,
Douglas D. II. Chambers, Frances, 1931-   III. Institute
for Research on Public Policy. IV. John Deutsch Memorial
for the Study of Economic Policy. V. Series.

HG3883.C3C36   332.1'52'0971   C83-090009-8

The Institute for Research on Public Policy/L'Institut de recherches politiques
2149 Mackay Street, Montreal, Quebec H3G 2J2

HG
3883
.C3
C 36
1983

Table of Contents

Foreword

The John Deutsch Round Tables on Economic Policy honour in name a distinguished Canadian economist who was intimately involved in debates on both domestic and international policy issues from the 1930s to the mid-1970s. John Deutsch entered these debates from an extraordinarily diverse series of perspectives. Early in his career he worked at the Bank of Canada; later he became Assistant Deputy Minister of Finance, responsible for international economic relations, then Secretary of the Treasury Board of Canada; and in 1963 he was appointed the first Chairman of the Economic Council of Canada. He held academic appointments at the University of British Columbia and Queen's University and was Principal of Queen's from 1968 to 1974. He served on many of the leading commissions of his time, including, to name only some, the Rowell-Sirois Commission in the late 1930s, the Royal Commission on Newfoundland Finances (1957), the Special Commission of Inquiry into the Unemployment Insurance Act (1961), the Royal Commission on Higher Education in New Brunswick (1961), the study of Maritime Union (1968), the Commission on Post-Secondary Education in Ontario (1969), an advisory committee on energy for Ontario (1971), and a United Nations commission on the effects of multinational corporations (1973).

A forum that brings together the research and viewpoints of academic and non-academic economists is most appropriate to his memory, as is the term 'round table'. John Deutsch strongly believed that a much wider consensus existed on a policy issue than pronouncements by leading spokesmen on the issue might imply, because there are pressures — whether in public office or in an academic appointment — to differentiate one's position from other experts on the issue. It followed that, in order to advance collective understanding of an issue, greater efforts should be made to bring together people who have thought seriously about the issue and to foster discussion in an atmosphere that minimizes the incentive to battle from entrenched positions.

The purpose of the round tables, held at the Donald Gordon Centre, Queen's University, is to promote analysis and discussion of economic policy issues of significant international and national concern to Canada by professional economists in business, government, and universities, and to facilitate the dissemination of this analysis to policy makers. The round tables are intended not only to encourage academic economists to work on difficult policy topics, but also to provide a forum to facilitate interaction among government, business, and academic economists. Initially three round tables have been planned, and they are a sequel to two successful experimental sessions held at Queen's University in the spring of 1978 and 1979.

The sponsorship and organization of the initial set of John Deutsch Round Tables was a joint venture of The Institute for Research on Public Policy and the John Deutsch Memorial for the Study of Economic Policy at Queen's University. John Deutsch was actively involved in the establishment and early development of the Institute. The John Deutsch Memorial was established at the time of his death in 1976. Douglas Purvis (Queen's University) has assumed responsibility for the organization of the conference program's overall editing of the proceedings. The Institute for Research on Public Policy contributed the valuable assistance of Frances Chambers, John Curtis and David Dodge. Others who have been particularly helpful in advising on the first round table include Pierre Fortin (Laval University), Charles Freedman (Bank of Canada), Guy Glorieux (Banque nationale du Canada), John Grant (Wood Gundy), and Ron Wirick (University of Western Ontario). Additional funding for the first of three round tables was sought from a variety of sources and grateful acknowledgement of financial support is made to the Alberta Treasury, the Bank of Canada, the federal Department of Finance, McLeod, Young, Weir Ltd., the Royal Bank of Canada, and Wood Gundy Ltd.

David C. Smith   Gordon Robertson
John Deutsch Memorial for   President
the Study of Economic Policy   The Institute
Queen's University   for Research on Public Policy

Avant-propos

Les *John Deutsch Round Tables on Economic Policy* veulent honorer la mémoire d'un éminent économiste canadien qui a participé activement au débat portant sur les questions de politiques tant intérieure qu'internationale de 1930 à 1975. John Deutsch jouissait d'une variété extraordinaire de perspectives pour se lancer dans de tels débats. Il a travaillé, au début de sa carrière, à la Banque du Canada pour ensuite être nommé sous-ministre adjoint des Finances, responsable des relations économiques internationales, et sub- séquemment secrétaire du Conseil du Trésor du Canada; en 1963, il était nommé premier président du Conseil économique du Canada. Il a été professeur à l'université de la Colombie-Britannique et à l'univer- sité Queen's, et a été principal de l'université Queen's de 1968 à 1974. Il a siégé à plusieurs des grandes commissions de son époque, y compris, pour n'en nommer que quelques-unes, la Commission Rowell-Sirois à la fin des années 1930, la Commission royale sur les finances de Terre-Neuve (1957), la Commission spéciale d'enquête sur la loi sur l'assurance-chômage (1961), la Commission royale sur l'enseignement supérieur au Nouveau-Brunswick (1961), l'Étude de l'Union maritime (1968), la Commission sur l'enseignement post- secondaire en Ontario (1969), un comité consultatif sur l'énergie en Ontario (1971), et une commission des Nations Unies sur les effets des entreprises multinationales (1973).

Un forum qui permet à des économistes, universitaires ou non, de présenter leurs recherches et leurs points de vue sous la forme de « table ronde » fait honneur à sa mémoire. John Deutsch croyait fermement qu'il existait un consensus beaucoup plus vaste, par rapport à toute question de politique, que les déclarations des premiers intéressés pouvaient le laisser entendre, et ce en raison des pressions — que l'on soit dans la fonction publique ou dans une université — voulant que notre position diffère de celle des autres experts. Il jugeait donc qu'il fallait, afin de favoriser la compréhension générale d'une question, consentir davantage d'efforts pour réunir les gens qui avaient réfléchi sérieusement à une question et pour encourager la discussion dans une atmosphère qui minimiserait les risques de voir chacun se retrancher dans sa position.

Ces tables rondes, tenues au centre Donald Gordon de l'université Queen's, veulent favoriser l'analyse et la discussion des questions de politique économique de portée internationale et nationale pour le Canada par des économistes professionnels de l'entreprise, de l'État et des universités, et faciliter la diffusion de cette analyse auprès des décideurs. Elles cherchent non seulement à encourager les économistes universitaires à s'attaquer aux difficiles questions de politique, mais aussi à fournir un forum qui facilitera l'interaction entre les économistes de l'État, de l'entreprise et de l'université. On a prévu, dans un premier temps, trois tables rondes qui donnent suite à deux séances expérimentales fort réussies tenues à l'université Queen's aux printemps 1978 et 1979.

Cette première série de *John Deutsch Round Tables* a été parrainée et organisée conjointement par l'Institut de recherches politiques et le John Deutsch Memorial for the Study of Economic Policy de l'université Queen's. John Deutsch a participé activement à la création et aux premières activités de l'Institut. Le John Deutsch Memorial a été créé lors de sa mort en 1976. Douglas Purvis (université Queen's) a assumé la responsabilité de l'édition des actes de la conférence. L'Institut de recherches politiques a fourni l'aide précieuse de Francis Chambers, de John Curtis et de David Dodge. Pierre Fortin (université Laval), Charles Freedman (Banque du Canada), Guy Glorieux (Banque nationale du Canada), John Grant (Wood Gundy) et Ron Wirick (université de Western Ontario) ont été des conseillers précieux pour l'organisation de la première table ronde. Nous nous sommes adressés à plusieurs sources pour aider au financement de la première série de tables rondes, et nous remercions le gouvernement de l'Alberta, la Banque du Canada, le ministère fédéral des Finances, McLeod, Young, Weir Ltd, la Banque royale du Canada et Wood Gundy Ltd de leur aide financière.

David C. Smith
John Deutsch Memorial for
the Study of Economic Policy
Université Queen's

Gordon Robertson
Président
L'Institut
de recherches politiques

Acknowledgements

I would like to acknowledge the help and support I have received in the transition from the trial of April 1978 to the reality of the John Deutsch Round Tables. My colleague Dick Lipsey gave timely counsel and advice at all stages. David Smith gave support and encouragement, and was of invaluable help in arranging the seed money for the early efforts and establishing more secure financing to put the series on an ongoing basis. The Bank of Canada, primarily through Charles Freedman and George Freeman, provided help in a variety of ways: financing, audience participation, and formal papers. Michael Parkin was involved in organizing the first two conferences; Ronald Wirick did most of the editing of the second volume, and in general provided energy and ideas in abundance. David Dodge was instrumental in getting The Institute for Research on Public Policy involved, and John Curtis and Frances Chambers of the Institute have been most helpful. Finally, the advisory panel has been a great help in planning future conferences and in the preparation of the 'Summary of Discussion' sections of the present volume.

Douglas D. Purvis

The Contributors*

Russell BOYER
Dr. Boyer is a member of the Economics Department at the University of Western Ontario. Following a career as a physicist in the American space program in the 1960s, he received his doctorate in economics from the University of Chicago where he studied under Canadians Harry Johnson and Robert Mundell. He is an important contributor to the professional journals in the area of international finance, focusing especially on exchange-rate analysis.

Neil BRUCE
Dr. Bruce is a member of the Economics Department at Queen's University. He is a graduate of the University of Victoria and earned his Ph.D. in economics at the University of Chicago. He is a specialist in the areas of public finance and international economics and has contributed widely to professional journals in these areas.

Frances CHAMBERS
Mrs. Chambers is an economist with the International Economics Program of The Institute for Research on Public Policy. She received a masters degree from the London School of Economics where she specialized in international trade and balance-of-payments analysis. She has been assistant economic adviser with the Bank of Montreal, a sessional lecturer at Sir George Williams University, and has engaged in research for Canada Mortgage and Housing Corporation and the Department of Employment and Immigration.

Thomas COURCHENE
Dr. Courchene is professor of economics at the University of Western Ontario. He has written extensively in many areas of economics and is widely known for his contributions to discussion of economic policy in Canada, specializing in monetary and regional policy. His recent book,

---

* At the time of the conference, October 1980.

The Strategy of Gradualism, is a follow-up to his highly acclaimed *Money, Inflation, and the Bank of Canada*.

John CUDDINGTON
Dr. Cuddington, a member of the Economics Department at Stanford University, is a graduate of Simon Fraser University and the University of Wisconsin. He is a specialist in the area of international economics, focusing on the macro-economic issues pertaining to balance-of-payments adjustment.

Donald DALY
Dr. Daly is professor of economics in the Faculty of Administrative Studies at York University. He is a graduate of Queen's University and received his doctorate in economics from the University of Chicago. Prior to joining York in 1969 he had worked with the federal government on economic forecasting, economic growth, and management for many years. His research has emphasized the competitive position of Canadian manufacturing, and the scope for both business and government to improve economic performance.

Robert DUNN
Dr. Dunn is professor of economics at The George Washington University. He is a specialist in international capital markets and the role of foreign investment, with special interest in Canadian-American practice. He is the author of several studies dealing with Canada's experience with fixed and flexible exchange rates, the role of capital markets, and the potential for investment distortions arising from exchange-rate rigidities.

John FLOYD
Dr. Floyd is a professor in the Department of Political Economy at the University of Toronto. Prior to that appointment he was a member of the Economics Department at the University of Washington where he went following his education at the Universities of Saskatchewan and Chicago. He has written widely in the areas of portfolio balance, capital movements, and international economic adjustment.

Pierre FORTIN
Dr. Fortin is professor of economics at Laval University. Since receiving his doctorate from the University of California at Berkeley, he has specialized in labour economics. He is widely known as a commentator on Canadian economic policy, with special emphasis on Quebec's economic problems, and for his analysis of employment and unemployment patterns.

Charles FREEDMAN

Dr. Freedman is chief of the Monetary and Financial Analysis Department at the Bank of Canada. He received his Ph.D. from the Massachusetts Institute of Technology and taught economics at the University of Minnesota. His research has focused on monetary economics, and his publications include major studies on the Eurodollar market and on the Canadian exchange rate.

Tim HAZLEDINE

Dr. Hazledine is president of his own consulting firm, Tim Hazledine Economics. A native of New Zealand, he received his doctorate from the University of Warwick in England. He has worked as an economist for Agriculture Canada and the Economic Council of Canada. In 1980–1981, he was a visitor to the Department of Economics at Queen's University.

John HELLIWELL

Dr. Helliwell is professor of economics at the University of British Columbia and editor of the *Canadian Journal of Economics*. He received his doctorate from Oxford University. He is well known for his research in macro-economics and energy policy. He was a main architect of the Bank of Canada's econometric model RDX2, and has since been actively engaged in modelling the implications for the Canadian economy of various domestic energy policies and international developments in energy prices.

Dale HENDERSON

Dr. Henderson is an assistant director in the Division of International Finance at the Board of Governors of the Federal Reserve System in Washington, D.C. He was educated at the London School of Economics and Political Science and Yale University. Most of his research has been in the areas of monetary economics and international finance.

Paul KRUGMAN

Dr. Krugman is a graduate of the Massachusetts Institute of Technology and taught at Yale University before returning to M.I.T. in his current position as a member of the economics faculty. He is one of the bright young stars of the economics profession and is widely known for his work on international trade and finance.

David LONGWORTH

Dr. Longworth is a member of the International Department at the Bank of Canada where he returned after pursuing his Ph.D. at the Massachusetts Institute of Technology. His work has focused primarily on analysis of flexible exchange rates and their interactions with key domestic variables.

Thomas MAXWELL
Dr. Maxwell, a graduate of Cambridge University, and Rhodes University, is vice-president and chief economist of the Conference Board of Canada. Prior to assuming that position, he was on staff in the Research Department at the Bank of Canada.

Douglas PURVIS
Dr. Purvis is professor of economics at Queen's University. He is a graduate of the University of Victoria and received his Ph.D. in economics from the University of Chicago. He has been a Visiting Economist at the Reserve Bank of Australia, the Cowles Foundation at Yale University, and the Institute for International Studies in Stockholm.

Hossein ROSTAMI
Mr. Rostami is a graduate student in the Department of Economics at Queen's University.

Brian SCARFE
Dr. Scarfe is chairman of the Department of Economics at the University of Alberta. He taught at the University of Manitoba for a number of years after receiving his doctorate from Oxford University. His recent book is entitled *Cycles, Growth, and Inflation*, and he has written widely in the areas of macro-economics and monetary theory. More recently he has been concerned with aspects of energy policy in the Canadian economy.

Gordon SPARKS
Dr. Sparks is a member of the Economics Department at Queen's University and is a graduate of the Universities of Toronto and Michigan. He has also taught at the Massachusetts Institute of Technology and served as an economist at the Bank of Canada where he helped build their econometric model RDX2. He has published a number of papers in his specialities of econometrics and monetary economics.

Introduction

by
Douglas D. Purvis and Frances Chambers

The inaugural session of the John Deutsch Round Tables on Economic Policy was held at the Donald Gordon Centre at Queen's University in the fall of 1980. Two broad areas of policy related to the Canadian balance of payments were discussed. The first included the strategy and tactics of setting and implementing monetary and exchange-rate targets. The second encompassed a variety of issues related to the causes and structure of Canada's large current-account deficit, the nature of the offsetting capital flows, and questions concerning the determination of the exchange rate.

The objective of the round tables, as noted in the Foreword by David Smith and Gordon Robertson, is to stimulate rigorous analysis of Canadian economic policy issues and to provide a forum in which academic, government, and business economists can come together to discuss the analysis and its implications for policy choices. The round tables are a sequel to two successful experimental sessions held at Queen's University in the spring of 1978 and 1979. These sessions had been organized in the belief that the scope for constructive criticism of current and proposed policies was much greater than might be thought, given the lack of public agreement among economists on key policy issues and the rather low profile of academic economists in major policy discussions. Papers on a wide range of policy issues were presented.[1] The ensuing discussion dealt not only with the papers but also with the broad issues pertaining to the role of policy criticism, policy advice, and policy formulation. The conclusion reached at the second of these conferences was that there was a need for a more formal forum for such interchange of ideas on Canadian economic policy. This series of John Deutsch Round Tables on Economic Policy is an attempt to meet that need.

In the series, it is planned that each round table will focus on a particular issue and consist of three or four major papers, as well as an introductory 'current events' session devoted to a topic of particular current interest and a 'wrap up' session that pulls together some of the themes common to the papers.

The plan of the inaugural round table on the Canadian balance of payments was to re-examine some of the conventional views of

Canada's balance-of-payments history with the purpose of exploring their implications for the future prospects of the Canadian economy and for the formulation of economic policy. These views or 'stylized facts' stem from the concept of Canada as an extremely open economy. This means, of course, that Canadian goods and capital markets are closely integrated into world markets, or are highly dependent upon them; moreover, the degree of integration has been growing steadily. This 'openness' of the Canadian economy has important implications for short-term movements in key macro-economic variables, such as prices and interest rates, as well as for long-run patterns of growth and development. It also raises the question of how much influence policy makers can actually exert over economic variables.

One of the important facts of Canadian economic history is that Canada has traditionally been a net borrower on international capital markets, particularly in terms of long-term capital flows and direct investment. As a result, there has been a net outflow of interest and dividend payments so that, in spite of frequent surpluses on the balance of trade, the current account has traditionally been in deficit.

Two basic relationships underlie the above statements and the organization of this first round table. The first is that Canada's international balance on current-account transactions, or exports minus imports of goods and services, must equal national saving, that is, private saving net of private investment plus the public-sector deficit.[2] Not surprisingly, then, many of the papers and much of the discussion focused on the government deficit and the determinants of net private saving as key explanatory variables.

The second basic relationship emphasizes that under a system of freely flexible exchange rates, the balance on current-account transactions must equal the balance on capital-account transactions; in the case of a country such as Canada, this means that the traditional deficit on current account has been matched by a surplus on capital-account transactions, that is, by an inflow of capital from abroad.

In line with these relationships, each of the balance-of-payments accounts, that is, trade, long-term capital, and short-term capital, was analysed separately, and a paper on the overall balance was also prepared. Not covered directly was the balance (deficit) on service transactions although many of its components were picked up in the discussion of long-term capital flows and the high levels of debt service that they have necessitated. In his comments on the final paper, *Dale Henderson* provided some salient comments on this organization as well as on the research strategies it evoked. He argued that, at a minimum, the two basic relationships "can be used as consistency checks for explanations and projections of movements in the balance-of-payments accounts. However, at times during the round table discussions, there was a tendency to claim more for simple analyses based on these relationships than they can deliver" (p. 226). Henderson also argued that the basic relationships indicate the importance of "undertaking direct analyses of the behavioural relations of the current and capital accounts such as those performed in some of the round table papers" (p. 226).

The round table opened with *Charles Freedman's* 'current events' paper, "Some Theoretical Aspects of Base Control." Freedman discussed theoretical aspects of the methods of achieving monetary targets and, in particular, whether the authorities should try to achieve their target by operating on interest rates, as is done in Canada, or on bank reserves, the mechanism adopted recently in the United States. In general, Freedman supported the Bank of Canada's use of operating on interest rates, that is, using M1 as the target and interest rates as the strategy; the commentators, however, preferred the use of some form of bank reserves as both the target and the means of achieving it.

This divergence of opinion raised such issues as the appropriate aggregate on which to target (e.g., M1 or M2), whether the uncertainty in the bond market has been a result of public uncertainty over central bank policy or a result of volatile American interest rates, and to the wider issue of whether the Bank of Canada really has the freedom to set or control domestic interest rates in view of the close integration of Canadian and American asset markets, the international mobility of capital, and the preoccupation with the exchange rate.

Discussion of the exchange rate provided a logical bridge to the main theme of the round tables — issues related to the Canadian balance of payments — and to *David Longworth's* paper on "Exchange Rates, Short-Term Capital, and Resource Allocation." His paper addressed the two questions: What factors influence the exchange rate in the short run? How do short-run fluctuations in the exchange rate influence the economy?

His theoretical framework distinguishes among four sources of activity in the foreign exchange market: arbitrage, speculation, intervention, and cover for future trade. The four are combined to form the so-called 'modern theory' of exchange-rate determination. His analysis focuses on the implications of each of the four related elasticities tending to infinity, yielding, respectively, interest-rate parity, forward rates as efficient predictors of future spot rates, fixed exchange rates, and purchasing-power parity. Longworth then examines empirically the 'modern theory' in the light of the Canadian experience of the 1970s. His results cast considerable doubt on the ability of simple monetary/portfolio-balance models to explain exchange rates. While covered interest parity 'virtually' holds, market efficiency is rejected; the forward exchange rate is not a good predictor of future spot exchange rates.

Longworth then constructs a simple model of the 'real economy' that distinguishes between traded and non-traded goods, and analyses the implications for resource allocation of changes in the 'real' exchange rate. His estimates imply that "holding foreign prices and domestic labour costs constant in the short run, an increase of 1 per cent in the exchange rate will change the ratio of output in the traded output sector to the non-traded output sector by about 0.22 per cent" (p. 82). He concludes, therefore, that "inefficiency in the exchange market could lead to a significantly large reallocation of resources domestically, which would be eventually reversed as the exchange rate returned to a level reflecting 'fundamentals' " (p. 82).

The conclusion that exchange-rate variability imposes real resource costs on the economy invited the question, not posed by the author but raised in the subsequent discussion, of whether such market inefficiency builds a case for official intervention in exchange markets and, if so, of the form that such intervention should take. That discussion focused on the impact of exchange-rate volatility and the role of monetary policy in mitigating the real effects of exchange-rate fluctuations on the economy. A number of participants argued that excessive short-run variations in the exchange rate should be avoided in the interests of producers in both the primary and manufacturing sectors. No real consensus was reached on the nature and degree of possible intervention; proposals made ranged from a crawling peg to *Pierre Fortin's* suggestion for "a more consistent, open, and understood exchange-rate strategy on the part of the Bank" (p. 97). Perhaps symptomatic of the whole discussion was the concluding comment of *Paul Krugman* that "we do not know very much about exchange-rate determination" (p. 102).

In the second major paper, *Robert Dunn Jr.* examines the role of long-term capital flows, both direct and portfolio, in Canada's balance of payments. He documents the well-known facts referred to above, as shown in his Table 2, that the long-term capital account has been in continuous surplus since 1960, while the short-term capital account has fluctuated regularly between surplus and deficit. Dunn also documents the rather sharp turn-around in direct investment in recent years; Canada has experienced negative net direct investment every year since 1974. This pattern, of course, is in sharp contrast to earlier experience, and Dunn attributes it to both increased foreign activity by Canadian firms and a world-wide reduction in American direct foreign investment.

Dunn's paper uses the basic relationships noted earlier as an organizing principle. He recognizes that the long-term capital account is simply (minus) the current account plus the short-term capital account plus central bank intervention. While he does offer interest differentials and "New York as a Canadian financial intermediary" (where Canada lends short and borrows long) as explanations of the long-term capital inflow, Dunn's basic premise is that the long-term capital account is largely autonomous. Hence, he views the current account and the short-term capital account as bearing the burden of short-run adjustment to disturbances in the economy.

Nevertheless, Dunn did suggest a long-run relationship between the current account and the long-term capital account, arguing that the surplus on the latter has been necessitated by the chronic deficit on the former. This view was particularly contentious; it was taken up by both discussants and provoked a lively discussion of current policy issues pertaining to the 'living beyond our means' explanation of trade-account deficits.

Many participants felt that the framework provided was inadequate to support such a conclusion and that further work would be necessary in order to really demonstrate the alleged causal relationship running from current-account deficit to capital inflows. One discussant, *Gordon Sparks*, used the Fisherian inter-temporal choice model to examine the interdependence of the two accounts; this model also allows an analysis of the impact of public-sector deficits on the current account. Another view put forward was that the issue of excess dependence on foreign capital could not be properly addressed until further examination had been made of the composition, and the shift in composition, of capital flows in terms of long-term loans versus direct investment. Also required would be an examination of the costs involved in shifting from one form to the other; these include, for example, the extent to which domestic capital formation is reduced by a reduction in foreign direct investment, the costs in terms of slower economic growth and/or lower levels of current consumption, as well as the relative merits of government borrowing abroad rather than domestically. In the words of one of the discussants, *John Cuddington*, in order to answer the question of whether our reliance on foreign capital is excessive, one must examine the whole domestic saving-investment process and the social worth of increased capital investment; the information gained by just "examining the balance-of-payments accounts will certainly not provide much guidance for policy-making purposes" (p. 138).

In the third paper, *Neil Bruce* with *Hossein Rostami* examine the recent concern about a 'chronic current-account deficit' in more detail. In particular, they address themselves to the view that the current-account deficit reflects a 'structural' imbalance in the Canadian economy with excessive concentration of exports in primary and semi-processed goods and imports in manufactured goods. Bruce and Rostami first develop the absorption model to argue that the current account surplus $(X - M)$ must equal the excess of national product, Y, over absorption of goods and services domestically, $C + I + G$. Hence, to the extent that structural problems are the source of our current-account deficit, they must lead to an increase in absorption relative to income. This argument is absent from the writing or the analysis of the advocates of the structuralist viewpoint, and Bruce and Rostami do not find any argument as to why the particular pattern of specialization that has evolved in Canada should cause absorption to rise relative to income. Hence, they conclude that the structuralist view is of dubious merit in understanding Canada's current-account deficit.

Bruce and Rostami go on to examine the patterns of specialization that have evolved, and introduce a novel and interesting method of decomposing 'structural' changes in Canadian foreign trade. They argue that there is very little evidence to support the view that there have been structural changes in Canada's pattern of trade; most changes in export and import values have reflected changes in volume and price, not changes in structure.

Bruce and Rostami stopped short of drawing any policy implications from their analysis. However, since they have rejected the structural explanation of Canada's deficit on current-account transactions, presumably they would also reject the usual structuralist remedies for chronic current-account deficits. Some of these ideas were picked up in the general discussion when it was agreed that it was not appropriate to draw implications for a Canadian industrial strategy by just examining the trade accounts.

While the first papers examined individual balance-of-payments accounts, in the final paper, "Canadian Post-War Balance of Payments and Exchange-Rate Experience," *Russell Boyer* looked at the overall balance of payments, the 'bottom line'. He examined the 1970s balance-of-payments and exchange-rate experience in the context of what might be called a 'monetary' framework but is probably more accurately labelled a 'general equilibrium framework'. Such a monetary approach is usually tested as a reduced form; Boyer asks the question whether the variables omitted in the models — in particular prices, interest rates, and the current-account balance — followed patterns that conform to the mechanisms of the monetary approach. The conclusion is that they did not.

Again, drawing on the basic framework set forth earlier, Boyer focuses on the role of the government deficit and concludes that fiscal influences had a central role in macro-economic developments in the external sector during the whole post-war period. This conclusion, he argues, is consistent with the monetary approach only under particular expectations assumptions concerning the financing of the deficit with an inflation tax.

Boyer also presents a novel interpretation of recent developments based on the 'currency substitution' hypothesis. *Dale Henderson* takes this up in his comments where he outlines a basic open-economy, macro-economic model and then examines its properties as various substitution elasticities take on extreme values. This, of course, links up rather nicely with the analysis done by David Longworth in the first paper.

Boyer's paper, and the subsequent discussion, raised a number of issues relevant to public policy. These include the extent to which it is appropriate to rely on monetary policy as opposed to fiscal policy, the impact of the size of the government deficit on the current-account deficit, how to channel Canadian savings into productive investment instead of government deficits, the responsiveness of Canadian prices to changes in the exchange rate, and the role that exchange-rate speculation plays in the successful implementation of public policy.

John Helliwell was given the important and difficult task of summarizing the conference. Not only did he summarize the key policy issues, but he put considerable effort into highlighting the suggested avenues for future research. As Helliwell's survey shows, Freedman's 'current events' paper actually fits into the overall conference quite well. Helliwell groups the Freedman and Longworth papers together as both deal with "the strategy and tactics of setting and implementing monetary and exchange-rate targets" (p. 241). The other three papers are grouped together as all "deal with the causes and structure of Canada's long-standing habit of having a trade deficit financed by long-term capital inflows" (p. 241). It would be hard to imagine anyone better suited than John Helliwell to handle the difficult task of summarizing a conference like this, and it is fitting that his masterly job concludes the volume.

Although specific conclusions and proposals can be found in the individual papers as well as in Helliwell's survey, some more general lessons can usefully be pointed to by way of introduction. How do the 'stylized facts' of Canadian foreign trade and investment experience noted at the outset stand up to the facts? Certainly this country is heavily concentrated in production and export of staples while dependent on manufactured imports. But that this is a source of Canada's current-account deficit seems highly suspect. It *may* indicate poor resource allocation, and hence it *may* lower Canadian national income, but there seems no reason to believe that it is a source of the current-account deficit. Bruce and Rostami also challenge the prevailing notion that there has been a persistent shift or structural change in the pattern of production and trade. The other commonly held explanation of the current-account deficit, that we are living beyond our means, also drew substantial criticism. In principle, it was felt that the capital inflows and the current-account deficit are simultaneous phenomena. If one were to have to choose a causal relationship, the view that the capital inflows are required to finance the deficit — the living beyond our means theory — appeared to receive much less support than the view that the current-account deficit is required in order to effect the net capital inflows.

Canada's integration into world, particularly American, capital markets was, of course, never questioned, but the nature of that integration and the policy implications of various issues such as informational efficiency and asset substitutability received considerable attention.

The conference was, in the mind of most participants, very successful; the papers were of high quality; the discussants were conscientious, critical, and constructive; the discussion from the floor was lively. We hope that the written volume will further understanding of what has become a rapidly changing situation and a matter of high policy priority.

Notes

[1] Copies of the proceedings of these two conferences are available from the Institute for Economic Research at Queen's University as "Issues in Canadian Public Policy" (I) and (II).

[2] Economists will recognize that this relationship arises from combining the goods market equilibrium condition, $Y = C + I + G + (X - M)$, with the household budget identity, $Y = C + S + T$, to yield the following fundamental macro-economic relationship for an open economy: $(X - M) = (S - I) - (G - T)$.

Introduction

La séance d'ouverture des *John Deutsch Round Tables on Economic Policy* a eu lieu au centre Donald Gordon de l'université Queen's à l'automne de 1980. La discussion a porté sur deux grands domaines de la politique ayant trait à la balance des paiements du Canada. Le premier comprenait la stratégie et les tactiques à utiliser pour fixer et atteindre des objectifs en matière de monnaie et de taux de change. Le second regroupait une variété de questions relatives aux causes et à la structure de l'important déficit du compte courant du Canada, à la nature des mouvements de capitaux compensatoires et aux questions relatives à la détermination du taux de change.

L'objectif de ces tables rondes, comme le remarquent David Smith et Gordon Robertson dans l'avant propos, est de favoriser une analyse rigoureuse des questions de politique économique canadienne et de servir de forum au sein duquel les économistes des universités, de l'État et de l'entreprise peuvent se rencontrer afin de discuter de l'analyse et de ses implications pour les choix politiques.

Ces tables rondes font suite à deux séances préliminaires réussies tenues à l'université Queen's aux printemps de 1978 et de 1979. L'organisation de ces séances s'appuyait sur une conviction voulant que les perspectives de critique constructive des politiques actuelles et projetées soient beaucoup plus vastes qu'on ne le laissait entendre, compte tenu du manque de consensus chez les économistes face aux grandes questions de politique et le peu d'influence exercée par les économistes universitaires dans les grandes discussions de politique. On y a présenté des communications traitant d'une vaste gamme de questions politiques[1]. La discussion qui a suivi a porté non seulement sur les communications, mais aussi sur les grandes questions entourant le rôle de la critique des politiques, les conseils en matière de politique et l'élaboration de politiques. Lors de la deuxième conférence, on a conclu au besoin d'un forum plus officiel pour l'échange d'idées sur la politique économique canadienne. Cette série de tables rondes John Deutsch sur la politique économique cherche à satisfaire ce besoin.

On prévoit que chaque table ronde de la série portera sur une question particulière, et comprendra trois ou quatre grandes communications ainsi qu'une séance d'introduction consacrée à un sujet d'actualité de grand intérêt et une séance de clôture qui permettra de faire le lien entre les communications.

La première table ronde sur la balance des paiements du Canada voulait réexaminer certaines des opinions classiques sur l'histoire de la balance des paiements du Canada afin d'en étudier les implications pour l'avenir de l'économie canadienne et pour l'élaboration de la politique économique. Ces points de vue ou « faits stylisés » découlent d'un concept du Canada vu comme une économie extrêmement ouverte. Cela signifie évidemment que les produits et les marchés de capitaux canadiens sont fortement intégrés ou assujettis aux marchés mondiaux; en outre, cette intégration va sans cesse croissant. Cette « ouverture » de l'économie canadienne est riche d'implications pour les futures situations à court terme des grandes variables macro-économiques telles que les prix et les taux d'intérêt ainsi que pour les profils de longue durée de la croissance et de l'expansion. Elle oblige aussi à se demander quelle influence les décideurs peuvent effective-ment exercer sur les variables économiques.

Une des données importantes de l'histoire économique canadienne, c'est que le Canada s'est traditionnellement présenté comme un emprunteur net sur les marchés de capitaux internationaux, par-ticulièrement en ce qui a trait aux mouvements de capitaux à long terme et à l'investissement direct. Par conséquent, on a connu une sortie nette des paiements d'intérêts et de dividendes à tel point que, malgré les surplus fréquents de la balance commerciale, le compte courant a traditionnellement accusé un déficit.

Deux relations fondamentales sous-tendent les déclarations précédentes et l'organisation de cette première table ronde. La première veut que la balance libre internationale du Canada en termes de transactions sur le compte courant, ou les exportations moins les importations des biens et services, soit égale à l'épargne nationale, c'est-à-dire les épargnes privées, déduction faite des inves-tissements privés plus le déficit du secteur public[2]. Il n'est donc pas surprenant que plusieurs des communications et une bonne part de la discussion aient insisté sur le déficit de l'État et sur les déterminants des épargnes privées nettes comme variables d'explication décisives.

La deuxième relation fondamentale fait ressortir que, en vertu d'un régime de taux de change flexibles, le solde des transactions sur le compte courant doit être égal au solde des transactions sur le compte de capital; dans le cas d'un pays comme le Canada, cela signifie qu'un surplus des transactions sur le compte de capital, c'est-à-dire des entrées de capitaux étrangers, a compensé le déficit traditionnel du compte des opérations courantes.

Conformément à ces relations, on a analysé séparément chacun des comptes de la balance des paiements, soit le commerce, le capital à long terme et le capital à court terme, en plus de préparer une communication sur la balance globale. On n'a pas traité directement de la balance (déficit) des transactions relatives aux services, bien qu'on ait abordé plusieurs de ses composantes dans la discussion des mouvements de capitaux à long terme et des hauts niveaux du service à la dette qu'ils ont entraînés. Dans ses commentaires relatifs à la dernière communication, *Dale Henderson* a présenté certaines observations pertinentes sur cette organisation ainsi que sur les stratégies de recherche qu'elle renferme. Il a prétendu que l'on pouvait au moins utiliser les deux relations fondamentales « comme mesure de compatibilité pour les explications et les projections des mouvements des comptes de la balance de paiement. Toutefois, on a parfois remarqué, au cours des discussions en table ronde, une tendance à vouloir faire dire davantage qu'elles ne le pouvaient aux simples analyses fondées sur ces relations » (p. 226). M. Henderson a aussi soutenu que les relations fondamentales témoignent de l'importance « d'effectuer des analyses directes des relations du comportement des comptes courant et de capital comme en ont fait part certaines communications au cours de la table ronde (p. 226).

C'est le texte « d'actualité » de *Charles Freedman* intitulé « Some Theoretical Aspects of Base Control » qui a ouvert la table ronde. M. Freedman a traité des aspects théoriques des moyens d'atteindre les objectifs monétaires et, en particulier, de la question de savoir si les autorités devraient tenter d'atteindre leur objectif en opérant sur les taux d'intérêt, comme c'est le cas au Canada, ou sur les réserves bancaires, comme ont récemment commencé à le faire les États-Unis. En général, M. Freedman était d'accord avec le recours de la Banque du Canada aux opérations sur les taux d'intérêt, c'est-à-dire l'utilisation de M_1 comme objectif et des taux d'intérêt comme stratégie; les commentateurs, cependant, auraient préféré utiliser un certain type de réserve bancaire à la fois comme objectif et comme moyen de l'atteindre.

Cette divergence d'opinion a permis de soulever des questions à savoir quelle agrégat utiliser comme cible (par exemple M_1 ou M_2), si l'incertitude du marché des obligations découlait de l'incertitude du public face à la politique de la Banque centrale ou provenait de la volatilité des taux d'intérêt américains, et, plus globalement, si la Banque du Canada a vraiment la liberté de fixer ou de contrôler les taux d'intérêt intérieurs compte tenu de l'intégration poussée des marchés de capitaux canadiens et américains, de la mobilité internationale du capital et de la préoccupation face au taux de change.

La discussion du taux de change a permis de passer au thème principal des tables rondes — les questions relatives à la balance des paiements du Canada — et à la communication de *David Longworth* intitulée « Exchange Rates, Short-Term Capital, and Resource Allocation ». Ce texte voulait répondre à deux questions. Quels facteurs influencent le taux de change à court terme? Comment les fluctuations à court terme du taux de change influencent-elles l'économie?

Son cadre théorique a distingué quatre sources d'activité sur le marché des devises : l'arbitrage, la spéculation, l'intervention et la couverture pour les échanges à venir. Les quatre s'unissent pour former ce qu'on appelle la « théorie moderne » de la fixation du taux de change. Son analyse insiste sur les implications de chacune de ces quatre élasticités connexes tendant à l'infinité et procurant respectivement : la parité des taux d'intérêt, les cours à terme comme indice efficace des taux de change au comptant, les taux de change fixes et la parité du pouvoir d'achat. M. Longworth fait ensuite un examen empirique de la « théorie moderne » à la lumière de l'expérience canadienne au cours des années 1970. Ses résultats sèment un doute sur la capacité des modèles d'équilibre monétaire/portefeuille simple d'expliquer les taux de change. Même si la parité des taux d'intérêt tient « en fait », on rejette l'efficacité du marché; le taux de change à terme prédit mal les futurs taux de change au comptant.

M. Longworth a échafaudé ensuite un modèle simple de l'« économie réelle » qui distingue entre les biens échangés et les biens non échangés, et a analysé les implications pour la répartition des ressources des changements du taux de change « réel ». Ces estimations laissent entendre que « le fait de maintenir constants les prix étrangers et les coûts de main-d'oeuvre intérieure à court terme signifiera qu'une augmentation de 1 % du taux de change modifiera le rapport entre le rendement du secteur des biens échangés et celui des biens non échangés d'environ 0,22 % » (p. 82). Il conclut donc que « l'inefficacité du marché des devises pourrait entraîner une réaffectation relativement importante des ressources au pays, qui serait éventuellement renversée lorsque le taux de change retournerait à un niveau reflétant les données fondamentales » (p. 82).

La conclusion voulant que la variabilité du taux de change impose des coûts réels en termes de ressources sur l'économie a soulevé la question, posée non par l'auteur mais au cours de la discussion qui a suivi sa communication, de savoir si une telle inefficacité du marché permet de prôner une intervention officielle sur le marché des devises, et, si tel est le cas, quelle forme une telle intervention devrait emprunter. La discussion a porté avant tout sur l'influence de la volatilité des taux de change et de la politique monétaire sur l'atténuation des effets réels des fluctuations du taux de change sur l'économie. Certains participants ont soutenu qu'il fallait éviter des variations excessives des taux de change à court terme dans l'intérêt des producteurs tant dans le secteur primaire que dans le secteur manufacturier. On n'en est arrivé à aucun consensus réel sur la nature et le degré d'une possible intervention. Les propositions allaient d'une lente indexation à la suggestion de *Pierre Fortin* voulant que la Banque adopte une stratégie du taux de change plus constante, plus ouverte et plus compréhensible » (p. 97). *Paul Krugman*, qui affirmait en terminant que « nous n'en savons pas vraiment beaucoup au sujet de la fixation du taux de change », a peut-être le mieux résumé la teneur de la discussion (p. 102).

Dans la deuxième communication principale, *Robert Dunn, Jr.* examine le rôle des mouvements de capitaux à long terme, que ce soient les capitaux directs ou ceux du portefeuille, dans la balance des paiements du Canada. Il documente les faits bien connus dont il a été question ci-dessus et qu'illustrent son tableau 2 : le compte de capital à long terme a connu un surplus permanent de 1960 à 1980, tandis que le compte de capital à court terme est passé régulièrement du surplus au déficit. M. Dunn documente aussi le revirement assez abrupt de l'investissement direct ces dernières années; depuis 1974, le Canada connaît chaque année des investissements directs nets négatifs; cette tendance contraste évidemment avec les expériences passées, et M. Dunn attribue ce contraste tant à l'activité accrue des entreprises canadiennes à l'étranger qu'à une réduction mondiale des investissements directs américains à l'étranger.

Le texte de M. Dunn s'appuie sur les relations fondamentales décrites auparavant. Il admet que le compte de capital à long terme est simplement (moins) le compte courant plus le compte de capital à court terme plus l'intervention de la Banque centrale. Même s'il présente l'écart des taux d'intérêt et « New York en tant qu'intermédiaire financier canadien » (où le Canada prête à court terme et emprunte à long terme) comme explication des entrées de capital à long terme, l'hypothèse fondamentale de M. Dunn veut que le compte de capital à long terme soit à peu près autonome. C'est donc, à son avis, le compte courant et le compte de capital à court terme qui portent le fardeau des rajustements à court terme face aux perturbations de l'économie.

Il reste que M. Dunn a laissé entrevoir une relation de longue durée entre le compte courant et le compte capital à long terme en soutenant que les surplus du deuxième ont été occasionnés par le déficit chronique du premier. Ce point de vue a prêté à forte controverse; les deux participants à la discussion l'ont relevé et se sont engagés dans un débat animé des questions politiques actuelles relatives à l'explication des déficits des comptes commerciaux qui veut que nous « vivions au-dessus de nos moyens ».

Plusieurs participants croyaient que le cadre explicatif présenté ne pouvait soutenir une telle conclusion et qu'il fallait effectuer des travaux supplémentaires afin de démontrer réellement la prétendue relation causale entre le déficit du compte courant et les rentrées de capitaux. Une des personnes participant à la discussion, *Gordon Sparks*, a utilisé le modèle de choix intertemporel de Fisher pour examiner l'interdépendance des deux comptes; ce modèle permet aussi une analyse des répercussions des déficits du secteur public sur le compte courant. On a soutenu également que la question de la dépendance excessive face au capital étranger ne pouvait trouver de réponse satisfaisante tant qu'on n'aura pas examiné plus en profondeur la composition (ainsi que ses transformations) des apports des capitaux en terme de prêt de longue durée par rapport aux investissements directs. Il faudrait de même étudier les frais encourus en passant d'une forme à l'autre; il s'agit notamment de la portée des réductions dans la formation du capital intérieur entraînées par une réduction de l'investissement étranger direct, des coûts en terme de ralentissement de la croissance économique ou de la consommation courante, ainsi que les mérites relatifs des emprunts de l'État à l'étranger ou au pays. Aux dires d'un des participants à la discussion, *John Cuddington*, afin de pouvoir savoir si notre dépendance du capital étranger est excessive, il faut examiner tout le processus d'épargne et d'investissement intérieur ainsi que la valeur sociale d'une augmentation des investissements en capital; les renseignements obtenus en « examinant tout simplement les comptes de la balance de paiement n'aideront certainement pas beaucoup à l'élaboration de la politique » (p. 138).

Dans la troisième communication, *Neil Bruce*, avec la collaboration de *Hossein Rostami*, examine plus en profondeur les préoccupations récentes face à « un déficit chronique du compte courant ». Ils se penchent en particulier sur le point de vue voulant qu'un déficit du compte courant témoigne d'un déséquilibre « structurel » au sein de l'économie canadienne avec une concentration excessive des importations des matières premières et des produits semi-finis et des importations de produits manufacturés. MM. Bruce et Rostami exposent tout d'abord le modèle d'absorption afin de démontrer que le surplus du compte courant $(X - M)$ doit être égal au surplus du produit national, Y, sur l'absorption au pays des biens et services, $C + I + G$. Par conséquent, dans la mesure où les problèmes structurels sont la source de notre déficit actuel du compte courant, ils doivent entraîner une augmentation de l'absorption par rapport au revenu. Cet argument est absent des écrits ou des analyses des partisans du point de vue structuraliste; MM. Bruce et Rostami ne voient aucun argument qui puisse démontrer que le profil particulier de spécialisation qui s'est dessiné au Canada doive entraîner une hausse de l'absorption relativement au revenu. Ils soutiennent donc que l'on peut douter de la valeur du point de vue structuraliste pour comprendre le déficit du compte courant du Canada.

MM. Bruce et Rostami examinent ensuite les profils de spécialisation qui se sont dessinés, et présentent une méthode nouvelle et intéressante pour analyser les changements structurels du commerce étranger du Canada. Ils soutiennent qu'il n'existe que très peu de preuves appuyant le point de vue voulant que le profil commercial du Canada ait subit des changements structurels; la plupart des changements des valeurs des exportations et des importations reflètent des changements de volume et de prix et non des changements de structure.

MM. Bruce et Rostami ne sont pas allés jusqu'à tirer les implications de leur analyse pour la politique. Toutefois, puisqu'ils ont rejeté l'explication structuraliste du déficit du Canada par rapport aux transactions sur le compte courant, on peut supposer qu'ils rejeteraient aussi les remèdes structuralistes habituels pour les déficits chroniques du compte courant. On a relevé certaines de ces idées au cours de la discussion générale lorsqu'on s'est entendu qu'il ne convenait pas de tirer des conclusions au sujet de la stratégie industrielle canadienne tout simplement en examinant les comptes commerciaux.

Tandis que les premiers textes examinaient les comptes particuliers de la balance des paiements, le dernier texte, intitulé « Canadian Post-War Balance of Payments and Exchange-Rate Experience » par *Russell Boyer*, porte sur la balance globale des paiements. Il a étudié l'expérience de la balance des paiements et du taux de change des années 1970 dans un cadre qu'on pourrait qualifier de « monétaire » mais qui pourrait mieux s'appeler un « cadre d'équilibre général ». On met habituellement à l'essai une telle approche monétaire sous une forme réduite; M. Boyer s'est demandé si les variables laissées de côté dans les modèles — en particulier les prix, les taux d'intérêt et la balance du compte courant — adoptaient des profils conformes aux mécanismes de l'approche monétaire. La conclusion a été négative.

S'inspirant toujours du cadre fondamental établi plus tôt, M. Boyer s'est penché sur le rôle du déficit de l'État et a conclu que les influences fiscales ont joué un rôle de premier plan dans l'évolution macro-économique du secteur externe au cours de la période d'après-guerre. Cette conclusion, prétend-il, est conforme à l'approche monétaire seulement si l'on tient compte de certaines hypothèses relatives aux attentes face au financement du déficit à l'aide d'un impôt sur l'inflation.

M. Boyer présente aussi une nouvelle interprétation des derniers événements fondée sur l'hypothèse de la substitution des devises. *Dale Henderson* donne suite à cette interprétation dans ses commentaires où il trace les grandes lignes d'un modèle macro-économique de base de l'économie ouverte pour ensuite examiner ces propriétés dans la mesure où certaines élasticités de substitution prennent des valeurs extrêmes. Cela rejoint évidemment, et de manière assez élégante, l'analyse effectuée par David Longworth dans la première communication.

La communication de M. Boyer et la discussion qui l'a suivie ont permis de soulever un certain nombre de questions relatives à la politique générale. Il s'agit entre autres de savoir dans quelle mesure il est convenable de s'appuyer sur une politique monétaire plutôt que sur une politique fiscale, quelles sont les répercussions de la taille du déficit de l'État sur le déficit du compte courant, comment orienter les épargnes canadiennes vers des investissements productifs plutôt que des déficits de l'État, la sensibilité des prix au Canada au changement du taux de change et le rôle de la spéculation sur le taux de change dans le succès de la mise en oeuvre de la politique générale.

John Helliwell s'est vu confier la tâche difficile et importante de résumer la conférence. Non seulement a-t-il résumé les grandes questions de politique, mais il a fourni de grands efforts pour mettre en relief les orientations possibles des recherches futures. Comme le démontre la vue d'ensemble de M. Helliwell, la communication « d'actualité » de M. Freedman cadre effectivement bien avec l'ensemble de la conférence. M. Helliwell a regroupé les communications de MM. Freedman et Longworth, puisque toutes deux traitent de la « stratégie et des tactiques pour fixer et mettre en oeuvre des objectifs en terme de monnaie et de taux de change » (p. 241). On a regroupé les trois autres communications vu que toutes traitent « des causes et des structures de l'éternelle habitude qu'a le Canada de financer un déficit commercial au moyen des mouvements du capital à long terme » (p. 241). Il serait difficile d'imaginer quelqu'un de plus compétent que John Helliwell pour résumer une conférence comme celle-là, et il convient tout à fait que son travail magistral serve de conclusion au volume.

Bien qu'il soit possible de trouver des conclusions et des propositions particulières dans chacune des communications ainsi que dans le résumé de M. Helliwell, on peut tirer des leçons plus générales en guise d'introduction. Comment les « faits stylisés » de l'expérience du Canada en matière de commerce à l'étranger et d'investissement dont il a été question au début se comportent-ils à la lumière de la réalité? Il est certain que ce pays s'est concentré fortement sur la production et l'exportation de denrées de base tout en demeurant dépendant des importations manufacturées. Mais on peut douter que cela soit la source du déficit du compte courant canadien. Il est *possible* que cela indique une mauvaise affectation des ressources et que cela *puisse* abaisser le revenu national du Canada, mais rien ne semble permettre de croire que ce soit là une source du déficit du compte courant. MM. Bruce et Rostami contestent aussi l'opinion courante voulant qu'il y ait eu un déplacement constant ou un changement structurel du profil de production et de commerce. L'autre explication habituelle du déficit du compte courant, c'est-à-dire celle qui veut que nous vivions au-dessus de nos moyens, s'est aussi attirée passablement de critiques.

En principe, on croit que les rentrées de capital et le déficit du compte courant sont des phénomènes simultanés. S'il nous fallait choisir une relation de cause à effet, il semble que le point de vue selon lequel les rentrées de capital sont nécessaires pour financer le déficit — la théorie de « vivre au-dessus de nos moyens » — semble avoir reçu beaucoup moins d'appui que le point de vue selon lequel le déficit du compte courant est nécessaire pour effectuer les rentrées nettes de capital.

On n'a évidemment jamais douté de l'intégration du Canada dans les marchés de capitaux mondiaux, et en particulier américains, mais la nature de cette intégration et ses implications en matière de politiques relatives à des questions telles que l'efficacité informationnelle et la substitution du capital ont attiré une assez grande attention.

La conférence a été, aux dires de la majorité des participants, très réussie; les communications étaient de qualité; les personnes participant à la discussion étaient consciencieuses, critiques et constructives; la discussion a été animée. Nous espérons que le compte rendu écrit permettra de comprendre davantage ce qui est devenu une situation en pleine évolution et une question prioritaire de politique.

Notes

[1] Les exemplaires des actes de ces deux conférences sont disponibles à l'Institute for Economic Research de l'université Queen's sous le titre « Issues in Canadian Public Policy » (I) et (II).

[2] Les économistes reconnaîtront que cette relation vient de la combinaison de la condition d'équilibre du marché des denrées, $Y = C + I + G + (X - M)$, et de l'identité du budget des ménages, $Y = C + S + T$, pour obtenir la relation fondamentale macro-économique suivante pour une économie ouverte : $(X - M) = (S - I) - (G - T)$.

Some Theoretical Aspects of Base Control

1

by
Charles Freedman*

1. Introduction

One can divide into two groups the decisions surrounding the implementation of a monetary policy based on the use of monetary aggregates as intermediate targets: one group is composed of strategic decisions, the other of tactical decisions. The former includes such questions as which monetary aggregate provides the most appropriate target (narrow versus broad aggregates) and how rapidly should the rate of growth of that target be brought down (gradualism versus cold-shower policies). Of the three principal contending approaches to interpreting a strategy of targeting on a monetary aggregate, one can be derived from the work of Poole (1970), one is related to the reduced-form types of equations, and the third can be thought of as a feedback mechanism in which interest rates respond in the appropriate direction to nominal income growth that is too rapid or too slow.[1]

The tactical questions presuppose that a choice has been made regarding the target rate of growth of a specific monetary aggregate over some horizon period. In this category of questions one can place the choice of fan versus band and the width of the fan or band (i.e., the difference between upper and lower targets), and the horizon over which the authorities attempt to bring the monetary aggregate back within the band should it move outside the limits. Perhaps the most important of these tactical questions is whether the authorities should try to achieve their monetary target by operating on interest rates, that is, by sliding up and down the demand curve for money, or by operating on the monetary base (or bank reserves).[2] A recent interchange on this question can be found in White (1979) and Courchene (1979).

In Canada the authorities have used interest rates as the proximate instrument in the achievement of the intermediate-run narrow money target; until October 1979 this was also the mechanism used in the United States. However, in October 1979, the Federal Reserve moved the focus away from the federal funds rate and towards reserve measures as a means of controlling the monetary aggregates.[3]

Switzerland, which appears to have opted for a system of base as both a target and an instrument, is used as an example by those who wish the authorities to drop monetary aggregates altogether and to focus only on base.[4] In Germany, central bank money has been used as a target, but a combination of interest rates and other control techniques has been used to achieve this target. Thus there is a variety of international experience to draw on in assessing the relative merits of different techniques.

In this paper I carry out a theoretical analysis of the implications of using base or bank reserves to control a monetary aggregate: that is, I examine the role of base as an instrument but not as a target. Most studies of such a form of control have focused on the stability and predictability of the money multiplier.[5] Adherents of base control and the money multiplier approach have tended to emphasize the 'supply of money' and have tended to downplay or ignore the demand for money. But it is the interaction of demand and 'supply' functions that determines both the resulting level of money and the level of interest rates. In some cases it is possible that rigid adherence to some forms of base control will lead to explosive (i.e., undamped) oscillations in interest rates and perhaps even in the monetary aggregate itself. Hence it is worth analysing the movements of interest rates in cases where the authorities are using base control to see whether this instability problem can arise. Furthermore, the analysis yields insights into the strengths and weaknesses of base control for achieving the monetary targets over a short-run horizon.

There are a number of limitations to the analysis to which attention should be drawn. First, it accepts as given the two-stage procedure in which base is used to target on an intermediate monetary aggregate and the latter, in turn, is related to the final target variable. However, Friedman (1975) has argued that, in general, there is no need for an intermediate monetary target and that the monetary instrument (base or interest rate) should be directed towards achieving the final target. Secondly, it is assumed that the authorities are trying to hit actual money and, hence, are not adjusting their targets to take into account the stochastic nature of money demand. This is in line with the prescription of most advocates of base control, although it may be non-optimal in cases where there are stochastic movements in the demand-for-money equation.[6] Thirdly, I offer no empirical work in this paper. The significance of some of the theoretical results discussed below will depend on whether the relevant conditions are fulfilled in practice or not. Fourthly, the analysis is limited to the financial sub-sector. I am thus implicitly assuming that over the period of time analysed in the paper (i.e., the short run), there is little or no effect on the real sector or price sector of movements in financial variables.[7] This limitation of the analysis can be removed by adding the other sectors to the model, but, at least in the more complex analysis with lags, the resulting model may not be analytically tractable and, hence, one might require recourse to computer simulations. Fifthly, I use only one interest rate in the model, thereby obviating the need to deal with the relationships between the one-day rate that is determined principally by the banking system in its attempt to adjust its reserve position, the 30- to 90-day rates that are more important in the demand-for-money equation, and the long-term rates that enter into investment functions. The oscillations of the one-day rate that are the focus of this paper would not be very important if they did not result in similar movements in the longer-term money-market and bond-market rates. However, recent theoretical work by Shiller (1979) and Pesando (1980) on the volatility of longer-term rates and the American experience of the past year suggest that there can be a great deal of volatility even in the longer-term rates engendered by sharp movements in the very short-term rates. The effect of the movements of one-day rates on longer-term rates makes the argument of this paper more general than might otherwise be thought. Finally, the models are all deterministic in nature. Introducing additive uncertainty to the initial model gives results similar to those found by Pierce and Thomson (1972).

2. The Models

Model 1: No Lags, One Bank Liability, No Currency
In this simple textbook case, money is defined as non-interest-bearing demand deposits held with the banks, and the banks are assumed to have no liabilities other than demand deposits. Reserve requirements are contemporaneous and all relationships are deterministic with no stochastic component. There are also assumed to be no lags in the demand-for-money equation.

$$RR(t) = dDD(t). \tag{1}$$
$$RT(t) = RR(t). \tag{2}$$
$$DD(t) = a - b\,i(t) + cY(t). \tag{3}$$
$$MA(t) = DD(t). \tag{4}$$

In equation (1), required reserves (RR) are a constant fraction of contemporaneous demand deposits (DD). Equation (2) sets out the equality of required reserves and total reserves (RT); that is, there are no excess reserves held by the banks. Note also that there are no borrowed reserves in this system and, therefore, that the central bank directly controls total reserves. In equation (3) the public's demand for demand deposits is expressed as a function of the one interest rate in the system (i) and of real income (Y).[8] Finally, the monetary aggregate on which the authorities are targeting (MA) is equal to demand deposits in this system. Throughout the paper, all coefficients are positive.

Solving (1), (2), and (4) one gets the following equation:

$$MA(t) = \frac{1}{d}(RT(t)). \tag{5}$$

This is a standard money multiplier result in which the target monetary aggregate is tightly linked to the reserve variable under the control of the central bank. An even more basic formulation would have an equation linking the supply of reserves to the asset side of the central bank's balance sheet and would thus relate changes in the money supply to open-market purchases and sales.

There is a second equation implicit in the system developed above, that linking the interest rate to total reserves.

$$i(t) = \frac{1}{b}(a + cY(t) - \frac{1}{d}RT(t)). \tag{6}$$

An increase in total reserves leads to an immediate decline in the interest rate. The smaller is either the reserve requirement, d, or the interest rate coefficient in the demand for money, b, the larger is the effect on the interest rate of a given change in reserves.

Even in the context of this very simple model, attention should be drawn to several important points. First, although reserves can be used to hit the target monetary aggregate, interest rates can be used equally well as shown by replacing DD by MA in the demand-for-money equation and then treating i as the instrument. Secondly, although the focus of the base- or reserve-control approach is on the supply of reserves, it is the case that the demand-for-money equation must always be satisfied. The public is induced to increase or decrease its holdings of money by interest-rate changes, and, indeed, it is these interest-rate changes that are the fulcrum of the effect of changes in the monetary aggregate on output, employment, the exchange rate, and prices in most macro-economic models.

A third element in this analysis is the implicit structure of the banking system assumed in this model. This structure may play an important role in determining whether or not a change in reserves leads towards or away from the new equilibrium, that is, whether or not the model is stable. In many base- or reserve-control models, there is implicitly or explicitly a banking-system balance sheet in which the banks hold liquid assets and reserves as their assets and demand deposits as their liabilities. Furthermore, in response to an increase (decrease) in reserves created by the central bank through open-market operations, the banks buy (sell) liquid assets thereby pushing down (up) interest rates and increasing (reducing) demand deposits. (Models in which the banks rely on liability management to adjust their balance sheets can give different results; this will be addressed in a future paper.)

One final element worth noting in this model is the absence of a money-supply equation. In this model and all the succeeding models, the crucial equation is that in which the supply of reserves created by the central bank is equated to the demand for reserves, which is a function of the magnitude of reservable deposits, the reserve requirement, and in some cases the desired holding of excess reserves. These supply and demand functions are the basic building blocks of the analysis and they can be related to the behaviour of the central bank and the banking system respectively. An alternative approach to analysing the model is to solve out for the monetary aggregate as a function of reserves as in equation (5). Instead of treating this result as one of the reduced-form equations of the model (along with equation (6)), it is often treated as a money-supply equation. Since the money supply combines the behaviour of the banks and the central bank (and indeed in some models the behaviour of the non-bank public and the government as well), it is not a supply equation in the usual sense of the word. This causes no problems as long as one realizes that the money supply defined in this way is an artificial construct and does not simply represent the behaviour of any single group in the model or the economy. None the less it seems to me to be much simpler to discuss the financial side of the economy in terms of the basic transactors whose behaviour is being modelled and I shall continue to do so throughout the analysis.[9]

Model 2: No Lags, One Bank Liability Plus Currency

Thus far it has been assumed that the target monetary aggregate consisted only of demand deposits and that the liabilities of the central bank consisted only of the reserves of the chartered banks. In fact, currency is part of the narrow monetary aggregate and it is also a liability of the central bank.

$$RR(t) = dDD(t). \tag{7}$$
$$B(t) = RR(t) + C(t). \tag{8}$$
$$DD(t) + C(t) = a - b\,i(t) + cY(t). \tag{9}$$
$$MA(t) = DD(t) + C(t). \tag{10}$$

In equation (8) the supply of base (B) is equated to the demand for base, which is the sum of required reserves and currency (C). The target monetary aggregate is the sum of demand deposits and currency, and the demand curve for these money balances is assumed to be the usual function of income and the interest rate.

Solving, one gets the following two equations:

$$MA(t) = \frac{1}{d}B(t) - (\frac{1}{d} - 1)\,C(t). \tag{11}$$

$$i(t) = \frac{1}{b}(a + cY(t) - \frac{1}{d}B(t) + (\frac{1}{d} - 1)\,C(t)). \tag{12}$$

To achieve the monetary aggregate target, the central bank must be able to respond to shifts between currency and demand deposits. For example, if d were equal to 0.1, a \$1.00 random shift from demand deposits to currency, with base unchanged, would lead to a \$9.00 decline in total money, and a corresponding increase in the interest rate. The appropriate response of the authorities to a \$1.00 shift from demand deposits to currency would be to increase base by \$0.90. In such a case, currency rises by \$1.00, reserves fall by \$0.10, demand deposits fall by \$1.00, and therefore the target monetary aggregate is unchanged.[10] In terms of the multiplier analysis, large random shifts between currency and demand deposits imply a very volatile multiplier. In contrast, if the interest rate is used as the instrument via the demand-for-money equation, then shifts between currency and demand deposits cause no operational difficulties.

A common way of treating currency in this type of model is to assume a stable relationship between currency and demand deposits held by the non-bank public.

$$C(t)/DD(t) = e. \tag{13}$$

Then the money supply equation becomes:

$$MA(t) = \frac{1+e}{d+e} B(t). \tag{14}$$

Thus the simplicity of the base-control relationship is re-established if the ratio of currency to demand deposits is constant, that is, if there are no random shifts between the two components of money.

Model 3: No Lags, Two Bank Liabilities, No Currency

In this model I assume that banks issue interest-bearing time deposits but that they do not use these time deposits to conduct liability management. One simple way of introducing these 'passive' time deposits into the analysis is to postulate that the banks move the time-deposit rate in line with movements of market rates of interest and accept the resulting volume of time deposits.

$$RR(t) = dDD(t) + tTD(t) \tag{15}$$
$$0 \leq t \leq d.$$
$$RT(t) = RR(t). \tag{16}$$
$$DD(t) = a - b\,i(t) + cY(t). \tag{17}$$
$$MA(t) = DD(t). \tag{18a}$$
$$MA(t) = DD(t) + TD(t). \tag{18b}$$
$$TD(t) = f + g\,i(t) + hY(t). \tag{19}$$

Required reserves are now a function of both demand deposits and time deposits (TD), with the reserve ratio on time deposits smaller than or equal to that on demand deposits. The target monetary aggregate can be specified either in terms of narrow money — that is, demand deposits in this model where currency does not exist (equation (18a)); or broad money — that is, demand deposits plus time deposits (equation (18b)). The level of time deposits demanded is directly related to the market rate of interest since a rise in the latter brings about a corresponding rise in the time-deposit rate and, hence, a shift from demand deposits to both market instruments and time deposits. Note that this argument implies that $b > g$ since some of the reduction of demand deposits in response to a rise in interest rates corresponds to a movement into market instruments. The demand for time deposits is also directly related to the level of nominal income.[11]

The reduced-form equations in this model are more complicated than those in the earlier models because of the movements between time deposits and demand deposits as interest rates increase. The equation corresponding to the use of narrow monetary aggregate as target is labelled (a) and that corresponding to the broad aggregate is labelled (b).

$$i(t) = \frac{d}{bd-tg}(a + \frac{t}{d}f + (c + \frac{th}{d})Y(t) - \frac{1}{d}RT(t)). \tag{20}$$

$$MA(t) = \frac{1}{d}RT(t) - \frac{t}{d}TD(t)$$

$$= \frac{1}{d}(1 + \frac{tg}{bd-tg})RT(t) - \frac{t}{bd-tg}(bf + ag)$$

$$- \frac{t}{bd-tg}(cg + bh)Y(t). \tag{21a}$$

$$MA(t) = \frac{1}{d}RT(t) + \frac{d-t}{d}TD(t)$$

$$= \frac{1}{d}(1 - \frac{(d-t)g}{bd-tg})RT(t) + \frac{d-t}{bd-tg}(ag+bf)$$

$$+ \frac{d-t}{bd-tg}(bh + cg)Y(t). \tag{21b}$$

Since $b > g$, as discussed above, and $d \geq t$ by our assumptions regarding the institutional framework, $bd > tg$. Hence the denominators of all the fractions are positive.

If the authorities' preferred aggregate is the narrow monetary aggregate, an increase in income with reserves constant will result in a decline in the monetary aggregate. This result occurs because the increase in income leads to an increase in the demand for time deposits both directly and through the induced increase in interest rates; the increase in time deposits means that fewer demand deposits can be supported by the given reserves. On the other hand, if the broader aggregate is the focus of policy, an increase in income with reserves constant leads to an increase in the monetary aggregate since the rise in time deposits more than offsets the decline in demand deposits when the latter bear a higher reserve requirement than the former.

It is clear that if the authorities wish to simplify their task of linking reserves with the preferred monetary aggregate, they should set t equal to zero if they pursue a narrow aggregate policy and set t equal to d if they pursue a broad aggregate policy. In both cases this would have the effect of simplifying the reduced-form equation for money to its most basic form; that is, $MA(t) = \dfrac{1}{d} RT(t)$. Thus the intuitively obvious conclusion is reached, at least for this simple model: impose a uniform reserve requirement on all the components of the monetary aggregate but do not impose a reserve requirement on deposits that are not included in the aggregate.[12] With a split reserve requirement or with reserves on deposits not included in the aggregate, the authorities must act to offset shifts among components by adjusting the volume of reserves.[13]

As pointed out above, with a split reserve requirement an increase in income leads to a fall in the narrow aggregate and an increase in the broader aggregate, if reserves are held constant. To keep the monetary aggregate constant in the face of an increase in income would require an increase in reserves if the authorities are targeting on the narrow aggregate and a reduction if the authorities are targeting on the broader aggregate. Using equation (19) one can see that this implies that with a rise in income, interest rates would increase more in the case of a broad aggregate target than in the case of a narrow aggregate target. This point has been an important element of the discussion about the choice of a narrow aggregate by the Bank of Canada. See White (1979).

Model 4: Lags, One Bank Liability, No Currency

I now turn to more realistic models of the economic environment in which lags in behaviour play a crucial role.

Model 4a: Economic Lags, No Borrowed or Excess Reserves

In this model the demand-for-money equation includes lagged interest rates as an explanatory variable in addition to current interest rates. This is in line with estimated equations of money demand in virtually all of which interest rates take some time to affect the quantity of money demanded.

$$RR(t) = dDD(t). \tag{22}$$
$$RT(t) = RR(t). \tag{23}$$
$$DD(t) = a - b_0 i(t) - b_1 i(t-1) + cY(t). \tag{24}$$
$$MA(t) = DD(t). \tag{25}$$

There would be no difficulty in generalizing the money-demand equation to incorporate a lagged income term or an error term.[14] Since there are no borrowed or excess reserves in this version of the model, the reserves equation retains its simple form of an equality between the supply of total reserves and the demand for required reserves. The reduced-form equations for the monetary aggregate and the interest rate are as follows:

$$MA(t) = \frac{1}{d} RT(t). \tag{26}$$

$$i(t) = \frac{1}{b_0}(a + cY(t) - \frac{1}{d} RT(t)) - \frac{b_1}{b_0} i(t-1). \tag{27}$$

The monetary aggregate retains its usual simple form in this model. The interest-rate equation, however, now contains a lagged dependent variable with a coefficient that is the ratio of the effect on the demand for money of the lagged interest rate to the effect of the current interest rate. Regardless of the relative magnitudes of these coefficients, this formulation implies a sawtooth movement of interest rates in response to a change in income with reserves constant or to a change in reserves with income constant. Furthermore, if, as is not unlikely in practice, b_1 is greater than b_0, that is, the lagged effects of interest-rate changes dominate the current effects,[15] then the coefficient on the lagged interest rate in equation (27) will be greater than one in absolute value and the movement of interest rates will follow a path of explosive oscillations. Thus a change in income or reserves (or in the error term for the demand for money if it were added to equation (24)) would lead to ever increasing upward and downward movements of the interest rates.[16]

The economics behind this result is fairly straightforward. Suppose nominal income began to increase and the authorities held total reserves constant. The increase in the demand for money in the face of an unchanged quantity of reserves supplied by the central bank would lead to a rise in the interest rate of $c\Delta Y/b_0$. If this new interest rate prevailed in the subsequent period, it would entail a further downward movement in the demand for money of the order $b_1 c\Delta Y/b_0$ because of the lagged effect of interest rates on money demanded. Hence interest rates have to fall in the second period. The lower interest rates of the second period would lead to an increase in the quantity of money demanded in the third period if left unchanged. Hence interest rates would have to rise in the third period. Whether these oscillations are damped eventually, leading to a stable equilibrium, or undamped, leading to explosive oscillations, depends on the ratio b_1/b_0, the relative size of lagged effects and current effects of interest rates on the demand for money, as shown above.

Model 4b: Economic Lags, Borrowed Reserves and Excess Reserves

In the U.S. institutional structure, borrowed reserves play an important role in the transmission of the policy impulse from the supply of
reserves to interest rates and monetary aggregates. With the introduction of borrowed reserves, one must divide total reserves into
non-borrowed reserves (RNB), which are under the control of the
central bank, and borrowed reserves (RB), which are created at the
initiative of the banks. Total reserves can also be defined as the sum of
required reserves and excess reserves (RE).

$$RT(t) = RNB(t) + RB(t). \tag{28}$$
$$RT(t) = RR(t) + RE(t). \tag{29}$$

The rest of the model remains as before with contemporaneous reserve
requirements and lagged responses of the demand for money to
interest-rate changes; that is, equations (22), (24), and (25) continue to
hold. To close the model, it is necessary to add a pair of equations
describing the demand for excess reserves and borrowed reserves by
the banking system.

$$RB(t) \quad \begin{cases} = q(i(t) - rdis(t)) & \text{if } i(t) \geq rdis(t) \\ = 0 & \text{if } i(t) < rdis(t). \end{cases} \tag{30}$$
$$RE(t) = p \qquad\qquad\qquad 0 < i(t). \tag{31}$$

As long as the market rate exceeds the discount rate $(rdis)$ charged
by the central bank on borrowings by the banks, there is a relationship
between borrowed reserves and the difference between the two rates.[17]
The greater is this differential, the larger is the amount of borrowing
by the banks. If the market interest rate falls below the discount rate,
I assume that all borrowing is repaid. Regardless of the level of
interest rates, the banks are assumed to hold a relatively small and
fixed amount of excess reserves. I also assume that the banks would
not be willing to hold more excess reserves unless the marke interest
rate fell very close to zero. At such very low interest rates, however,
the demand for excess reserves becomes almost infinitely elastic, as
was the case in the 1930s.[18]

Solving this model for the case in which the market rate is above the
discount rate and the banks are borrowing reserves from the central
bank gives the following pair of equations:

$$i(t) = \frac{q}{q+db_0}rdis(t) + \frac{1}{q+db_0}(p + ad + cdY(t) - RNB(t))$$
$$- \frac{db_1}{q+db_0}i(t-1). \tag{32}$$

$$MA(t) = \frac{1}{q+db_0}(b_0 RNB(t) + b_1 RNB(t-1) - qb_0 rdis(t)$$
$$-qb_1 rdis(t-1) + cqY(t) + qa - (b_0 + b_1)p)$$
$$-\frac{db_1}{q+db_0}MA(t-1). \tag{33}$$

In comparison with equation (27), in which there was no discount window, one can see that the coefficient on the lagged dependent variable is now smaller than before and, therefore, the system is less likely to be explosive. The coefficient on the lagged dependent variable can be written as $b_1/(b_0 + \frac{q}{d})$ as compared to b_1/b_0 in the earlier case. The damping in the oscillation arises from the fact that any increase in money demanded can now be offset not only by rising interest rates but also by increased borrowing at the discount window, which permits the monetary aggregate to increase in the short run. Nevertheless the sawtooth movement in interest rates continues to hold and the monetary aggregate now also follows the same sawtooth movement.

It is worth emphasizing that holding non-borrowed reserves constant in this case does not imply that the monetary aggregate will return to its target value after a shock to the system such as an increase in income. This can be seen by solving for the equilibrium equations corresponding to equations (32) and (33).[19]

$$i = \frac{1}{q+d(b_0+b_1)}(q\,rdis + p + ad + cdY - RNB). \tag{34}$$

$$MA = \frac{1}{q+d(b_0+b_1)}((b_0+b_1)RNB - q(b_0+b_1)rdis + cqY + qa$$
$$-(b_0+b_1)p). \tag{35}$$

An increase in income leads to an increase in interest rates and an increase in the monetary aggregate even after the system settles down. The reason is that the higher interest rate (relative to the discount rate) results in an increase in borrowing from the central bank that allows the monetary aggregate to expand. In this version of the model, therefore, an increase in income leads to an increase in the interest rate, which is not sufficient to bring money back to its target.[20] If the authorities wish to keep money on target in the relatively short run, they will have to push up the interest rate from the level that is consistent with a constant amount of non-borrowed reserves, either by reducing the level of non-borrowed reserves or by raising the discount rate. Thus an element of discretion is re-introduced into the system in that the central bank has to decide on the horizon over which the monetary aggregate should return to its target and the combination of discount rate increase and decrease in non-borrowed reserves needed to achieve this result.[21]

Rather than pursuing this general model further, I wish to examine more closely the economics of the slightly simpler model in which b_0 equals zero; that is, interest rates affect money only with a lag. In the case of the model with no discount window, this assumption would imply that the interest rate was indeterminate. In the case of a model with a discount rate, the solution to the system is as follows:

$$i(t) = rdis(t) + \frac{ad+p}{q} + \frac{cd}{q}Y(t) - \frac{1}{q}RNB(t) - \frac{db_1}{q}i(t-1). \tag{36}$$

$$MA(t) = \frac{b_1}{q}RNB(t-1) - b_1 rdis(t-1) + (a - \frac{b_1 p}{q}) + cY(t)$$

$$- \frac{db_1}{q}MA(t-1). \tag{37}$$

Suppose income were to increase and hence cause an increase in money demanded. The increase in the quantity of money demanded results in an increase in required reserves. The banks would drive up the interest rate either by trying to sell liquid assets or by trying to increase their borrowing in the federal funds market. Interest rates would continue to increase until the banks were prepared to increase their borrowing from the central bank by the amount of the increase in required reserves. In the next period this increase in interest rates would lead to a reduction in the demand for money and, hence, a fall in required reserves and thus a fall in interest rates. Unlike the earlier models, the equilibration of the amount of reserves supplied by the central bank and that demanded by the banks is brought about in the first instance not by an adjustment of money demanded (and hence required reserves) as a result of interest-rate movements, but by an increase in borrowing at the discount window. Indeed no adjustment of the current level of demand deposits demanded is possible in this model given that b_0 is equal to zero; that is, there is no response of money demanded to interest rates in the current period. The increase in the interest rate is initially determined, therefore, by the magnitude of q since that represents the response of borrowed reserves to changes in interest rates.[22]

It is important to realize that in these models the apparent direct linkage between non-borrowed reserves and the monetary aggregate no longer exists. For example, as can be seen from equation (37), a change in non-borrowed reserves in the current period has no effect on the aggregate until the following period; the monetary aggregate will then oscillate until a new short-run equilibrium is reached. And in this particular case it is very clear that the linkage from non-borrowed reserves to the monetary aggregate operates via the rise in interest rates and borrowed reserves in the current period to the demand for money in the following period. Whether it is useful to call such a relationship a money-supply curve is a moot point. What is clear is that the relationship is a good deal more complex than in the earlier models. It is also clear that because of the lag between non-borrowed reserves and the monetary aggregate, it is not possible to hit the monetary target period by period in this model even if one were willing to accept the implied movements of interest rates. It follows, therefore, that total reserves are also not controllable in this model. As discussed above, in the more general model with b_0 not equal to zero, the authorities might be able to achieve their target each period, but only by manipulating non-borrowed reserves and the discount rate appropriately and accepting possibly explosive oscillations in interest rates.

In circumstances where the excess reserves provided by the central bank exceed the frictional level (p in equation (31)) desired by the banks, it may easily be the case that the interest rates will settle at just above zero. This result will occur, for example, when there is a lag in the demand for money. A decline in income leads to a decline in money demanded and required reserves; banks will try to lend federal funds or buy liquid assets, thereby driving down interest rates. With lower interest rates and a constant discount rate, the banks will repay their borrowings to the central bank. If the fall in required reserves is large, there will be a substantial increase in excess reserves and the banks will probably not be willing to hold these large excess reserves at interest rates much above zero.[23] I am thus arguing that there is a serious asymmetry in the base-control mechanism that arises from the difference between the demand for borrowed reserves and the demand for excess reserves, with the former very sensitive to market rates of interest and the latter very insensitive to market interest rates. This asymmetry becomes significant when current rates of interest have little effect on the current quantity of money demanded.

Formally, the model of positive excess reserves can be treated by setting q equal to zero in equations (32) and (33). The equations collapse (except for terms in p) to equations (26) and (27); that is, the discount window ceases to matter. If, in addition, b_0 is very small or indeed zero, then interest rates will fall towards zero very rapidly and the authorities will still not necessarily be able to achieve the aggregate target over any short horizon.

Model 4c: Institutional Lag, Borrowed Reserves and Excess Reserves

In this version of the model I introduce lagged reserve accounting of the sort currently being used in the United States and Canada. I continue with the U.S. institutional environment of borrowing at the discount window but drop the economic lags in the demand for money. Since the results correspond fairly closely to those in the case of an economic lag, we can treat them in fairly cursory fashion.

$$RR(t) = dDD(t-1). \tag{38}$$
$$DD(t) = a - b\,i(t) + cY(t). \tag{39}$$
$$MA(t) = DD(t). \tag{40}$$

Required reserves are now a function of demand deposits one period earlier where the period is defined in terms of the length of the accounting lag. In the case of the United States, for example, this period is two weeks. The equations describing reserve behaviour, that is, equations (28), (29), (30), and (31), are the same as in the previous model.

Solving in the usual fashion for the situation in which equation (30) holds, one gets the following:

$$i(t) = rdis(t) + \frac{1}{q}(p + ad + cdY(t-1) - RNB(t)) - \frac{db}{q}i(t-1). \quad (41)$$

$$MA(t) = a - \frac{bp}{q} - b\,rdis(t) + \frac{b}{q}RNB(t) + cY(t) - \frac{db}{q}MA(t-1). \quad (42)$$

These results are formally similar to those in the case of a one-period economic lag in the demand for money and contemporaneous reserve requirements (equations (36) and (37) above), although with slightly different lag structure. The economic interpretation is somewhat different, however. Suppose there is an increase in income that leads to an increase in money demanded. There is no effect on required reserves in the current period and hence no change in the interest rate in the current period. In the next period, however, required reserves increase. If the central bank holds non-borrowed reserves constant, the banks will find themselves short of reserves. The attempt by the banks to increase their reserves will lead to an increase in the interest rate as banks attempt to purchase federal funds, and to sell liquid assets to the public. As the short-term interest rate rises relative to the central bank discount rate, banks will turn to the central bank and borrow reserves, and the shortage of reserves will therefore disappear. As a result of the increase in interest rates, there will be a decline in demand deposits held at the banks. This in turn will lead to a decline in required reserves in the following period, which will lead to a fall in interest rates and a rise in demand deposits held at the banks. The by-now familiar sawtooth will be the outcome of this system.[24]

Turning to the situation in which there are positive excess reserves in the system, there is no longer any reduced-form relationship between interest rates or the monetary aggregate and non-borrowed reserves. If the central bank increases non-borrowed reserves in such a situation, the extra reserves entail an increase in the excess reserves of the banking system, since required reserves are predetermined and are not affected by movements in current demand deposits. With the banks unwilling to add excess reserves to their portfolio at interest rates much above zero, interest rates will clearly fall to very low levels in such circumstances. This scenario becomes of practical significance in a situation where nominal income falls or grows more slowly than the targeted rate of growth of money. The fall in income leads to a fall in current demand deposits that, in turn, leads to a decline in the following period's required reserves. With non-borrowed reserves constant, this implies an increase in excess reserves with the consequent fall in interest rates to very low levels as described.[25]

3. The New Federal Reserve Procedures

As part of its 6 October 1979 program, the Federal Reserve announced that it was "placing greater emphasis in day-to-day operations on the supply of bank reserves and less emphasis on confining short-term fluctuations in the federal funds rate."[26] Although the details of the new operating procedures were not spelled out by the Federal Reserve in its 6 October 1979 press release, they have since been set out in a staff paper entitled "The New Federal Reserve Technical Procedures for Controlling Money."[27] In this section of the paper I set out my interpretation of these procedures in the light of the analysis of the earlier sections. Although I rely heavily on the staff paper for the Federal Reserve's own views on how the system is being implemented, the evaluation I am offering is based in large part on the experience of the first year of the operation of the reserves control system.

The principal steps in the new methods of controlling the monetary aggregates can be characterized as follows:

1. Set growth rates for those aggregates for which the Federal Reserve establishes targets, that is, M1A, M1B, and M2. In compliance with the Humphrey-Hawkins Act, target growth rates are set over a one-year horizon.
2. Given these targeted growth paths and expectations as to desired excess reserves, the growth of certificates of deposit and that of other reservable liabilities not in the targets, the growth of currency, and the split of deposits between member banks and non-member banks, the Federal Reserve calculates the implied path for the family of reserve measures such as total reserves, monetary base, non-borrowed reserves. The Federal Reserve is prepared to supply whatever reserves the banks are required to hold against certificates of deposit and other deposits that are not components of the narrower monetary aggregates, that is, M1A, M1B, and M2.

Two comments are in order here. First, the Federal Reserve is engaged in a reserves control process rather than a base control process for the reason outlined in Section 2 (Model 2). A random shift from demand deposits to currency would lead to much larger movements of the monetary aggregates under a system of base control than under a system of reserves control. Secondly, in Section 2 (Model 3), I argued that in an optimal system, reserves would be imposed only against deposits included in the monetary aggregates and that reserve requirements against these deposits would be uniform. Given that there are reserves in the American system against deposits that are not in the monetary aggregates and that reserve requirements against the deposits within the aggregate are far from uniform, the Federal Reserve must allow for growth in the former types of deposits and for shifts within the latter types of deposits. It is easiest to think of the Federal Reserve adjusting non-borrowed reserves to deal with these 'nuisance' elements.[28]

3. The planned path of non-borrowed reserves is calculated from the path of total reserves by initially assuming a level of borrowing near that prevailing in a recent period.

4. Although total reserves are the principal overall objective of reserve setting, only non-borrowed reserves are directly under the control of the Federal Reserve through open-market operations.

5. Suppose, for example, M1A began to grow faster than targeted. Given the path for non-borrowed reserves, the increase in required reserves would lead the banks to attempt to raise funds in the federal funds market and hence bid up the federal funds rate and to borrow more at the discount window. The higher interest rates would eventually feed back on M1A and slow down its growth rate. In the interim period, while the higher interest rates are having their effect on M1A, required reserves, and hence total reserves, will remain above their initial targeted path. Thus during that period the Federal Reserve can control only the supply of non-borrowed reserves and not that of total reserves.

6. If the Federal Reserve wished to speed up the effect of its policy and bring total reserves down more quickly, it could lower the non-borrowed reserve path and/or raise the discount rate. Both these actions would have the effect of raising interest rates more than otherwise and hence would reduce the growth of M1A (and thus of required reserves and total reserves) more quickly than using the strategy of holding non-borrowed reserves to their initial path and leaving the discount rate unchanged.

The analysis of Model 4b throws some light on this aspect of the analysis. As shown there, holding non-borrowed reserves to their target path is likely not to have a sufficiently large effect on interest rates to bring the monetary aggregate back to its target in a relatively short period of time. Hence the Federal Reserve can speed the impact of its actions on the monetary aggregate (and therefore on total reserves) by increasing the discount rate or reducing the level of non-borrowed reserves. The Federal Reserve must thus make a choice between a fairly automatic policy in which it adheres to a target path for non-borrowed reserves while allowing the monetary aggregates and total reserves to deviate from their target paths for lengthy periods of time (a long-horizon policy), or a policy with substantial discretion over non-borrowed reserves and discount rates that aims at bringing the monetary aggregates and total reserves back to their target path in a short period of time (a short-horizon policy). One element entering the decision between long-horizon and short-horizon policy is the substantially greater credibility the Federal Reserve would achieve by controlling the aggregates and total reserves over a shorter time period. Offsetting this, however, is the increase in interest-rate volatility from choosing a shorter horizon. Indeed, as indicated in the various models in Section 2 (Model 4), if the Federal Reserve tries to hit its aggregate targets over too short an horizon period, it might create an explosive oscillation of interest rates. Furthermore, with the lag structures at work in the economy, it is possible that both interest rates and the monetary aggregates will display ever-increasing cycles.[29]

The principal conclusion of this part of the analysis is that the choice of horizon is crucial. A relatively short horizon for bringing monetary aggregates and total reserves back to their target path would imply very sharp movements in interest rates and non-borrowed reserves and possibly even explosive oscillations in these variables. With a longer horizon, interest rates and non-borrowed reserves would be less volatile, but total reserves and monetary aggregates would remain above target for a longer period of time following the increase in income.

Another aspect of the control system that has become apparent over the year is the asymmetry on the upside and on the downside. As noted above (Model 4), with non-borrowed reserves remaining on their target path, an increase in income would lead to a rise in interest rates, and, in the short run, the size of this increase would be dependent on the response of borrowed reserves to the differential between the interest rate and the discount rate. Conversely, if income fell substantially and non-borrowed reserves remained on their growth path, then interest rates would fall, borrowed reserves would be repaid, and the system would likely move into a position in which it was holding excess reserves. With banks generally unwilling to hold more than frictional amounts of excess reserves even when interest rates are relatively low, the interest rates have to fall to very low levels to induce the banks to hold the excess reserves. Furthermore, the fall in interest rates would probably be very rapid. The asymmetry between the two cases arises because the demand for borrowed reserves depends on the differential between the interest rate and the discount rate, whereas the demand for excess reserves above a minimum frictional level is zero for all interest rates above a very low level. This asymmetry implies that the Federal Reserve would have to live with total reserves (and non-borrowed reserves) below target paths for a longer period of time than it would like unless it was prepared to see interest rates fall to very low levels. Since such an outcome is unlikely to be palatable, the Federal Reserve will not be able to follow an automatic non-borrowed reserves path when the monetary aggregate falls substantially below its target.

4. The Canadian Institutional Structure

Detailed descriptions of the way in which cash setting by the Bank of Canada affects the excess reserves of the chartered banks and thus influences short-term interest rates in Canada can be found in Dingle *et al.* (1972) and White and Poloz (1980). The model underlying these descriptions can be characterized as a disequilibrium model and hence does not fall into the same category as the equilibrium models discussed in this paper. None the less it is possible to capture important elements of the Canadian structure by adding one equation to the set of equations used in earlier models.

The flavour of the type of analysis of the Canadian system coming out of the Bank of Canada is suggested by the following quotation from Clinton and Lynch (1979):

> ... Suppose for example the Bank were to embark upon a more expansionary policy. Initially, the chartered banks would be confronted with an excess supply of cash reserves. In their efforts to eliminate the excess they would buy assets, causing interest rates to decline and the money supply to increase, just as in the familiar textbook credit multiplier. However, because of the lagged reserve requirement, expansion of the banking system does not bring about a reduction in excess reserves. Thus, there is no definite limit on the expansion of the system that will follow from a given increase in excess reserves. As long as an excess supply remains in the system a disequilibrium persists and the banks continue to expand. Analytically the problem is that if the demand for excess reserves is not a function of the level of this month's deposits or interest rates then the demand for total reserves is a predetermined function of lagged deposits, and the supply of reserves is given by monetary policy. Equilibrium thus requires the mutual coincidence of two predetermined variables and the system is overdetermined. In practice the process is typically brought to a halt not by a self-equilibrating market mechanism but by the central bank itself withdrawing the excess, having achieved its desired effect on short-term interest rates or some other proximate target. The point to note is that at the end of the month the level of bank reserves will not necessarily indicate an expansionary policy (pp. 18−19).

It is of interest to try to describe this type of behaviour in the context of the types of financial models developed earlier in this paper.

$$RR(t) = dDD(t-1). \tag{43}$$
$$RT(t) = RNB(t). \tag{44}$$
$$RT(t) = RR(t) + RE(t). \tag{45}$$
$$DD(t) = a - b_0 i(t) - b_1 i(t-1) - b_2 i(t-2) + cY(t). \tag{46}$$
$$MA(t) = DD(t). \tag{47}$$
$$RE(t) = p \qquad 0 < i(t). \tag{48}$$

Required reserves are a function of lagged demand deposits under the system of lagged reserve requirements in use in Canada. I ignore for the sake of simplicity the fact that there are reserves against time deposits.[30] Total reserves are equal to non-borrowed reserves and also to the sum of excess reserves and required reserves. Although there is occasional borrowing by the chartered banks from the Bank of Canada, this usually occurs at the end of an averaging period and is often the result of an unexpected clearing swing against a bank on the last day of the averaging period. Without going into detail on this point, I believe that it is fair to characterize the Canadian system as an excess reserves system despite occasional borrowings.[31] Demand deposits are assumed to respond to interest-rate movements with a distributed lag. The monetary aggregate is defined in terms of demand deposits. Of course, in Canada, the narrow aggregate that the authorities use as an intermediate target is M1, the sum of currency and demand deposits, but once again, for the sake of simplicity, I ignore currency in the discussion that follows. Finally, the excess reserves desired on average by the banking system are equal to a constant, p. In practice, in Canada, the average amount of excess reserves is normally on the order of less than 0.05 of 1 per cent of statutory deposits or about $60 million.

As can easily be seen by attempting to solve the model, there is no determinate equilibrium for interest rates or the monetary aggregate if one were to treat RNB as the driving variable of the model. To characterize what actually happens in the Canadian system, albeit crudely, one has to add a disequilibrium equation that links the change in interest rates to the difference between the actual amount of excess reserves in the system and the desired holdings of the chartered banks. Thus equation (48) is replaced by the following equation.

$$i(t) - i(t-1) = -s(RE(t) - p). \tag{49}$$

If excess reserves exceed (fall short of) those desired by the banks (i.e., p), interest rates fall (rise). The coefficient s reflects the magnitude of the change in interest rates in each period to the excess or shortfall in excess reserves. Note that if excess reserves are held above the desired level indefinitely, interest rates will eventually fall to levels close to zero as in the earlier equilibrium models. It is the fact that it takes time for such a fall to occur that is the crux of the Canadian system, since the surplus of excess reserves will be removed by the Bank of

Canada when interest rates reach the desired levels, that is, well before they reach zero.

One can now sketch out the mechanism used by the Canadian authorities to achieve monetary aggregate targets.[32] Suppose the aggregate is initially on target[33] but that nominal income subsequently begins to grow at a faster rate than that consistent with the targets. The level of money demanded will rise above the target as a result of the income increase. The authorities then decide to raise interest rates to the level required to bring money back to target.[34] Because of the lags in the money demand equation and the danger of instrument instability or excessive volatility of interest rates, the increase in interest rates is designed to bring money back to target, not immediately but in a reasonable period of time where the latter is determined from the properties of the money demand equation. To achieve this increase in interest rates, the authorities temporarily reduce the amount of reserves to the system, reducing the amount of excess reserves below the desired level, and thus forcing the banks to sell liquid assets and bid aggressively for large blocks of time deposits. Both these actions result in an increase in short-term interest rates. When the desired level of interest rates is reached, the reserves previously removed are returned to the system, the banks no longer are short of funds, and interest rates remain at their new level. This in turn eventually brings money back to its target value.

The movement of total reserves over the period under discussion is largely the result of the movements of other variables and is therefore of little interest to policy makers. There are four elements affecting the level of reserves in the example. First, as a result of the increase in money demand required, reserves rise in the following period and hence total reserves increase. Secondly, the reduction in excess reserves is mirrored by a decline in total reserves but the amounts involved are very small (i.e., s is large). Thirdly, until the higher interest rates influence the quantity of money demanded, total reserves will remain high. Fourthly, when money demand falls back to the target, required reserves will fall and so will total reserves.

To make these points in a slightly more concrete fashion we can use the system of equations (43) to (47) and (49). Suppose nominal income rises in period t by one unit. The monetary aggregate rises in period t by c units. Suppose the policy makers decide in period $(t+1)$ that the cause of the increase in money demand was a rise in income and it was not simply random noise. If b_2 were larger than the sum of b_0 and b_1, it would not be possible to re-achieve the target money balances in less than three periods without introducing explosive oscillations in interest rates. Hence the authorities would act to increase the interest rate in period $(t+1)$ by $c/(b_0 + b_1 + b_2)$ and hold it there, thereby aiming at bringing money back to target in period $(t+4)$. To achieve the higher interest rate in period $(t+1)$, non-borrowed reserves and hence excess reserves would be reduced by $\dfrac{1}{s}\left(\dfrac{c}{b_0+b_1+b_2}\right)$ during period $(t+1)$. Once the interest rate rose to its new level, these reserves would be put back into the system.

Using these elements one can calculate the movement in total reserves brought about by the change in income as follows. In period t, there is no change in total reserves since the increase in demand deposits affects required reserves only with a lag. The change in total reserves in period $(t+1)$ is composed of an increase of dc units in required reserves (one unit increase in income results in c units increase in demand deposits, which in turn causes an increase of dc units in required reserves). Offsetting this in part is the decline in excess reserves set into motion by the authorities of $\dfrac{1}{s}\dfrac{c}{b_0+b_1+b_2}$ units that is needed to raise interest rates. Thus the net increase in total reserves in period $(t+1)$ is $cd - \dfrac{1}{s}\dfrac{c}{b_0+b_1+b_2}$. In period $(t+2)$ these excess reserves are put back into the system, but required reserves fall because of the effect of the increase in interest rates on money demanded in period $(t+1)$. Hence, compared to the initial position in period t, total reserves are higher by $cd - cd\,\dfrac{b_0}{b_0+b_1+b_2}$. In period $(t+3)$ required reserves are pushed down further by the effect of the continuing high interest rates on demand deposits in period $(t+2)$. Thus, compared to the initial position, total reserves are higher by $cd - cd\,\dfrac{b_0+b_1}{b_0+b_1+b_2}$. Finally, in period $(t+4)$ total reserves are back to their initial equilibrium since money returned to its initial value in period $(t+3)$. As can be seen by this outline, the movement of total reserves is very much a resultant of other behavioural actions and hence is not a useful guide to central bank actions.

Clearly the above characterization is very crude. The relationship between excess reserves and interest rates is much more complex than indicated, as can be seen in the two articles cited at the beginning of this section. None the less two principal conclusions can be drawn from the analysis. First, there is a recursive element in the Canadian policy structure that runs from (1) movements of the monetary aggregate, to (2) the desired setting of interest rates intended to re-establish the target levels of the monetary aggregate at some future date, to (3) the temporary setting of excess cash in order to achieve the desired level of interest rates. Secondly, the movement of total reserves is a combination of the movements in required reserves resulting from the movement in deposits of the previous period and of the temporary movements of excess reserves needed to achieve changes in interest rates. In sheer size the former overwhelm the latter[35] and hence total reserves are not a variable that can be used to interpret central bank actions.

5. Conclusions

In this paper I have examined some of the implications of the rigid version of base control. It seems clear in the case of those models that incorporate either institutional or economic lags that base control may entail very sharp and possibly explosive oscillations of very short-term interest rates. These in turn are likely to lead to sharp oscillations in longer-term money-market and bond-market rates. There may be forms of base control that are sufficiently flexible to avoid the problems discussed in this paper. I believe that it is incumbent on the proponents of base control to specify with some precision the kind of less rigid rules for base control that would give sensible results. Furthermore, they must consider whether changes in institutional structure would be needed to make their system workable and whether the new rules would be likely to lead to the requisite changes in behaviour by market participants. Finally, they must show that this type of system would perform better than the system currently in place. It is only in the context of a well-defined proposal for base control embedded in a moderately realistic model of the financial system (i.e., one with lags and stochastic error variables) that the debate can proceed.

Notes

* The views expressed in this paper are those of the author and no responsibility for them should be attributed to the Bank of Canada. The author would like to thank Gordon Thiessen whose probing comments aided the development of many of the ideas discussed in this paper.

[1] A recent theoretical analysis of these questions of strategy can be found in Freedman (1981).

[2] In one sense this formulation of the problem is inaccurate since the authorities operate on reserves (or excess reserves in Canada) to influence interest rates even when the latter are used to affect the monetary aggregate. None the less, in a more basic sense the distinction remains, since in a base control system the authorities aim at money directly via the movement of base without using interest rates as a proximate instrument. This does not mean, however, that interest rates play no role in bringing about the movement of money in response to a change in base, as will be seen below.

[3] A detailed discussion of the new procedures can be found in Board of Governors of the Federal Reserve System (1980) and Axilrod and Lindsey (1981). The former has been excerpted and discussed in Lang (1980). The study of short-run procedures is also a current issue in the United Kingdom; see United Kingdom (1980).

[4] Comments by Karl Brunner at Federal Reserve Bank of Boston Conference, October 1980. But see Büttler et al. (1979) in which base is treated as the instrument for achieving the desired money target.

[5] See, for example, Clinton and Lynch (1979) and the references cited therein. More recent studies include Johannes and Rasche (1979) and Büttler et al. (1979).

⁶ The magnitude of these random movements in the very short run is a significant element in the controversy whether to use base or interest-rate control to achieve monetary aggregate targets. If the demand for money were volatile in the very short run but stable over an intermediate run, the Poole analysis would imply use of interest rates in the very short run to control the monetary aggregate in the intermediate run.

⁷ In the Canadian case this assumption is particularly suspect since there is a very quick linkage from interest rates to exchange rates and then to prices.

⁸ The price level is assumed to be constant throughout the analysis.

⁹ This point becomes more substantive when one reaches the case of lagged reserve accounting where the notion of a money supply based on the reserves of the banking system becomes much more difficult to conceptualize, whereas the notions of the demand for and supply of reserves continue to hold without modification. This point will be developed in Section 2 (Model 4b) below when lagged reserve accounting is introduced.

¹⁰ If the central bank finds it difficult in the short run to track shifts between currency and deposits, a case can be made for focusing on a reserve path rather than a base path. A shift of $1 from demand deposits to currency in the former case leads to a $1 increase in money, whereas in the latter it leads to a $9 decline in money. See Board of Governors of the Federal Reserve System (1980).

¹¹ We assume that interest rates on demand deposits are fixed, and that all assets are gross substitutes. In this formulation income is proxying for both income and wealth, which would be introduced separately in a correctly specified equation. One could also model the ratio of time deposits to demand deposits.

¹² This simple conclusion might have to be modified for a model in which the banks conduct liability side management rather than liquid asset management. Note also that in certain cases reserve requirements are imposed for equity or efficiency reasons that are unrelated to the question of monetary control.

¹³ The problems created by imposing reserves on deposits that are not part of the target monetary aggregate or by non-uniform reserve requirements are much easier to handle in a system with lagged reserve requirements than in a system with contemporaneous reserve requirements.

¹⁴ The careful reader will note that if the lag structure of the demand for money with respect to income were identical to that with respect to interest rates, the oscillation of interest rates in response to an increase in income would disappear in some of the models of this section. If the mean lag on income were shorter than that on interest rates, a result found in some demand-for-money equations, the oscillation results would continue to hold, however. Perhaps more important, an increase in the price level in those models of money demand in which prices affect money with no lag, or a movement in the error term in the demand-for-money equation, will give rise to the types of oscillations described. Hence the result is more general than indicated in the text.

¹⁵ In making this assertion I have implicitly defined the time period in which the analysis is cast as the period over which proponents of base control wish to achieve control over the money supply. This period is sufficiently short that the statement in the text holds.

¹⁶ This argument and the corresponding ones in the rest of this section of the paper are closely related to the notion of instrument instability in Holbrook (1972). The fact that the authorities are using reserves rather than interest rates to control money does not cause the problem of potentially explosive oscillations of the interest rate to disappear. It simply reappears in a slightly different guise. Discussion of the possibility that interest-rate movements could be explosive can also be found in Pierce and Thomson (1972), Ciccolo (1974), and Lombra and Struble (1979).

¹⁷ The coefficient q is at least partly related to the way in which the discount window is administered. Thus the 'reluctance' of banks to borrow from the central bank can be influenced by the behaviour of the central bank. One could also add a constant to

equation (30) to represent a certain small amount of borrowing that takes place even when the interest rate falls below the discount rate, but this would not change the analysis.

[18] Although the behavioural equation from the point of view of the banks treats borrowed reserves as a function of the level of the interest rate (relative to the discount rate), from the point of view of the system as a whole it is preferable to think of borrowed reserves as the given factor and interest rates as endogenously determined. With the central bank setting non-borrowed reserves, required reserves a function of income and mainly lagged interest rates, and a constant level of excess reserves, borrowed reserves are almost a residual of the system. Thus in the analysis that follows I will consider separately the case in which banks have positive borrowed reserves and that in which the movements of non-borrowed reserves and required reserves result in the banks having no borrowed reserves on their balance sheet, that is, an excess reserves case.

[19] Recall that I am assuming that there is no effect on income of changes in interest rates in the period under study. Hence the notion of equilibrium must be interpreted as a temporary position before the influence of financial variables on the real economy begins to take effect.

[20] Eventually, of course, the higher interest rates will lead to a slow-down in income growth, which will bring the monetary aggregate back to its target.

[21] In the simple model that we are using, if the authorities were to float the discount rate on market rates, then equations (32) and (33) basically collapse to equations (26) and (27), and the monetary aggregate is always on target; that is, the discount window becomes irrelevant if the margin between the market rate and discount rate never moves. Recall, however, that the oscillation of interest rates may well be explosive in equation (27).

[22] In this model, floating the interest rate on the discount rate leads to an indeterminacy of the interest rate, as can be seen from equation (36). The reason is that with a floating discount rate there is no way to equilibrate a shortage of reserves caused by an increase in money demanded since neither the public nor the banks respond to a movement in current rates.

[23] Floating the discount rate will make no difference to the outcome since interest rates must fall sufficiently to induce the banks to hold the excess reserves, and the discount rate is not an argument in the demand function for excess reserves.

[24] In principle, the central bank could prevent the sawtooth in money and interest rates from arising by offsetting the increase in income by the appropriate decline in non-borrowed reserves. This, however, requires perfect information regarding the movement of income.

[25] One can easily combine the one-period lag in the demand for money and lagged reserve accounting. The resulting interest-rate pattern is one in which interest rates oscillate every second period. More complicated models with n period lags can be constructed by the interested reader. The resulting nth order difference equations may be difficult to solve but are very likely to give cyclical movements that may well be undamped.

[26] *Federal Reserve Bulletin* (October 1979), p. 830.

[27] Board of Governors of the Federal Reserve System (1980). This paper has been discussed in Lang (1980).

[28] Note that it is much easier to deal with these problems in a system with lagged reserve accounting than in one with contemporaneous reserve accounting.

[29] Adding an expenditure sector and a price sector to the model may, under certain circumstances, strengthen the conclusion in the text regarding an unstable cyclical response. Suppose, for example, that the authorities are following a short-horizon policy that has caused interest rates to increase sharply in response to an increase in the monetary aggregate, which resulted from an increase in the rate of growth of nominal income. It may be the case that at the same time as the lagged effects of the

high interest rates drive the monetary aggregate below its target, they also slow down the growth of real income and perhaps prices and, hence, intensify the downward movements of the monetary aggregate. Thus the possibility of explosive oscillations in the monetary aggregate and interest rates may be increased by introducing the interrelationship of the financial sector and the real and price sectors into the model.

[30] In any event the Bank of Canada is willing to supply whatever reserves are required to support these time deposits since they are not part of the target monetary aggregate.

[31] The purchase and resale arrangements (PRA) between the money market dealers and the Bank of Canada also do not vitiate this judgement.

[32] See White (1976) for an early account of this mechanism.

[33] For purposes of simplicity I ignore the existence of the band in the analysis that follows.

[34] There may be a lag at this point because of the need to decide whether the increase in money was random, in which case there should be no interest-rate change, or was a result of an increase in income.

[35] This is particularly the case since required reserves also move in response to movements in time deposits and Government of Canada deposits.

References

Axilrod, Stephen H. and Lindsey, David E. (1981) "Federal Reserve System Implementation of Monetary Policy: Analytical Foundations of the New Approach." *American Economic Review* 71 (May): 246–52.

Board of Governors of the Federal Reserve System. (1980) "Appendix B: Description of the New Procedures for Controlling Money," appended to "Monetary Policy Report to Congress Pursuant to the Full Employment and Balanced Growth Act of 1978." 19 February. Washington, D.C.

Büttler, H.-J.; Gorgerat, J.-F.; Schiltknecht, H.; and Schiltknecht, K. (1979) "A Multiplier Model for Controlling the Money Stock." *Journal of Monetary Economics* 5 (July): 327–41.

Ciccolo, John H. (1974) "Is Short-Run Monetary Control Feasible?" In Federal Reserve Bank of New York, *Monetary Aggregates and Monetary Policy*, pp. 82–91. New York.

Clinton, Kevin and Lynch, Kevin. (1979) "Monetary Base and Money Stock in Canada." Bank of Canada Technical Report No. 16. Ottawa: Bank of Canada.

Courchene, Thomas J. (1979) "On Defining and Controlling Money." *Canadian Journal of Economics* 12 (November): 604–15.

Dingle, J.F.; Sparks, G.R.; and Walker, M.A. (1972) "Monetary Policy and the Adjustment of Chartered Bank Assets." *Canadian Journal of Economics* 5 (November): 494–514.

Freedman, Charles. (1981) "Monetary Aggregates as Targets: Some Theoretical Aspects." Bank of Canada Technical Report No. 27. Ottawa: Bank of Canada.

Friedman, Benjamin M. (1975) "Targets, Instruments, and Indicators of Monetary Policy." *Journal of Monetary Economics* 1 (October): 443–73.

Holbrook, Robert S. (1972) "Optimal Economic Policy and the Problem of Instrument Instability." *American Economic Review* 62 (March): 57–65.

Johannes, James M. and Rasche, Robert H. (1979) "Predicting the Money Multiplier." *Journal of Monetary Economics* 5 (July): 301–25.

Lang, Richard W. (1980) "The FOMC in 1979: Introducing Reserve Targeting." *Federal Reserve Bank of St. Louis Review* 62 (March): 2–25.

Lombra, Raymond and Struble, Frederick. (1979) "Monetary Aggregate Targets and the Volatility of Interest Rates: A Taxonomic Discussion." *Journal of Money, Credit and Banking* 11 (August): 284–300.

Pesando, James E. (1980) "On Expectations, Term Premiums, and the Volatility of Long-Term Interest Rates." NBER Working Paper No. 595. Cambridge, Mass.: National Bureau of Economic Research.

Pierce, James L. and Thomson, Thomas D. (1972) "Some Issues in Controlling the Stock of Money." In Federal Reserve Bank of Boston, *Controlling Monetary Aggregates II. The Implementation*, pp. 115–36. Boston.

Poole, William. (1970) "Optimal Choice of Monetary Policy Instruments in a Simple Stochastic Macro Model." *Quarterly Journal of Economics* 84 (May): 197–216.

Shiller, Robert J. (1979) "The Volatility of Long-Term Interest Rates and Expectations Models of the Term Structure." *Journal of Political Economy* 87 (December): 1190–1219.

United Kingdom. Parliament. (1980) *The Green Paper on Monetary Control*. Cmnd. 7858.

White, William R. (1976) "The Demand for Money in Canada and the Control of Monetary Aggregates: Evidence From the Monthly Data." Bank of Canada Staff Research Study No. 12. Ottawa: Bank of Canada.

White, William R. (1979) "Alternative Monetary Targets and Control Instruments in Canada: Criteria for Choice." *Canadian Journal of Economics* 12 (November): 590–604.

White, William R. and Poloz, Stephen S. (1980) "Monetary Policy and Chartered Bank Demand Functions for Excess Cash Reserves." *Canadian Journal of Economics* 13 (May): 189–205.

Comment

by
Thomas J. Courchene*

My comments are of two sorts. The first general area focuses on some concerns, often rather trivial by their very nature, relating to the various theoretical models that appear in the paper. Implicitly, this assumes that Dr. Freedman's analysis is appropriate to the task at hand and I am only amplifying on his assumptions or assertions. The second thrust of my comments begins from a slightly different perspective and one that Freedman may not accept. Basically, I view his paper only in part as an exercise in theory. It is also an exercise in persuasion in the sense that he is coming down rather negatively on base or reserve control and on my past arguments in support of base control. The difficulty with this is that Freedman has not, in my opinion, come to grips with the essence of what I perceive to be reserve control. It might still be the case that base control comes off as a distinct second best, but the issue is not addressed adequately in his present paper.

I begin with some comments relating to his text.

1. Notes on the Freedman Models

Strategic versus Tactical Decisions

Freedman's distinction between what he calls "strategic decisions" (e.g., choosing the appropriate money aggregate) and the lower level of "tactical decisions" (e.g., how this aggregate should be controlled) does not sit well with me because I have always felt that the Bank of Canada's preference for an interest-rate control mechanism has effectively forced it to choose M1 as the definition for money (because only M1 has a consistent and negative interest-rate elasticity, a necessity for interest-rate control).[1] I have always argued for an aggregate that is broader than M1 and have likewise believed that base control is a necessary condition for the Bank to even consider such a broader aggregate. Hence, although I will have little to say about the choice of broader aggregates in what follows, my arguments in support of base control are, in effect, arguments for abandoning M1 as the chosen definition for money.

Interest Elasticities Assumptions

Freedman's models imply that $b > g$; that is, the M1 interest elasticity is greater than the M2 elasticity (see his Model 3). Empirical work over the recent past has, in general, shown that b is greater than g (for reasons that in part appear in note 1). Indeed for some such tests, g is negative (i.e., M2 is positively related to the general level of short rates), leading to the suggestion made by some Bank of Canada researchers that in order to increase the rate of growth of M2 (or, more generally, a broad aggregate), one would have to *increase* interest rates. I want to focus on this for a while because I think that it is symptomatic of a general problem emanating from some of the research in this area. First of all, it is easy to explain why this elasticity might be 'perverse' — the own rate set by chartered banks on these deposits rises more than the general level of interest rates, or at least more than the rate on the close substitutes. This can occur because the Bank of Canada will *automatically* supply the reserves required to support the increase in these deposits; that is, it is not controlling M2. However, I think that it is poor economics to draw conclusions from empirical work, based on current operating procedures, and to apply them to alternate operating procedures. Specifically, I would hypothesize that if M2 (i.e., something broader than M1) *were* controlled via the reserve base with high penalty rates, one would find a very strong *negative* correlation between M2 and the general level of interest rates. This is the Heisenberg principle in another guise: new information about how the system actually operates would change the system itself. If I go to an exclusive restaurant with some of my establishment acquaintances, I am likely to pay close attention to the prices on the menu. If, however, we agree beforehand to divide the bill evenly, my ordering preferences will no longer coincide with my previous 'preference ordering': knowledge about the system affects behaviour. This critical issue will arise later in the discussion of the Clinton-Lynch paper referred to by Freedman and also in the context of Freedman's overall approach to modelling base control or reserve control.

Reserve Requirements (Model 3)

Freedman notes:

> It is clear that if the authorities wish to simplify their task of linking reserves with the preferred monetary aggregate, they should set t [the reserve requirement on time deposits] equal to zero if they pursue a narrow aggregate policy and set t equal to d [the reserve requirement on demand deposits] if they pursue a broad aggregate policy (p. 26).

Freedman is correct as long as he is referring to controlling a broad aggregate. From a theoretical standpoint, however, differing reserve requirements may be exactly what one wants if the aggregate to be controlled is the *monetary base* or the *reserve base*. Suppose the 'moneyness' of time deposits is one third that of demand deposits. Then it would be appropriate to have the reserve requirements for demand deposits set at three times the level of those for time deposits. The reserve base would be set to grow at, say, 6 per cent, and the manner in which the resulting deposits were allocated between demand and notice deposits would presumably be a matter of indifference. I mention this only to point out that differential reserve requirements do not automatically rule out either base control or a monetary aggregate different from M1.

On the more practical level, however, it probably *is* the case that uniformity of reserve requirements is desirable. In this context, I have never understood why the Bank of Canada did not take a very strong stand against the provisions of the new Bank Act whereby reserve requirements on different classes of deposits are not only different but invariable. It is ridiculous to tie the hands of the Bank in this manner. Yet I suspect that once the Bank Act is law, the Bank will use this provision as the backbone of the argument of why base or reserve control is not feasible. Obviously, this is a very personal observation and not really a comment that can be directed against Freedman's paper.

One Interest Rate

There is a problem in Freedman's paper in that there is only one interest rate in the model. To be sure, he does introduce an 'own' rate for time deposits. None the less, the variable i relates to the entire maturity structure. There is no reason why the federal funds rate on one-day reserves in the United States need mirror movements in the short-term interest rates, let alone long-term rates. Implicitly, if not explicitly, the interest rate on day-to-day money is identified with the i in the model. Henry Wallich of the Federal Reserve Board of Governors argues (1980) that one aspect of the learning process associated with base control must be a severing of this umbilical link between the federal funds rate and the rates on longer maturities. Freedman's analysis takes on a different perspective if one breaks the link between this federal funds rate (i.e., the rate for inter-bank lending of reserves) and the short-term rate, i, since the *instrument variability* in the federal funds market is no longer as serious a problem if it is not reflected in variations further along the maturity spectrum.

Instrument Variability (various places)

I have always been confused by the fact that once the Bank opted for controlling monetary aggregates, the publications emanating from the Bank pay a great deal of attention to *instrument variability*. What about *target variability*? The Bank is on record as saying that the path of M1 over a period of a month or several months is not of much import (1979 *Annual Report*). Yet movements of M1 in the United States above target for as short a period as one month can and do generate changes in expectations and in the behaviour of interest rates. I am not trying to downplay the importance of instrument variability, but rather I am suggesting that some concern ought to be focused on target variability as well. This point relates to the previous one in the sense that interest-rate variability is a more serious problem if it implies movements in general interest rates than if it implies movement in the equivalent of a federal funds rate. More generally, the thrust of Freedman's analysis of base control is really directed more at what it does to the likely pattern of interest rates *in the short term* than what it might imply for the pattern of money growth and, therefore, interest rates *in the longer term*.

2. Comments on the Overall Approach

Now to the more troublesome areas. Briefly put, I simply do not accept Freedman's views that these models have much at all to say about base control. They do not even come to grips with what I understand to be the principles underlying reserve base control. The heart of the matter is that *there are no money-supply functions in the models*, at least as I interpret what a money-supply function should be. My interpretation of reserve control is that the central bank announces the rate of reserve growth and the chartered banks generate the appropriate money supply or else pay the consequences via penalty-rate borrowing from the Bank of Canada. This conception of reserve control is far removed from the modelling that appears in Freedman's paper. I want to elaborate on this point.

I will assume a lagged reserve-settlement period since Freedman feels that this is a major blow at any attempt in the direction of reserve control. The central bank is following a growth rule for reserves that it will make available freely. Call this $\overline{RS}$. In period t, $\overline{RS}_{t+1}$ is *known* to the banks. The chartered banks face the following decision in period t: make demand deposits in period t adjust so as to coincide with $\overline{RS}_{t+1}$, that is,

$$\frac{1}{d}\overline{RS}_{t+1} = DD_t$$

or

$$\frac{1}{d}\overline{RS}_{t+1} = a - b_{i_t} + cY_t \tag{1}$$

to use Freedman's notation. The banks would influence i (which may be a range of own and market rates) so that current-period demand deposits correspond to the reserves that the Bank is going to supply next period to service these deposits. I need a few more assumptions. First, the chartered banks have to know, on a daily basis, what is the total level of demand deposits in the system. In our progressively electronic era, this does not seem to be a serious restriction. Secondly, individual banks will have to make projections as to their likely shares of reserves in period $(t+1)$. They will already know whether the 'system' is over or under the limits from the previous assumptions and from the knowledge that $\overline{RS}_{t+1}$ is known and fixed. Finally, the banks would have to know what the penalty rate would be: it could be set as a certain fraction above short-term rates that prevail in $(t+1)$, the precise fraction depending positively on the excess of required reserves in $(t+1)$ relative to $\overline{RS}_{t+1}$. These short-term rates would also have to be predicted by the banks. I have not modelled this system, but it seems to me that it does not differ in principle from the problems that beset a contemporaneous reserve settlement system. The addition of random shocks on the real side will mean that the banks will not be able to hit their desired DD exactly, but neither will they be able to under a contemporaneous settlement period.

Yet Freedman, in commenting on his version of the lagged settlement period model (Model 4c), suggests:

> . . . Suppose there is an increase in income that leads to an increase in money demanded. There is no effect on required reserves in the current period and hence no change in the interest rate in the current period (p. 32).

While the first part of the second sentence is correct, the second part reflects the myopic mechanistic approach he has taken to the reality of a lagged settlement system. The banks in my model know very well that if income increases, they had better curtail demand deposit growth or they will be in serious trouble in period $(t+1)$. I cannot accept that Freedman can have much to say about reserve control when he refuses *intentionally* to include a money-supply function. I do not want to get bogged down in semantics here. Perhaps the purist might not refer to this as a money-supply equation. But an equation like (1) above (where the chartered banks set i to ensure that the reserves they require in period $(t+1)$, that is, DD in period i, correspond closely to $\overline{RS}_{t+1}$ and more closely the higher is the penalty rate), is the pivotal adjustment mechanism under reserve control. This does not, of course, imply that the model I suggest would be stable. But surely it is a more realistic model. The 'sawtooth' behaviour that Freedman gets from this lagged reserve model is a result of his not allowing the banks in his model to be 'forward looking'. They are apparently oblivious to the problem that we, the readers, know will beset them in period $(t+1)$. I am sure that Freedman would take issue with someone who attempted to evaluate interest-rate control in the context of a model where there did not exist a well-defined, demand-for-money function. Surely the essence of reserve base control must presuppose a well-defined supply-of-money function that, at a minimum under a lagged settlement period, requires that the chartered banks be able to incorporate period $(t+1)$ in their operating horizon.

Two further comments are required here. The approach I have outlined implies that *all* interest rates be set by the private sector (except the penalty rate). The Bank of Canada would *not* engage in excess reserve management by providing reserve 'cushions', and so forth. Its job, *à la* Patinkin, would be to control a *nominal* magnitude, the reserve base, and nothing more. If it is not clear by now, the implicit assumption is that currency drains to the public would be completely offset.

Secondly, the 'model' here applies to the entire banking system. The behaviour for each bank would be more complicated because it would have to make assumptions about market shares, although with current technology it should be possible to get daily information on the level of reservable deposits in the system at any point in time. One concern that always seems to arise in this context is that on an individual bank basis, such a system would be inherently unstable. What might be true for the system breaks down for individual banks. Would one also conclude that individual gas stations cannot possibly exist without being 'unstable'? Once one assumes that banks do adopt a forward-looking strategy, I think that these system-versus-individual bank problems become much less important. One aspect that initially appeared intriguing was the following. Suppose that $RR > \overline{RS}$, that is, suppose that required reserves in $(t+1)$ were greater than the reserves the central bank would make available. Which bank in the system would be forced to do the borrowing? This is really a non-issue because the penalty rate would also become the inter-bank borrowing rate for the settlement period, so that the cost of funds to a bank that finds itself short is the same whether it gets these funds from a surplus bank or from the Bank of Canada.

Enough of my musings without laying out the formal model. The essential point that I want to make is that Freedman should attempt to incorporate this sort of forward-looking money-supply approach in his modelling exercise.[2] I have focused on the case with a lagged reserve settlement period, which is supposedly the 'problematical' case. Presumably the problems are less with a contemporaneous system. And I would expect that the 'sawtooth' nature of his solutions arising from lags in the demand-for-money equation would also be modified if he allowed banks to optimize over more than the current period.

3. The U.S. Experience

Freedman provides a rather convenient summary of the U.S. experience with reserve control. I want to comment on only one aspect of this experience, namely the *variability* of interest rates. According to Wallich (1980), the principal reason that the Federal Reserve went to reserve control was that the federal funds rate exhibited too much inertia. It was *not* variable enough and, therefore, was not effective enough in controlling monetary aggregates. Therefore, one should expect to find more variability in interest rates under reserve control — *that was why reserve control was instigated!*

The interesting question becomes: What is the definition of too much variability? Interest rates in the United States certainly have exhibited a yo-yo pattern over the past year. There is one episode in which I think it is necessary to exert some caution prior to coming to a conclusion with respect to interest-rate gyrations and that is the period over which rates hit their peak of 20 per cent or so, that is, in the early months of 1980. Over December and January, world oil prices made their second major upward jump of the decade. Gold prices were rising. Over this same period the U.S. inflation rate hit 18 per cent (largely because of the peculiarities of the U.S. Consumer Price Index calculation procedure). Moreover, the Russians moved into Afghanistan and expectations were rampant in terms of an inflationary arms build-up in the United States. I think that this was the closest the Americans have ever come to losing faith in the value of their currency. Interest rates went to 20 per cent. I think that rates in this range were needed. What would have happened under the old interest-rate control regime?

I recognize that analysis should not be conducted on an episode-by-episode basis or else theory tends to be relegated to the background. All that I am suggesting here is that in focusing on the U.S. experience with reserve control, some attention should be paid to this rather unusual period when assessing the variability or instability of interest rates under base control.

4. The Canadian Experience

Freedman presents a most enjoyable and enlightening discussion of how the Bank conducts interest-rate control. We are all in his debt for this effort.

I have two comments on this section. The first one is that I really do not have much sympathy for the Clinton and Lynch (1979) study, which Freedman quotes at length. I believe that Clinton and Lynch are falling prey to the Heisenberg principle. They investigate behaviour under the current operating procedures (i.e., lagged reserve settlement periods) on a monthly and quarterly basis and generate conclusions relating to reserve control (an *entirely different* operating procedure). To be sure, they do make a statement in the introduction to the effect that their analysis might not hold under altered operating environments. But the implications they draw are not so conditional. They argue:

> ...if (a) "money" is defined as privately held bank deposits, (b) the base concept is limited to net bank reserves, and (c) monthly data are used, we expect rejection of the hypothesis that base causes money and acceptance of the hypothesis that money causes base (p. 20).

The empirical work confirms their expectation. But so what? This is how the base is calculated. There are *no economic implications* of such a finding. Yet the authors go on to suggest that this lends support to an interest-rate control mechanism. This is hardly surprising: if total reserves are allowed to be determined by the public's demand for money, then it is certainly the case that one would not find any causal influence running from the reserve base to the money supply.

5. The Rationale for Reserve Control

The reason why some economists are in favour of base or reserve control is that they deem it to be preferable to interest-rate control. However, there may also be a pragmatic reason: interest-rate control of M1 may well become progressively more problematical. This is so for two reasons. First, the role of DD in the Canadian financial system is undergoing major changes. Computerization has led to a great many innovations that have tended to reduce the reliance on DD. One example of this is the move by the chartered banks to manage their large corporate accounts on a daily basis, even to the point of converting idle DD into overnight interest-bearing corporate notice deposits. More recently, the Bank of Montreal has introduced 'in-house, real-time terminals' that offer corporations immediate access to all their accounts and the ability to move these deposits from one account to another. This is especially significant for nation-wide corporations like Sun Life. They can have instant access to the amounts in their various accounts across the country and move them at will. What impact is this going to have on DD? My belief is that the velocity of DD is going to increase rapidly and the Bank will end up monitoring a progressively smaller aggregate. The solution might be to define money somewhat broader than M1. However, this immediately involves one in the problems with 'own' rates of interest. The Bank will no longer be able to control, via interest-rate control, the opportunity cost of holding these interest-bearing components of the new aggregate. This, then, is the first problem I foresee with the current interest-rate control system; namely, that the Bank may want to define money more broadly, but that would make interest-rate control extremely difficult unless it also has some control over the 'own' rates of interest in the M2 components.

The second pragmatic concern is that the chartered banks are progressively moving in the direction of 'paying interest' on DD. Some of this is direct payments and some of this is in the form of services rendered. If these 'payments' move in tandem with the general rate of interest, then this, too, will pose problems for interest-rate control because the zero interest fulcrum is gone and the Bank will have a much more difficult time in influencing the opportunity cost of DD and, therefore, of influencing the demand for money. I would expect this issue to become more serious as we experience an 'inflow' of new chartered banks as a result of the new Bank Act legislation.

These, of course, are not theoretical issues and certainly do not relate directly to Freedman's paper. But they are important from a policy perspective. And it seems to me that the research emanating from the Bank is geared more towards justifying current operating procedures than attempting to prepare some groundwork for an alternative operating procedure that may be in the works. Alternatively, the Bank might adopt a policy of ensuring that real interest rates remain positive as a mechanism for controlling inflation. Indeed, some analysts are suggesting that this may well be its recent approach. But that is another story.

Notes

* I want to thank John Helliwell for helping me sort out some of the many problems that beset the first draft of these comments. No doubt many still remain. Some of the more technical points have been deleted from this version.

[1] In turn, this is so because of the existence of the zero own rates of interest on the components of M1. It is probably the case that the components of the broader aggregates (e.g., corporate notice deposits) are *more* interest sensitive than, say, demand deposits, relative to their close substitutes. However, the Bank of Canada cannot control the opportunity cost of these interest-bearing deposits relative to their close substitutes: this is a chartered bank decision. But because of the zero-interest-rate fulcrum, a rise in short-term rates implies a rise in the opportunity cost of holding M1 balances. In turn this leads to a negative and systematic M1 interest-rate elasticity compared to the M2 interest-rate elasticity. Hence the Bank will have a great deal of difficulty controlling M2 via an interest-rate mechanism that operates through the demand for money.

[2] A good start in the direction is the recent paper by Timothy Lane, "A Simple Perfect Foresight Model of the Money Supply Process," (London: University of Western Ontario, December 1980).

References

Clinton, Kevin and Lynch, Kevin. (1979) "Monetary Base and Money Stock in Canada." Bank of Canada Technical Report No. 16. Ottawa: Bank of Canada.

Wallich, Henry C. (1980) "Techniques of Monetary Policy." Remarks to a Meeting of the Missouri Valley Economic Association, Memphis, Tennessee, 1 March.

Comment

by
John E. Floyd

Dr. Freedman has presented a stimulating theoretical analysis of some of the implications of base control. I find myself in agreement with Freedman on virtually all the technical aspects of his paper; his conclusions follow from his assumptions, as one expects in competent analysis. My comments are thus directed to the feasibility of base control in the Canadian context, focusing not so much on the validity of Freedman's conclusions as on their applicability to current problems in Canada.

First, I would like to address the question of base versus interest-rate control. The notion that the money supply can be controlled by manipulating interest rates appears to be an exclusively central bank preoccupation. I have never seen the approach advocated from any other quarter, academic or otherwise. Let me advance the view that attempting to use interest rates as a control variable is likely to lead to confusion and error in the implementation of monetary policy and that the money supply can be properly controlled only by operating on the monetary base.

Freedman treats interest-rate control as a method of changing the stock of money by moving the economy along its demand function for money. I am sure he recognizes that the demand function for money is only one equation in the macro-economic equilibrium of the economy and that the determination of interest rates involves other factors as well. Interest rates are determined by the demand for credit as well as the supply, and the demand for credit depends on consumption, investment, and other real variables. While ignoring these factors presents few difficulties in the simple models Freedman develops, it is worrying to see this done in Bank of Canada reports and technical studies that suggest that analysis of the demand function for money alone can supply the necessary information for interest-rate control decisions. Indeed, the Bank of Canada has chosen M1 as the monetary target rather than M2 on the grounds that the demand for the narrow aggregate is more responsive to interest rates and income.

This alleged greater responsiveness of M1 to interest-rate changes points to another problem with interest-rate control. It turns out that a rise in interest rates causes depositors to shift their holdings from demand to time deposit instruments in response to the differential in returns. This causes M1 to decline and M2 to rise. Such shifting of deposits probably accounts for the strong negative relationship between M1 and interest rates and the poor and sometimes positive observed relationship between interest rates and M2. By focusing on the relationship between interest rates and M1, the Bank thinks it is controlling the *level* of money in the system when, to a greater or lesser degree, it is controlling the *composition* of money holdings instead.

Further difficulties arise from the fact that Canada is an open economy whose asset markets are integrated with those in the rest of the world. This has fatal implications for interest-rate control. In the extreme (and admittedly unrealistic) perfect capital mobility case, Canadian real interest rates would be determined abroad and entirely independent of Bank of Canada control. Of course, observed nominal rates could vary relative to foreign rates in response to asset holders' expectations about the relative rates of domestic and foreign inflation. But the Bank of Canada could affect nominal rates only by influencing expected inflation, a difficult task that would require the generation of expectations of long-term monetary contraction to lower interest rates and of future monetary expansion to raise them.

While no one would seriously argue that capital is perfectly mobile internationally, it is hard for me to believe that the Bank of Canada can have much effect on the general level of domestic interest rates. No doubt it can influence the treasury bill and other individual interest rates for short periods. However, markets adjust quickly and Canadian asset markets are fully integrated with those abroad. Since changes in domestic rates will surely lead to substantial portfolio shifts, how can one seriously believe that the Bank of Canada, as it claims, sets domestic interest rates?

In any event, the relationship between domestic interest rates and the quantity of money is much flatter — bigger changes in money are associated with given interest-rate changes — than would be indicated by the demand function for money. For this reason, Freedman's models are not applicable to the Canadian economy at all and the problems of interest-rate instability and sawtoothed oscillations raised by his models are not to be taken seriously. Moreover, it is clear that the heavy emphasis of Bank of Canada research on the demand function for money is completely misplaced.

The conclusion from this is that the Bank should operate on the monetary base and ignore interest rates (and, incidently, exchange rates as well) if it wants to successfully stabilize Canadian monetary growth.

I now turn to the so-called lag problem with base control. Bank of Canada economists argue that since required reserves depend on last month's deposits, there is no mechanism by which a change in current deposits can bring about equilibrium. Excess reserves in the system will lead the banks to expand loans and deposits, but the increase in deposits will not lead to an increase in required reserves. The excess reserves will not be eliminated and the system will expand indefinitely. Base control becomes impossible.

As Courchene has just pointed out, this argument assumes that the banks have a zero time horizon. A smart bank, faced with an increase in its reserves, will not expand its current deposits out of line with the anticipated availability of reserves next period. To do so would necessitate borrowing next period from the Bank of Canada at penalty rates. When reserves are declining, such borrowing would provide a natural way for the system to meet current reserve requirements until deposits can be adjusted in subsequent periods. As long as it can be assumed that the chartered banks think ahead, there does not seem to me to be any problem.

Finally, I would like to comment briefly on the implementation of base control. The obvious approach is to try to manipulate base money on a month-to-month basis to produce a target level of the money supply. The required change in base money would be calculated using last period's money multiplier, or perhaps forecasts of the current period's multiplier. The approach is similar to the recently adopted U.S. policy of attempting to control the money supply by manipulating unborrowed reserves.

The problem with this simple-minded view is that the M1 and M2 money multipliers are not invariant to current changes in the monetary base. In some current work, Jack Carr and I have been finding that changes in the monetary base are associated with opposite changes in the money multiplier that wipe out one third of the effect on M1 and virtually all the effect on M2 in the current period. Evidently, it takes deposits a while to adjust to reserves with the result that base money changes affect the money supply only with a lag. To determine how long it takes the system to adjust, we regressed the month-to-month changes in the money multipliers on the current and lagged changes in base money. We found that the cumulative effect is insignificant after twelve months. Also, it is difficult because of multicolinearity to determine the timing of the system's response to base money changes. The conclusion is that we have a long and perhaps variable lag problem in using base money to fine-tune the money supply just as we have in using the money supply to fine-tune the economy. It would seem that the only feasible approach is a growth rule for base money.

How one should implement base control in the Canadian context turns on matters of judgement. For what it is worth, I will give you my opinion. I would target on M2 rather than M1. The argument that M1 is more responsive to interest rates and income is irrelevant: what counts is the causal effect of the aggregate on economic activity. Moreover, as Courchene has noted, with the recent institutional developments in banking, the M1 definition is getting narrower and narrower. I would take a three-year moving average of the M2 multiplier on a month-to-month basis and use it in combination with a target rate of growth of M2 to establish a target level for base money each month. Setting base money on target, month by month, would give it a virtually constant rate of growth. This would not result in a constant rate of growth of M2, of course, because the money multiplier would vary from month to month. But systematic variations in the multiplier would be neutralized eventually since they appear in the moving average. Depending on how the multiplier varied, the procedure might be more or less inflationary than anticipated. If, after a year or so, it became clear that the resulting rate of M2 growth was too inflationary or deflationary, I would introduce a pre-announced gradual adjustment of the target rate of base money growth over, say, a six-month to one-year period. Such 'fiddling' with the target growth rate is not objectionable as long as it is infrequent and in a direction that will obviously be viewed by the public as stabilizing. What is to be avoided is 'fiddling' to accomplish interest rate, exchange rate, and other objectives that conflict with the objective of stabilizing the money supply.

To the extent that this procedure stabilizes the actual and expected inflation rate — which I think it would — it will stabilize nominal interest rates and result in less switching back and forth between time and demand deposits. The money multipliers will thus tend to be stabilized and the growth rates of M1 and M2 will become more similar. This will reduce the variability of M2 in relation to target and make the decision to focus on an M2 rather than an M1 target less serious.

Summary
of
Discussion

The general discussion focused on the choice of the appropriate instrument for achieving monetary targets, the extent of the central bank's freedom of action to influence interest rates in view of the high degree of international asset market integration and the perceived importance of maintaining an appropriate exchange rate and, in particular, upon the role expectations play in the public's response to central bank signals.

Jack Galbraith led off on the subject of appropriate instruments by suggesting that interest-rate control reflects an indifference to the monetary base that is not shared by people in the financial markets. In his opinion, erratic behaviour of the monetary base leads to unsettled expectations. He felt that this was a major reason for the U.S. Federal Reserve's shift to monitoring reserves as a means of controlling monetary aggregates, and he proposed setting a target growth rate for the monetary base in Canada.

Charles Freedman responded with the comment that 'base watchers' misunderstand the system. He agreed that the Bank of Canada views itself as targeting on money, but conceded the validity of Tom Courchene's point that in some circumstances targeting on money would be inappropriate. However, he maintained that, at the moment, base was unimportant. He added that using multiple targets, as in the United States, for example, is a way of avoiding any responsibility whatsoever and that the Bank, by focusing on one target (M1), was playing the game honestly. The fact that base does not seem to behave nicely seemed irrelevant to Freedman as long as the Bank has achieved its target.

Tom Courchene criticized Freedman for predicting the effect on income of controlling M2 using evidence gleaned from the current behaviour of M2 in relation to income. Courchene felt that a shift to control M2 would alter the system; banks would no longer be willing to occasionally 'buy the whole commercial paper market' and experience rapid run-ups in their M2. He argued that if they knew they were going to be penalized, they would operate differently, and that this casts doubt on some of the policy implications of the empirical work cited by Freedman.

The question of the Bank's ability to exert independent control over interest rates was raised by *John Floyd*, who also criticized Freedman for focusing on nominal interest rates that ignore expectations about inflation. He felt that conducting monetary policy through interest rates was not feasible given the current international mobility of financial capital. *Pierre Fortin* also wondered whether stability in interest rates had been sacrificed in favour of exchange-rate stability. Freedman defended the Bank's ability to influence real interest rates and cited the fact that there often is an uncovered differential between the paper rates in the two countries. One example occurred in early 1979 when Canada chose not to have the kind of interest-rate volatility as the United States and accepted a certain amount of fluctuation in the exchange rate instead. Freedman conceded, however, that the Bank's freedom of action is limited by its choice of focusing, to some extent, on the exchange rate in the short run, although he felt that the money-supply target is dominant in the longer run. But he argued that it is a choice — a choice that can be justified in terms of feed-through from exchange rates to prices. Freedman emphasized that, in his view, a statement that the Bank cannot control interest rates, even in the short run, is incorrect.

The issue of expectations dominated the remainder of the discussion. Fortin questioned the Bank of Canada's course of controlling the money supply without also trying to convince the public that wider variations in interest rates are necessary to control inflation and, possibly, output. *Ron Wirick* also regarded the issue of expectations as critical. He felt that policy must formulate not only tactical decisions but also strategic decisions with the explicit intention of attempting to influence those expectations.

In response to these comments, Freedman voiced scepticism about the rational expectations view, which holds that by announcing the expected rate of growth in money supply, people's expectations will be reduced. He viewed as more realistic a notion that you have to use 'economic slack' (unemployment) and the price nexus to bring down the rate of inflation, a very long process. Further, he argued that monetary policy alone cannot combat inflation and unemployment, even in the long run; other policies, micro policies, are very important. He felt that policy makers are faced with a lot of unhappy choices and that the least unhappy one is to continue with a monetary policy that has reasonable, long-run possibilities. Freedman saw a monetary target as imposing some discipline; it produced an objective against which performance can be measured. The tactical question, he concluded, is really how rigidly that particular growth path should be imposed. Fortin's work was cited as evidence that argues that the Bank should not be too rigid in its pursuit of monetary targets.

On the same theme of expectations, *John Grant*, speaking from the perspective of an investment dealer, argued that over the previous eight months, the private sector could have sold a great deal of corporate long-term debt in the bond market if the bond market had not been, by its own account, totally demoralized. He argued that bond buyers did not know what to think and that if there had been any expectations management, it had been in the direction of totally wiping out expectations beyond the next five minutes.

Freedman conceded that this was a tough question to answer satisfactorily. The expectations theory of interest rates implies that movements in short rates that are not expected to last any length of time should not have much effect on long rates. But the evidence is that long rates have moved much more than can be explained by the expectations theory, so the question remains: Why has the long rate been so volatile? Freedman suggested two possible answers. One is that the market is irrational. The other one is that the expectations theory assumes that movements of short rates or the exchange rate or of dividends are from a stationary process. When rates go up by 20 per cent, and there is a possibility that they are not going to come back down, then it is no longer irrational for long rates to move with short rates. In any event, he conceded that the market has not been paying much attention to the fact that the Bank has had the monetary aggregate on target for five years.

Courchene wondered what there was to the above statement that the monetary aggregate has been on target, since he could cite episode after episode when he felt the Bank had made major mistakes. One was in 1977, just before Canada lifted wage and price controls; the money supply was much below target, and had been for a long period of time. Courchene agreed with Governor Bouey who, in his annual report, had argued that the demand for money had shifted permanently downward, and that the Bank might have to adjust its target downward. But Courchene noted that, instead, the money supply rose from the bottom of the target range to the top over quite a short period of time. Courchene argued that there are certain critical times when expectations can be influenced and one of them is when controls are being lifted. By letting the money supply grow at such a critical time and at a rate of growth that may have been 15 per cent or more, Courchene felt that a difficult situation may have been aggravated. He felt that a second mistake, also related to expectations, occurred in 1978 when the Bank of Canada could have rationalized its growth targets in terms of the money supply; instead it chose to focus on the exchange rate. Nevertheless, the money supply remained within the target range. He contended that the episode did something very negative to those people on Bay Street who had been convinced that the Bank was following targets, and, consequently, the Bank had to start its 1975 exercise of convincing people all over again in 1978 and 1979.

A general discussion ensued related to the ability of monetary policy to influence expectations directly via 'announcement' effects. The consensus, from the available evidence, was that it cannot. One problem noted, however, was that there is no way of testing whether there had been an Anti-Inflation Board (AIB) effect separate from the introduction of monetarism since both had occurred at the same time. There was evidence of a significant effect of the AIB on wage settlements, and most participants agreed with Wirick that these could be explained best as expectations effects; hence there could have been an anticipations effect from the introduction of monetarism, but it is difficult to disentangle the impacts of the two events. It was agreed, however, that given the reduction in expectations, whatever the cause, monetary policy had failed to take advantage of the situation. A number of explanations for this failure were offered, including the inflexibility of a gradualist strategy and the usual problem that wage-price controls are too often viewed as substitutes for, rather than complements to, conventional anti-inflationary policies.

Exchange Rates, Short-Term Capital, and Resource Allocation

2

by
David Longworth*

1. Introduction

The key price determined in the international sector of any macro model is the exchange rate because of its effect on aggregate economic activity, prices, income distribution, and the allocation of resources. Because of the pervasive influence of the exchange rate, it is essential to understand the factors determining exchange-rate movements in order to analyse the impact of macro-policy initiatives in an open economy.

In this paper these factors are examined in the general 'modern theory' framework of Tsiang (1959) and McCormick (1977), extended to multiple lengths of forward exchange contracts. This framework distinguishes among arbitrage, speculation, intervention, and covered future trade schedules.

By making certain simplifying assumptions, the number of factors potentially influencing exchange-rate movements can be reduced. One such simplifying assumption is that the stock of short-term capital does not affect the exchange rate. If this were true, then the current account and other balance-of-payments flows would have no direct effect on the exchange rate. In particular, one channel whereby official intervention could affect the exchange rate would be removed.

Dornbusch (1980a) has recently discussed "Exchange Rate Economics: Where Do We Stand?" concentrating on theory and the movement of the U.S. dollar *vis-à-vis* other major currencies. The present paper deals with where we stand with respect to our knowledge of the Canadian–U.S. exchange market. In particular, by reviewing the literature and presenting some new evidence, it deals with the following:

1. What simplifying assumptions can fruitfully be made.
   a. Which elasticities can be assumed to be infinite? (Can we assume purchasing-power parity, covered interest parity, and an infinitely elastic speculative schedule?)
   b. Can the exchange market be considered efficient?
   c. Are past empirical approaches to forward rate determination useful?

2. What recent exchange-rate modelling approaches are worth pursuing.

3. What implications inefficiency in the exchange market would have for shifts in the domestic allocation of resources.

The paper proceeds as follows. Section 2 summarizes previous research on exchange-rate determination and Canadian short-term capital flows. Section 3 outlines the framework to be used and introduces the arbitrage, speculation, intervention, and covered future trade schedules. A detailed description of the framework is given in the Appendix. Section 4 discusses the implications of infinite elasticities in the four schedules and provides evidence on purchasing-power parity, covered interest parity, and efficient markets. The empirical implementation of the modern theory of foreign exchange is critiqued in Section 5. The role of expectations in exchange-rate determination is discussed in Section 6. Section 7 presents some preliminary results on the effect of the exchange rate on resource allocation. Section 8 concludes the paper.

2. The Relationship Between Exchange Rates and Short-Term Capital Flows

If capital flows are infinitely elastic with respect to expected returns, the stock of short-term capital will have no effect on the exchange rate. In this case it would suffice to look at reduced-form exchange-rate models that (implicitly) make the infinite elasticity assumption.

On the other hand, for the case of a less than infinite elasticity, there is a large literature on models where the exchange rate is determined by the requirement that balance-of-payments flows sum to zero. This is consistent with an asset market approach if capital flows are derived from stock demands. In these models, the short-term capital equation, which is often inverted to solve for the exchange rate, depends upon the current and expected exchange rates among other determinants.

Empirical reduced-form models for the Canadian–U.S. exchange rate may be categorized as follows:

1. Purchasing-power-parity monetarist (see, for example, Dornbusch (1978) for a theoretical description; an empirical example for the Canadian dollar–U.S. dollar exchange rate is to be found in Freedman and Longworth (1980), where there is also a critique of this type of model as applied to the Canadian experience)

2. Other monetarist (Girton and Roper, 1977, criticized by Sargen, 1977; Knight, 1976)

3. Efficient markets models (reflecting the theory as presented in Levich, 1979 and Dornbusch, 1978; an empirical example for Canada is found in Longworth, 1980b)

4. Other (such as Freedman's (1979) eclectic model, which emphasized expectations and which could not find a significant role for the stock of short-term net foreign assets).

There are great weaknesses in the explanatory power of the above models for the 1970s (see Freedman and Longworth, 1980), probably due largely to the difficulty in capturing the way market participants formed their expectations. There is some evidence that expectations formation is myopic, not very forward looking. Speculators may not be willing to have large uncovered positions over long periods of time. This, however, is equivalent to saying that elasticities are not infinite and that we should be concentrating on another class of model.

Models of short-term capital flows that either are or can be imbedded in complete balance-of-payments sectors are of two major types: flow demand models and stock demand models. Flow demand models relate short-term flows to the levels of interest-rate differentials and are theoretically unappealing, even though often apparently consistent with the data. Empirical flow models for Canada include those of Rhomberg (1960), Arndt (1968), Helliwell (1969), Caves and Reuber (1971), and Helliwell and Maxwell (1972). Models of stock demands, which either relate flows to changes in interest-rate differentials[1] or more properly the stocks themselves to interest-rate levels, are represented by Helliwell and Maxwell (1972), Choudhry *et al.* (1972), Haas and Alexander (1979), and the portfolio balance model of Martin and Masson (1979).[2] The dynamics of exchange-rate changes in stock models when subjected to shocks (especially interest-rate shocks) are discussed in Bank of Canada (1980).

One major empirical weakness of these models is the formulation of the expected future exchange rate that enters the speculative schedule. The arbitrage schedule may be properly formulated, but one must know what determines the *level* of the forward rate. As will be shown below in Section 5, the reduced-form approach to the determination of the forward rate by those following the modern theory approach is likely to be severely flawed under the conditions of almost perfect arbitrage and highly variable exchange rates.

Recent theory developed by Frankel (1979) and Dornbusch (1980b) shows that in an optimizing model with perfect markets and no default risk, there is no justification for a risk premium related to the stock of net foreign claims; that is, the stock of net foreign claims has no direct influence on the exchange rate in their models (although unexpected changes in it might affect expectations and thereby the exchange rate). However, where there are institutional or legal constraints on speculation, or sizeable 'country' default risks (see Buiter (1980) on international asset risk), one may be able to theoretically justify the use of models where the stock of short-term assets has an important role.

In the next two sections it is shown that the question as to whether reduced-form (infinite elasticity) exchange-rate equations should be used is related to whether covered interest parity holds and whether the forward rate is the expected future spot rate.

3. Exchange-Market Equilibrium

This section examines the theory of foreign exchange and exchange-market equilibrium developed by Tsiang (1959) and McCormick (1977). In the theory there are four roles in the exchange market: that of arbitrageur, speculator, commercial trader, and official foreign exchange trader. At any one time one person or firm may be playing a number of roles in the market.

The Appendix contains a detailed development of the theory when there are a large number of forward markets (for different maturities) and stock demands for arbitrage and speculative capital. If these demands can be suitably approximated by dealing with 90-day rates alone, the results in the Appendix may be summarized as follows.

First, the stock of arbitrage capital (K_A) is equal to the stock of speculative capital (K) plus the stock of official forward intervention (K_G) plus the stock of future trade contracts (K_T):

$$K_A = K + K_G + K_T. \tag{1}$$

If r and r^* are the domestic and foreign interest rates, respectively, expressed at quarterly rates, s is the log of the spot rate, and f is the log of the 90-day forward rate, then the stock demand for arbitrage capital may be denoted:

$$K_A = k_1 (r^* - r - s + f), \quad k_1 > 0. \tag{2}$$

Similarly, if s^e denotes the expected log of the spot rate 90 days hence, the speculative schedule may be written:

$$K = k_2 (s^e - f), \quad k_2 > 0. \tag{3}$$

Then from the three above equations one can derive the following expression for the spot rate:

$$s = s^e - (r - r^*) - K_A \left(\frac{k_1 + k_2}{k_1 k_2}\right) + \frac{K_T + K_G}{k_2}. \tag{4}$$

Since the stock of arbitrage capital is identically the stock of short-term capital, this says that the spot rate is the expected spot rate discounted by the interest-rate differential and adjusted by a linear combination of the stock of short-term capital, the stock of future trade contracts, and the stock of official forward intervention.

It will be found useful to express the total demand for foreign exchange for current trade (oTo) and future trade K_T as

$$K'_T = K_T + oTo = k_3(p - p^* - f), \quad k_3 > 0, \tag{5}$$

where p and p^* are the logs of domestic and foreign contract prices for goods. Also, the total demand for foreign exchange for intervention purposes (including intervention in the spot market oGo) might be represented as

$$K'_G = K_G + oGo = k_4(s^t - s), \quad k_4 > 0, \tag{6}$$

where s^t is a target exchange rate.

Since $oGo + oTo = -(oAo + oSo)$ where the latter two terms are respectively the flows of arbitrage and speculative capital in the spot market, one can rewrite (4) using (5) and (6) as

$$s = s^e - (r - r^*) - (K_A)\left(\frac{k_1 + k_2}{k_1 k_2}\right) + \frac{k_3(p - p^* - f) + k_4(s^t - s) + oAo + oGo}{k_2}. \tag{7}$$

The expression will be useful in evaluating the effect of infinite elasticities in the next section.

4. The Implications of Infinite Elasticities in Various Balance-of-Payments Schedules

Introduction

This section considers the implications of infinitely elastic intervention, trade flows, speculation, and arbitrage. These implications correspond to the 'building blocks' of simplified theories of exchange-rate determination. Evidence on whether the implications hold true is examined in the following subsections.

From the stock equilibrium condition (7) it can easily be seen that (if there is only one infinite elasticity at a time):

a. If K'_G is infinitely elastic $(k_4 \to \infty)$ with respect to deviations of the exchange rate from a target value, then the exchange rate is effectively fixed.[3]

b. If K'_T is infinitely elastic $(k_3 \to \infty)$ with respect to the ratio of contract prices adjusted by the forward rate, then the forward rate will follow purchasing-power parity (*PPP*) as measured by contract prices. (If the forward rate is also the expected future spot rate — see below — the spot rate will approximately follow *PPP* with respect to measured prices at the time of completion of transactions.)

c. If arbitrage schedule K_A is infinitely elastic $(k_1 \to \infty)$ with respect to deviations from covered interest parity $(r^* - r - s + f)$, then covered interest parity holds $(f - s = r - r^*)$. (But this does not determine the *level* of either the spot or the forward rate.)

d. If the speculative schedule K is infinitely elastic with respect to the difference between the forward rate and the expected future spot rate ($k_2 \to \infty$), then the forward rate will be the expected future spot rate.

If the speculative schedule were a function of the difference between the forward rate and the expected future spot rate adjusted for a risk premium[4] not dependent on the stock of speculative capital, then with an infinitely elastic speculative schedule the forward rate would, of course, be the expected future spot rate adjusted for a risk premium.

Empirical Evidence on Purchasing-Power Parity

If purchasing-power parity held in the short run, the ratio of Canadian prices (costs) to U.S. prices (costs) should have been a good predictor of the Canadian–U.S. exchange rate. However, as can be seen from Figure 1, this was not the case. Both labour costs and broadly based price measures of *PPP* would have predicted a steady depreciation of the Canadian dollar from 1973 to 1976, yet the depreciation occurred only in 1977–1978. Although there is evidence of a return towards *PPP*, deviations from it have been substantial and prolonged; there have been large changes in the real exchange rate (the nominal exchange rate adjusted for relative price or cost movements).

Empirical Evidence on Covered Interest Parity

The early evidence on covered interest parity in Canada was indirect, as part of tests of the modern theory of forward exchange-rate determination (Stoll, 1968; Kesselman, 1971; and Haas, 1974). Pippenger (1978) has done the most extensive study of interest arbitrage and concludes that the arbitrage schedule has an elasticity that is near zero in the short run and near infinity in the long run. The early studies refer to the float of the 1950s. Pippenger considers the 1959–1964 and 1971–1975 periods.

When testing the interest-parity hypothesis, the correct choice of interest rates, the proper timing of the data, and the recognition of certain technical factors — the week-end effects and the Thursday-Friday effects (Levi, 1978) — are very important.

Researchers have found that covered interest parity holds (to within transactions costs) in Euro-currency markets. The domestic Canadian financial instrument that appears to be the closest to a perfect substitute for a Euro-Canadian dollar deposit is the chartered bank deposit rate on large-scale fixed term deposit receipts (sometimes referred to as large notice deposits or certificates of deposit). Therefore one would expect that use of the Canadian notice deposit rate and the Eurodollar rate for the corresponding maturity would be appropriate for testing for covered interest parity.

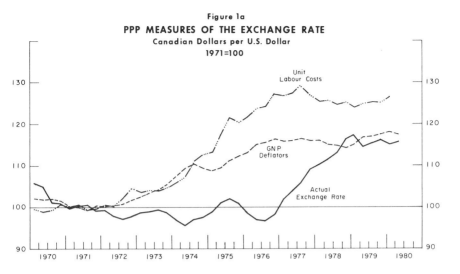

Figure 1a
PPP MEASURES OF THE EXCHANGE RATE
Canadian Dollars per U.S. Dollar
1971=100

Figure 1b
REAL EXCHANGE RATES
Canadian Dollars per U.S. Dollar
1971=100

Given the large variability of both interest rates and exchange rates in recent years, the data should pertain to the same point in time. Monthly averages for interest rates are not always averages of all the banking days of the month and, therefore, are not comparable with monthly averages of daily exchange-rate data. Thus it is preferable to use daily data — ideally data recorded at the same point in time. Unfortunately the data available to test the interest-parity theorem do not meet this requirement. The data used in the regressions reported below are the average over the day of all transactions for the Canadian notice deposit rate, a bid quote for the Eurodollar rate, and closing rates for the spot and forward exchange rates. In these provisional examinations, the interest-rate data are unadjusted for technical factors concerning the number of days for which interest is actually paid.

Table 1 presents the results of two regressions: deviations from covered interest parity are regressed on a constant, and the forward premium (in logarithmic form) is regressed on a constant and the appropriately defined interest-rate differential. In a statistical sense covered interest-rate parity is rejected, yet the mean deviations (see equation 1.1) and standard errors are economically small. Neither is there any evidence of first-order autocorrelation, such as might be in evidence if there were lagged adjustment to covered interest-rate parity. In the second regression, failure to account for the technical factors and other measurement error may be the cause of an estimate of b, the coefficient on the interest-rate differential, which is significantly less than one.

Since data for the net stock of short-term capital are only available on an end-of-quarter basis, one must use quarterly data to test whether deviations from covered interest parity are related to the net stock of short-term capital. Since the Winnipeg Agreement imposed

Table 1
INTEREST-RATE PARITY THEOREM:
DAILY DATA FOR 1979

Equation 1.1: $\quad f^t - s - 1n\,(1 + \dfrac{t \cdot r}{36500} + 1n\,(1 + \dfrac{t \cdot r^*}{36000})) = a \quad t = 30, 60, 90$

t	a	$\bar{R}^2$	S.E.E.	D.W.	N
30	.0002* (.00004)	—	.0006	2.0443	221
60	.0004* (.00004)	—	.0006	2.0178	221
90	.0006* (.00005)	—	.0007	1.9431	221

Equation 1.2: $\quad f^t - s = a + b\,\{1n(1 + \dfrac{t \cdot r}{36500}) - 1n(1 + \dfrac{t \cdot r^*}{36000})\}$

t	a	b	$\bar{R}^2$	S.E.E.	D.W.	N
30	.0002* (.00004)	.6960* (.0567)	.4048	.0005	1.8549	221
60	.0004* (.00004)	.8019* (.0326)	.7324	.0005	2.0141	221
90	.0005* (.00005)	.8337* (.0279)	.8022	.0006	1.8866	221

Notes:
1. * for a denotes significantly different from 0 at the 5% level.
  * for b denotes significantly different from 1 at the 5% level.
  * for $D.W.$ denotes significantly autocorrelated at the 5% level.
2. The r^*'s are London Eurodollar bid rates. Canadian rates are Canadian chartered bank deposit rates.
Standard errors are in brackets throughout this paper.

interest-rate ceilings on Canadian dollar certificates of deposit from June 1972 to January 1975, that rate was probably not the appropriate interest rate to use for that period. Therefore the regressions in Table 2 are also presented using the Canadian finance paper rate and the U.S. commercial paper rate. Although there is significant first-order autocorrelation — likely due to the change in appropriate interest rates — the stock of short-term capital scaled by wealth is insignificant. This tends to point to a very elastic arbitrage schedule.

Table 2
INTEREST-RATE PARITY THEOREM:
QUARTERLY DATA

Equation 2: $f^{90} - s - 1n\ (1 + \dfrac{90 \cdot r_{90}}{36500}) + 1n\ (1 + \dfrac{90 \cdot r^*_{90}}{36000}) = a + b\ (\dfrac{Ks}{NW})$

Sample: 71Q1—79Q4   Estimation by Cochrane-Orcutt

$Ks^{1)}$	$r,r^{*2)}$	a	b	ρ	$\overline{R}^2$ $(S.E.E.)$	D.W.	N
KIDEN	CCD, EURO	.0021* (.0006)	−.0002 (.0004)	.3292 (.1654)	.0721 (.0017)	2.0284	36
KTOTAL	CCD, EURO	.0023* (.0006)	.0002 (.0003)	.3012 (.1662)	.0842 (.0017)	1.9729	36
KIDEN	CFP, USCP	−.0006 (.0004)	.0001 (.0003)	.4340* (.1601)	.1515 (.0010)	1.7898	36
KTOTAL	CFP, USCP	−.00003 (.0004)	.0002 (.0002)	.3755* (.1623)	.1750 (.0010)	1.7655	36

Notes:
1. KIDEN   is the net stock of identified short-term capital.
   KTOTAL is the net stock of short-term capital including errors and omissions.
   NW   is a proxy for North American wealth.
2. CCD   is the Canadian certificate of deposit rate.
   EURO   is the Euro U.S. dollar rate.
   CFP   is the Canadian finance paper rate.
   USCP   is the U.S. commercial paper rate.
   (All rates used are 90-day rates.)
3. *   denotes significantly different from 0 at the 5% level.

Empirical Evidence on Efficiency

If the foreign exchange market is efficient (see, for example, Levich, 1979), then there should be no mathematical expectation of an extraordinary gain from foreign exchange trading. In particular, since the expected return on a speculative forward contract is proportional to the difference between the forward rate and the expected future spot rate, in an efficient market where the speculative schedule is perfectly elastic and there is no other theoretical justification for a risk premium, the forward rate should be an unbiased predictor of the future spot rate. Since the current spot rate is known at the time the contract is entered into, it is also true that the forward premium should be an unbiased predictor of the future change in the spot rate. Also, even if there is a risk premium that is uncorrelated with the forward premium, then when the change in the logarithm of the spot rate is regressed on a constant and the forward premium (in logarithmic form), the coefficient on the forward premium should be insignificantly different from one. These and other tests of efficiency were considered for the 1970–1978 period by Longworth (1981). There it was found that for certain sub-periods, market efficiency could be rejected for the Canadian-U.S. exchange rate. For almost every sub-period the change in the spot rate is *negatively* related to the forward premium, and the current spot rate is a better predictor of the future spot rate than is the current forward rate.

The empirical work presented in Table 3 below updates the work mentioned above through April 1980.

The following periods were chosen for study:

a. The entire period

b. The period commencing in 1971 after the exchange rate had adjusted following its floating in June 1970

c. The last three-and-one-half years

d. The period since August 1978, a period in which the exchange rate had far less variation than in the previous two-year period.

Equation 3.1 examines the forecasts of the forward rate alone. For the period as a whole the forward rate appears to be very good; there is no evidence of bias. However, evidence for periods (c) and (d) indicates that for the recent past a linear function of the forward rate significantly improves upon the forward rate itself.

Equation 3.2 looks at the forecasting ability of the lagged spot rate. The coefficients a and b look much as they do in equation 3.1, as one would expect given the link in the levels of the spot and forward rates through interest parity. It is interesting to note, however, that the standard errors of the regressions using the spot rate are marginally less than those using the forward rate.

Equation 3.3 looks at the forward premium as a predictor of the change in the spot rate. With efficient markets a_2 is hypothesized to be 1. The addition of the data from 1979 and early 1980 now makes it possible to reject market efficiency for the period as a whole. Under the hypothesis of no risk premium, a_1 should be near 0 and therefore efficiency could be rejected for the latest three-and-one-half-years' period as well. The tendency for the forward premium to be *negatively* related to the future change in the spot rate remains pronounced.

In equation 3.4 the lagged forward and spot rates are both admitted as predictors. Both are significant, but, as might have been expected

Table 3
END-OF-MONTH DATA

Equation 3.1: $s_t = a_1 + a_2 f_{t-1}$

Period	a_1	a_2	D.W.	S.E.R.	$\bar{R}^2$
70.07 − 80.04	.0006	1.0049	2.14	.0121	.9663
	(.0013)	(.0173)			
71.01 − 80.04	.0008	1.0042	2.15	.0123	.9664
	(.0014)	(.0178)			
77.01 − 80.04	.0139*	.9144**	2.13	.0139	.9024
	(.0062)	(.0481)			
78.08 − 80.04	.1148*	.2754*	1.81	.0137	.0378
	(.0321)	(.2061)			

Equation 3.2: $s_t = a_1 + a_2 s_{t-1}$

Period	a_1	a_2	D.W.	S.E.R.	$\bar{R}^2$
70.07 − 80.04	.0011	1.0011	2.16	.0119	.9670
	(.0013)	(.0171)			
71.01 − 80.04	.0014	1.0002	2.19	.0122	.9673
	(.0013)	(.0174)			
77.01 − 80.04	.0160*	.8992*	2.17	.0136	.9069
	(.0059)	(.0408)			
78.08 − 80.04	.1109*	.2997*	1.86	.0136	.0567
	(.0315)	(.2020)			

Equation 3.3: $(s_t - s_{t-1}) = a_1 + a_2(f_{t-1} - s_{t-1})$

Period	a_1	a_2	D.W.	S.E.R.	$\bar{R}^2$
70.07 − 80.04	.0013	− .2198**	2.16	.0120	0
	(.0011)	(.7109)			
71.01 − 80.04	.0016	− .3431**	2.18	.0122	0
	(.0012)	(.7331)			
77.01 − 80.04	.0041**	− .1096	2.13	.0144	0
	(.0024)	(1.9078)			
78.08 − 80.04	.0011	−3.8140	2.26	.0169	.0028
	(.0038)	(3.7111)			

Equation 3.4: $s_t = a_1 + a_2 f_{t-1} + a_3 s_{t-1}$

Period	a_1	a_2	a_3	t on $a_3=0$	D.W.	S.E.R.	$\bar{R}^2$
70.07 − 80.04	.0012	− .2185**	1.2187**	1.684	2.16	.0120	.9668
	(.0013)	(.7264)	(.7235)				
71.01 − 80.04	.0016	− .3546**	1.3532**	1.810	2.18	.0122	.9671
	(.1432)	(.7510)	(.7477)				
77.01 − 80.04	.0340*	−6.8533*	7.6216*	3.117	2.15	.0126	.9206
	(.0085)	(2.4926)	(2.4453)				
78.08 − 80.04	.1206*	−5.9131*	6.1393*	2.223	2.03	.0125	.2031
	(.0293)	(2.7903)	(2.7619)				

Note: * denotes significantly different from hypothesized value ($a_1=0$, $a_2=1$, $a_3=0$) at the 5% level
(** at the 10% level).

from the results of equation 3.3, the spot rate has a coefficient greater than one and the forward rate has a corresponding negative coefficient.

The evidence indicates that the Canadian-U.S. exchange market has been inefficient and that this situation has not changed in the recent past. This does not necessarily indicate a low elasticity of the speculative schedule, however. Indeed, the volatility in the exchange rate is suggestive of a highly elastic speculative schedule, given a highly elastic arbitrage schedule and relatively smooth changes in interest-rate differentials. However, it appears that expectations have been consistently wrong. The question of expectations is dealt with at more length in Section 6 below.

5. A Critique of the Empirical Implementation of the 'Modern Theory' of Forward Rate Determination

In the empirical implementation of the 'modern theory' of forward rate determination, a reduced-form equation derived from the speculative and arbitrage schedules is used to determine the forward exchange rate. In the case where there is no intervention in the forward market and no future trade contracts, the forward rate is estimated as a linear function of the future expected spot rate and the forward parity rate (the current spot rate adjusted for the interest-rate differential). The ratio of the reduced-form coefficients on the two explanatory variables is an estimate of the ratio of the elasticities of the speculative and arbitrage schedules.

Early work in the modern theory framework (Stoll, 1968; Kesselman, 1971; and Haas, 1974) using the treasury bill rates and the Canadian-U.S. exchange rate found that exchange-rate expectations as well as the forward parity rate helped to explain the current forward rate. Freedman, Longworth, and Masson (1977) found that the percentage difference between the spot and forward exchange rates was best explained by a number of Canadian-U.S. interest-rate differentials (for various financial instruments) and the change in the spot rate.

More recent work for the 1950s in a rational expectations framework (McCallum, 1977) showed that most of the explanatory power in the forward rate is coming from the forward parity rate. Kohlhagen (1979) and McCallum's subsequent comment (1979) showed that the forward rate can simultaneously be the forward parity rate and the expected future spot rate, and so tests of the modern theory may be misleading. The proponents of the modern theory claim that they are measuring the ratio of the elasticity of the arbitrage schedule to the elasticity of the speculative schedule, but in the situation envisaged by Kohlhagen and McCallum, the coefficients are functions of relative error variances.

This can be seen as follows. Measurement error and transactions costs may mean that the interest-parity condition holds to within a white noise error:

$$F = F^* + v, \tag{8}$$

where F is the forward exchange rate, F^* is the forward parity rate (the spot rate (S) adjusted for domestic and foreign interest rates, r and r^*: $S(1+r)/(1+r^*)$), and v is the error term. Simultaneously the forward rate may be the expected future spot rate (S^e) within measurement error (u):

$$F = S^e + u. \tag{9}$$

Now if one estimates the modern theory forward rate equation:

$$F = aS^e + bF^* + w, \tag{10}$$

$$\text{plim} \begin{bmatrix} \hat{a} \\ \hat{b} \end{bmatrix} = \begin{bmatrix} \dfrac{\sigma_v^2}{\sigma_u^2 + \sigma_v^2} \\ \dfrac{\sigma_u^2}{\sigma_u^2 + \sigma_v^2} \end{bmatrix} \tag{11}$$

Thus the estimated coefficients are functions of relative error variances. The above example can be generalized to the case where the forward rate is the expected spot rate plus exchange risk (X) plus white noise:

$$F = S^e + X + w. \tag{9'}$$

Then if equation 10 is estimated (because there is no suitable proxy for risk, for example):

$$\text{plim} \begin{bmatrix} \hat{a} \\ \hat{b} \end{bmatrix} = \begin{bmatrix} \dfrac{(Q_{ss}+Q_{sx})\,(2Q_{sx}+\sigma_v^2)}{Q_{ss}(Q_{xx}+\sigma_u^2+\sigma_v^2) - (Q_{sx})^2} \\ \dfrac{(Q_{ss})\,(Q_{xx}+\sigma_u^2) - 2Q_{ss}Q_{sx} - (Q_{sx})^2}{Q_{ss}(Q_{xx}+\sigma_u^2+\sigma_v^2) - (Q_{sx})^2} \end{bmatrix} \tag{11'}$$

where: $Q_{ss} = \text{plim} \left(\dfrac{S^{e\prime}S^e}{n}\right)$,

$$Q_{sx} = \text{plim} \left(\dfrac{S^{e\prime}X}{n}\right), \text{ and}$$

$$Q_{xx} = \text{plim} \left(\dfrac{X'X}{n}\right).$$

If S^e and X are uncorrelated in the limit, $Q_{sx} = 0$ and

$$\text{plim} \begin{bmatrix} \hat{a} \\ \hat{b} \end{bmatrix} = \begin{bmatrix} \dfrac{\sigma_v^2}{Q_{xx}+\sigma_u^2+\sigma_v^2} \\ \dfrac{Q_{xx}+\sigma_u^2}{Q_{xx}+\sigma_u^2+\sigma_v^2} \end{bmatrix} \tag{11''}$$

Expected exchange rates are difficult to measure, and in a world of volatile exchange rates any proxy is likely to have a large error variance. On the other hand, with the proper data and a perfectly elastic arbitrage schedule, the standard error of estimate in a regression of the forward rate on the forward parity rate will reflect transactions costs alone, which are likely to be small. Thus one would expect to find that a regression of the 'modern theory' type would yield a very high coefficient on the forward parity rate and a very low coefficient on the proxy for the expected future spot rate. As long as the arbitrage elasticity were quite high, this could happen even if the speculative elasticity were *greater than* the arbitrage elasticity.

An example of the above discussion is given in Table 4 using actual end-of-month Canadian data from January 1971 to April 1980. (Missing observations on end-of-month interest rates limit the number of observations to 100.) McCallum's (1977) rational expectation method is used for the expected future exchange rate. The following instruments are used for s_{t+1}: $r_t, r_t^*, r_{t-1}, s_{t-1}, f_{t-1}$. Equation 4.1 gives the results of a regression of f_t on the proxy for the expected future exchange rate. The constant term is insignificantly different from 0 and the slope coefficient is insignificantly different from 1. However, the standard error of estimate of the equation, at 1.21 per cent, is quite large. Ordinary least squares (OLS) estimates of the forward parity determination of the forward rate (equation 4.2) result in an equation with a standard error of only 0.07 per cent, or one seventeenth as large. The coefficients a and b are significantly different from 0 and 1 respectively, perhaps because of the use of the Canadian notice deposit rate during the period of the Winnipeg Agreement and the use of data unadjusted for technical factors. When the proxy for the expected future spot rate and the forward parity rate are combined in the same OLS regression, the results (equation 4.3) are little changed from equation 4.2, as the coefficient on the expected future spot rate proxy is small both economically and statistically.

Since spot and forward rates are determined simultaneously, s_t is an endogenous variable and thus equations 4.2 and 4.3 should be estimated by an instrumental variables (IV) method. Using the same instruments for s_t as for s_{t+1}, the results are presented in the IV rows of Table 4. Although the standard error of estimate increases substantially in equation 4.2, the point estimates of the coefficients are hardly changed at all. However, in equation 4.3 the point estimates change substantially as the two explanatory variables are now on equal footing. Nevertheless, the coefficient on the proxy for the expected future spot rate remains insignificantly different from 0.

A second criticism of the empirical implementation of the modern theory of forward rate determination is that expectations formation is not adequately dealt with. Expectations are affected by more than the

Table 4
THE MODERN THEORY
DETERMINATION OF THE FORWARD RATE
1971.01 – 1980.04

$$f_t = a + b\hat{s}_{t+1} + c\{s_t + 1n(1+\frac{30r}{36500}) - 1n(1+\frac{30r^*}{36000})\}$$

Equation	Method	a	b	c	$\bar{R}^2$	S.E.E.	D.W.
4.1	OLS	−.0007	.9902		.9672	.0121	2.3323
		(.0015)	(.0183)				
4.2	OLS	.0007*		.9965*	.9999	.0007	1.6959
		(.0001)		(.0011)			
4.2	IV	.0008		.9964	.9679	.0122	2.2106
		(.0014)		(.0181)			
4.3	OLS	.0007*	.0072	.9896	.9999	.0007	1.6811
		(.0001)	(.0061)	(.0060)			
4.3	IV	.0004	.2471	.7433	.9684	.0119	2.2520
		(.0015)	(.3447)	(.3443)			

Note: * denotes significantly different from 0 (for a) or from 1 (for c) at the 5% level.

past history of spot exchange rates, forward exchange rates, and interest rates. The increasingly large volume of literature on efficient markets makes it clear that 'news' is all important in changing exchange-rate expectations and that news about the current account is liable to be among the most important. The question of expectations formation is dealt with at more length in the following section. Suffice it to say here that even if markets are not efficient, the effect of news on expectations must be fully recognized in any model of exchange-rate determination.

6. The Role of Expectations in Exchange-Rate Determination

As is evident from equation (4) in section 3 above, with high speculative and arbitrage elasticities, the effect of the expected future spot rate on the current spot rate will be almost one-for-one, independently of how those expectations are formed. In a market that is not subject to capital controls or infinitely elastic exchange-market intervention, the exchange rate is likely to move quickly to reflect revised expectations due to new information or a reappraisal of old information.

Appraisal of information must rely on a model of what is important. If incorrect models are used by market participants, then there will be over- or under-reactions to certain news and thus the exchange market will appear to be inefficient. However, whether or not the exchange market is efficient, it is interesting to assess what types of information are important in causing changes in the exchange rate and what is the magnitude of the effect on the exchange rate for a unit unexpected change in an economic variable. If the market is inefficient, however, one would not believe that such marginal responses would continue to be stable over time.

The two types of news that have been commonly examined have been news about current-account balances or trade balances (Longworth, 1980b; Dornbusch, 1980a; and Hakkio, 1980); and news about changes in interest-rate differentials (Longworth, 1980b; Dornbusch, 1980a; and Frenkel, 1980). In addition, Dornbusch studied cyclical variables and Longworth studied new foreign currency bond issues.

Longworth concluded that, at least for some years of the current float, surprises about interest-rate differentials, the Canadian trade balance, and new foreign currency bond issues had significant effects on changes in the exchange rate. In particular, an increase in the interest differential in favour of Canada causes the Canadian dollar to *appreciate*. Frenkel (1980), on the other hand, in his study of the U.S. dollar/pound, dollar/franc, and dollar/DM rates, noted that if interest rates primarily reflect expected inflation, then an increase in the interest-rate differential will cause a *depreciation* of the currency. This indeed is the relationship he found for the three exchange rates he studied.

Using the covered interest-parity theorem, the theory of the term structure of exchange rates and the theory of the term structure of interest rates, one can derive an expression for the unexpected change in the interest-rate differential:

$$r_t^{30} - r_t^{*30} - E_{t-1}\left\{r_t^{30} - r_t^{*30}\right\}$$
$$= f_t^{30} - s_t \quad - E_{t-1}\left\{f_t^{30} - s_t\right\}$$
$$= f_t^{30} - s_t \quad - E_{t-1}\left\{f_{t-1}^{60} - s_{t-1} - (f_{t-1}^{30} - s_{t-1})\right\}$$
$$= f_t^{30} - s_t \quad - f_{t-1}^{60} \quad + f_{t-1}^{30}$$

In Table 5, we repeat three of the equations from the tests of efficiency in Table 3 with the addition of the above innovation in the interest-rate differential. With the exception of the two shorter periods for equation 5.1, the results may be summarized as follows: there is an economically significant but statistically insignificant appreciation in the value of the Canadian dollar for an unexpected increase in the interest-rate differential. Perhaps in an equation including news in other economic variables, a statistically significant coefficient could be obtained. There is room for further research in this area.

One interpretation that could be put on the results in Table 5 is the following. Although there is an economically large response to

Table 5
THE EFFECT OF INNOVATIONS IN INTEREST RATES
ON THE EXCHANGE RATE

Equation 5.1: $s_t = a_1 + a_2 f_{t-1}^{30} + a_4 \{ f_t^{30} - s_t - f_{t-1}^{60} + f_{t-1}^{30} \}$

Period	a_1	a_2	a_3	a_4	$\bar{R}^2$ / S.E.E.	D.W.
70.07 − 80.04	.0006 (.0013)	1.0058 (.0174)		−.8703 (1.2754)	.9661 (.0121)	2.1387
71.01 − 80.04	.0009 (.0014)	1.0050 (.0179)		−.7879 (1.3140)	.9662 (.0124)	2.1530
77.01 − 80.04	.0143 (.0062)	.9102** (.0493)		1.1481 (2.2649)	.9004 (.0141)	2.1613
78.08 − 80.04	.1311* (.0339)	.1671* (.2191)		3.1121 (2.4026)	.1639 (.0135)	1.9169

Equation 5.2: $(s_t - s_{t-1}) = a_1 + a_2 \, (f_{t-1}^{30} - s_{t-1}) + a_4 \, (f_t^{30} - s_t - f_{t-1}^{60} + f_{t-1}^{30})$

Period	a_1	a_2	a_3	a_4	$\bar{R}^2$ / S.E.E.	D.W.
70.07 − 80.04	.0014 (.0011)	− .3184** (.7191)		−1.1804 (1.2680)	0 (.0119)	2.1537
71.01 − 80.04	.0017 (.0012)	− .4310** (.7413)		−1.1085 (1.3012)	0 (.0122)	2.1784
77.01 − 80.04	.0042* (.0025)	− .2120 (2.2128)		− .2525 (2.6573)	0 (.0146)	2.1228
78.08 − 80.04	.0005 (.0037)	−9.0638 (5.0197)		−5.6403 (3.7637)	.0642 (.0164)	2.2163

Equation 5.3: $s_t = a_1 + a_2 f_{t-1}^{30} + a_3 s_{t-1} + a_4 \{ f_t^{30} - s_t - f_{t-1}^{60} + f_{t-1}^{30} \}$

Period	a_1	a_2	a_3	a_4	$\bar{R}^2$ / S.E.E.	D.W.
70.07 − 80.04	.0014 (.0014)	− .3107** (.7337)	1.3118** (.7308)	−1.1844 (1.2754)	.9667 (.0120)	2.1561
71.01 − 80.04	.0017 (.0014)	− .4354** (.7581)	1.4348** (.7549)	−1.1062 (1.3093)	.9670 (.0122)	2.1772
77.01 − 80.04	.0383* (.0090)	−8.9992* (2.9304)	9.7387* (2.8796)	−3.2255 (2.3819)	.9223 (.0124)	2.0903
78.08 − 80.04	.1170* (.0333)	−6.6193 (3.9945)	6.8684 (4.0373)	− .8255 (3.2527)	.1594 (.0128)	2.0376

Note: * denotes significantly different from hypothesized value ($a_1 = 0$, $a_2 = 1$, $a_3 = 0$, $a_4 = 0$) at the 5% level (** at the 10% level).

changes in interest-rate differentials, an increase in the interest-rate differential (forward premium) has lagged effects in that the exchange rate has a tendency to continue appreciating with a positive interest-rate differential. Thus the market might be inefficient because either:

a. The initial response to a change in the interest-rate differential is too small (and thus there needs to be continuing effect), or

b. The initial response is correct, but the total response is too large.

This latter type of inefficiency could result from, for example, the belief of the market in a flow model (rather than a stock model) of exchange-rate determination.

7. The Effect of the 'Real' Exchange Rate on the Composition of Output

If the exchange market is inefficient, then the incorrect price signal will cause a misallocation of resources across countries and across industries within a country. Since the effect of exchange-rate changes on trade across countries has been extensively examined elsewhere, this section will consider only the latter subject — in a traded/non-traded output framework. The work presented here is an extension of Freedman and Longworth (1980), where the model is developed in more detail.

In a perfectly competitive industry, a rise in the output price relative to the price of inputs of an industry will cause it to move along its supply curve and produce more output. Since traded outputs are by definition able to be sold on world markets, their price will be strongly influenced (perhaps determined) by the foreign price, which will be primarily a function of the world price of raw materials (PRM) and foreign unit labour costs (ULC^*). Since raw materials may be inputs as well as outputs, there is no theoretical presumption regarding the effect of their price on output supply. However, since Canada is a net exporter of raw materials, an increase in raw materials prices will increase the average output price more than the average input price. Supply should therefore be an increasing function of the domestic price of raw materials ($PRM \cdot S$) relative to domestic unit labour costs (ULC) and a decreasing function of ULC relative to $ULC^* \cdot S$ where S is the exchange rate.[5]

If labour is the only variable input in the non-traded output sector, then labour resources will be transferred between sectors when the price of traded output rises relative to unit labour costs, and simultaneously the composition of output will shift towards the traded output sector.

If markets could be completely characterized by perfectly competitive behaviour in the short run, this would be the end of the story. However, the short-run behaviour in many industries is characterized by setting the price and producing the quantity demanded. Thus relative shifts in the demand schedules for the two sectors caused primarily by changes in foreign income (proxied by U.S. real GNP:GNPUS) will cause a change in the composition of output. Over the longer run, however, supply factors will likely dominate; that is, it is only short-run deviations in demand that are hypothesized to have an effect. A time-trend is therefore entered in the regression to represent trend demand.

The results are presented in Table 6. In equation 6.1, the traded output sector is defined as the output (real domestic product) of goods industries plus the complementary industries of transporting and retailing those goods. Government is excluded from the non-traded output sector on the grounds that its output is largely policy determined. In the last three equations, only subsets of the traded-goods producing industries themselves are included in the numerator, and all other industries are included in the denominator. In equation 6.2, agriculture and fishing are excluded from the numerator since their output is a function more of climate and government regulation (in the case of fishing and agricultural products marketed through certain marketing boards). Equation 6.3 examines manufacturing alone, and equation 6.4 considers the five major traded-goods industries.

Table 6
THE EFFECT OF THE 'REAL' EXCHANGE RATE
ON THE COMPOSITION OF OUTPUT

$$LN\left(\frac{RDPTR}{RDPNTR}\right) = a + bLN\left(\frac{PRM \cdot S}{ULC}\right) + cLN\left(\frac{ULC}{ULC^* \cdot S}\right) + dTIME + eLN(GNPUS) + \rho u_{t-1}$$

Equation	a	b	c	d	e	ρ	$\frac{\bar{R}^2}{S.E.E.}$	D.W.
6.1	−2.538*	.088*	−.108	−.0086*	.381*	.561*	.971	1.87
	(1.222)	(.027)	(.064)	(.0013)	(.155)	(.145)	(.0111)	
6.2	−4.534*	.129*	−.087	−.0092*	.625*	.656*	.975	1.52
	(1.081)	(.024)	(.059)	(.0011)	(.140)	(.135)	(.0091)	
6.3	−3.806*	.125*	−.101**	−.0072*	.532*	.565*	.960	1.57
	(.989)	(.020)	(.052)	(.0010)	(.126)	(.141)	(.0090)	
6.4	−4.110*	.113*	−.126*	−.0086*	.597*	.489*	.974	1.53
	(.900)	(.017)	(.045)	(.0009)	(.114)	(.167)	(.0087)	

Note: It is the definition of the dependent variable that differs across equations. The following definitions are used:

RDPTR: Real domestic product index for: RDPNTR: Real domestic product index for:

Equation
6.1   Agriculture, forestry, fishing, mining, manufacturing, transportation of goods, retailing of goods.   Everything else excluding government.
6.2   Manufacturing, forestry, mining.   Everything else.
6.3   Manufacturing.   Everything else.
6.4   Agriculture, forestry, fishing, mining, manufacturing.   Everything else.

  * denotes significantly different from 0 at the 5% level.
 ** denotes significantly different from 0 at the 10% level.

The results are fairly uniform across equations. The price of raw materials relative to unit labour costs is highly significant with an elasticity of about .12. The relative unit labour cost term (or the inverse of the 'real' exchange rate) has an elasticity of about .10 and is significant (at least at 10 per cent) in the latter two equations. The foreign demand term is also statistically significant.

The results imply that holding foreign prices and domestic labour costs constant in the short run, an increase of 1 per cent in the exchange rate will change the ratio of output in the traded output sector to the non-traded output sector by about 0.22 per cent. Thus it appears that inefficiency in the exchange market could lead to a significantly large reallocation of resources domestically, which would be eventually reversed as the exchange rate returned to a level reflecting 'fundamentals'. Further research would be necessary to measure the cost of such resource shifts to the Canadian economy in the 1970s.

Conclusions

This paper considered the empirical validity of a number of assumptions that are frequently made in models of exchange-rate determination. Short-run purchasing-power parity, efficient markets, and the empirical approach to the modern theory of forward exchange-rate determination were rejected as useful approaches to explaining the behaviour of the Canadian–U.S. exchange rate in the 1970s. On the other hand, covered interest parity appeared to be a good approximation to reality, but of course it does not explain the level of the spot rate.

Even though the efficient market model is rejected, it may be true that the forward rate is, at least up to a small risk premium, the market's expected future spot rate. However, given that there is no independent measure of market expectations, this may be an untestable proposition. The rapidity with which the market responds to new information tends to indicate a very highly elastic speculative schedule. However, the inefficiency of the market that was found may indicate myopic rather than forward-looking behaviour. It may be that the speculative schedule for long maturities (say greater than six months) is not very elastic with respect to deviations from the expected future spot rate. In terms of the general model presented in Section 3, perhaps something is lost by aggregating over all the forward markets and treating only one speculative schedule. If there are institutional or legal constraints on long-term exposure in the foreign exchange market, then the 'long-term' speculative schedule may not be very elastic and thus may be very different from the 'short-term' speculative schedule.

With a highly elastic speculative schedule, even if only at the short end, 'news' is going to cause most of the variation in the exchange rate in the short run. Any empirical exchange-rate model that attempts to explain more than the broad trends in market movements must thus determine what information is considered to be important by the market. The equations presented in this paper concentrated on the role of the interest-rate differential. A careful examination of continuing level effects of the trade balance or lagged effects of trade-balance announcements would be a useful extension of the work presented here.

As market participants revise their opinions of the effect of economic variables on the exchange rate, as would be necessary if the world were moving to rational expectations, coefficients in exchange-rate equations will shift. Thus empirical work on exchange-rate equations is likely to be only suggestive, never definitive.

Inefficiency in the exchange market causes improper price signals to be sent forth and so resources are misallocated across countries and between the traded output and non-traded output sectors of an economy. These effects may be economically large.

Appendix

The Modern Theory of Foreign
Exchange With Stock Demands

Following McCormick (1977), let A, G, S, and T represent respectively the excess demands for foreign exchange for covered interest arbitrage, official intervention, speculation, and trade (including long-term capital flows).[6] These four demands are 'pure' demands in the sense that they represent the demands by persons, firms, or governments acting in a particular role. Thus we consider pure covered interest arbitrage, pure intervention, pure speculation (using forward market and converting gains in the spot market), and pure trade (where no exchange risk is carried or, in the case of long-term capital flows, assumed not to be covered).

Subscripts before letters denote the dates that contracts are entered into; subscripts after letters denote the date of maturity of the contract.

Equilibrium in the spot market on day 0 is expressed as follows:

$$oAo + oSo + oTo + oGo = 0. \tag{1}$$

Equilibrium in each of the i-day forward markets on day 0 is expressed as follows:

$$oAi + oSi + oTi + oGi = 0 \quad i = 1, \ldots, N. \tag{2}$$

Summing over the forward markets to the maximum maturity (N days):

$$\sum_{i=1}^{N} oAi + \sum_{i=1}^{N} oSi + \sum_{i=1}^{N} oTi + \sum_{i=1}^{N} oGi = 0. \tag{3}$$

Arbitrageurs enter into an offsetting forward transaction for every spot transaction and thus:

$$oAo = -\sum_{i=1}^{N} oAi. \tag{4}$$

Speculators are assumed to convert the proceeds of their maturing forward contracts in the spot market:

$$oSo = -\sum_{i=-N}^{-1} iSo. \tag{5}$$

Adding equations (1) and (3) with the substitutions (4) and (5) gives:

$$\sum_{i=1}^{N} oSi - \sum_{i=-N}^{-1} iSo + \sum_{i=0}^{N} oTi + \sum_{i=0}^{N} oGi = 0. \tag{6}$$

The implications of flows on stocks are now considered. The change in the stock of net (uncovered) speculative positions is given by:

$$\Delta K = \sum_{i=1}^{N} oSi - \sum_{i=-N}^{-1} iSo. \tag{7}$$

Substituting (7) into (6) gives:

$$\Delta K + \sum_{i=0}^{N} oTi + \sum_{i=0}^{N} oGi = 0, \tag{8}$$

which implies:

$$Ko = -\sum_{j=-\infty}^{o} \sum_{i=0}^{N} jTj+i - \sum_{j=-\infty}^{o} \sum_{i=0}^{N} jGj+i. \tag{9}$$

This says that the stock of speculation against the domestic currency is equal to the negative of the net sum of all past and present trade contracts and long-term capital flows and official intervention.[7]

The demand for the stock of net speculative contracts maturing on day i (K_i) is a function of the difference between the log of the expected spot rate on day i (s_i^e) and the log of the current forward rate for day i ($_o f_i$) and appropriate wealth and risk variables:

$$K_i = K_i(s_i^e - {}_o f_i, \dots). \tag{10}$$

Now,

$$K = \Sigma K_i = \Sigma K_i(s_i^e - {}_o f_i, \dots). \tag{11}$$

Since covered interest arbitrage together with a smooth term structure of interest rates will tend to make $_o f_i$ smooth over i and since s_i^e is also likely to be smooth over i, equation (11) can be approximated by choosing a small number of i, and may be *very roughly* approximated by choosing the 90-day maturity for which the plurality of contracts are written:

$$K = K(s_{90}^e - {}_0f_{90}, \dots). \tag{12}$$

The stock of arbitrage capital, K_A, can be related to the stock of speculative capital, K, by taking a double summation on equation (2) recalling that the maximum length of forward contracts is N:

$$K_A = -\sum_{i=-N+1}^{0} \sum_{j=1}^{i+N} iAj = \sum_{i=-N+1}^{0} \sum_{j=1}^{i+N} iSj + \sum_{i=-N+1}^{0} \sum_{j=1}^{i+N} iTj$$

$$+ \sum_{i=-N+1}^{0} \sum_{j=1}^{i+N} iGj. \tag{13}$$

The double summation on iSj is exactly K since it accounts for all the speculative contracts in existence. The double summation on iTj is the stock of forward cover for future trade. Similarly the double summation on iGj is the stock of forward intervention.

The demand for arbitrage capital for contracts maturing on day i (K_{Ai}) is a function of wealth,[8] risk, and deviations from covered interest arbitrage $({}_0r_i^* - {}_0r_i + s_0 - {}_0f_i)$ where r and r_i^* are the domestic and foreign interest rates respectively, expressed as fractions for the holding period.

Now

$$K_A = \sum_i K_{Ai} = K_{Ai}({}_0r_i^* - {}_0r_i + s_0 - {}_0f_i, \dots). \tag{14}$$

Again, assuming smoothness over deviations from covered interest parity and a plurality of contracts at the 90-day maturity, we can approximate the demand for arbitrage capital by:

$$K_A = K_A({}_0r_{90}^* - {}_0r_{90} + s_0 - {}_0f_{90}, \dots). \tag{15}$$

The demand for the stock of forward cover for future trade K_T can be represented by the demand function:

$$K_T = \sum_{i=-N+1}^{0} \sum_{j=1}^{i+N} iTj({}_ip_j - {}_if_j - {}_ip_j^*, \dots), \tag{16}$$

where ${}_ip_j$ and ${}_ip_j^*$ are the logs of contract prices at time i for payments at time j in the domestic and foreign country respectively. Since past contracts must be taken as given, and taking prices as given in the short run, K_T is a function of the vectors of current forward rates ${}_0f_i$. Again we concentrate on ${}_0f_{90}$ to provide an approximation

$$K_T = K_T({}_0f_{90}, \dots). \tag{17}$$

Taking K_G, the stock of forward intervention, as an exogenous variable and using the notation:

$$r^* = {}_o r_{90}^*$$
$$r = {}_o r_{90}$$
$$s = s_o$$
$$f = {}_o f_{90}$$

and assuming the arbitrage and speculative schedules are linear through the origin with slopes k_1, k_2 (>0) respectively, we may write

$$K_A = k_1(r^* - r - s + f) \tag{18}$$

$$K_A - K_T(f) - K_G = K = k_2(s^e - f) \tag{19}$$

$$s = s^e - (r - r^*) - \frac{K_A}{k_1} - (\frac{K_A - K_T(f) - K_G}{k_2})$$

$$= s^e - (r - r^*) - K_A (\frac{k_1 + k_2}{k_1 k_2}) + \frac{K_T(f) + K_G}{k_2}. \tag{20}$$

Since the stock of arbitrage capital is identically the stock of short-term capital, this says that the spot rate is the expected spot rate discounted by the interest-rate differential and adjusted by a linear combination of the stock of short-term capital, the stock of forward cover for future trade, and the stock of forward intervention.

Notes

* The views expressed in this paper are those of the author and no responsibility for them should be attributed to the Bank of Canada. The author would like to thank Judy DiMillo and Kim McPhail for valuable research assistance and Kevin Clinton, John Conder, Chuck Freedman, Paul Masson, and Doug Purvis for useful comments.

[1] If $\frac{K}{W} = a + b(r - r^*)$, $F = \Delta K = a\Delta W + bW\Delta(r - r^*) + b(r - r^*)_{-1} \Delta W$, which is only roughly

approximated by $F = a\Delta W + c\Delta(r - r^*)$ since W is variable.

[2] See Masson (1980) on stability of portfolio balance models.

[3] The evidence for Canada is that intervention has been of the leaning-against-the-wind variety (Longworth (1980a), estimated over $1970 - 1977$) rather than being directed to a target exchange rate.

[4] Theoretical justifications for risk premia are discussed in Frankel (1979), Dornbusch (1980b) and Buiter (1980).

[5] The price of output, P_Q, can be represented by

$$P_Q = (PRM \cdot S)^\alpha (ULC^* \cdot S)^\beta (ULC)^{1 - \alpha - \beta},$$

where domestic unit labour costs are allowed to affect prices in the cases of imperfect substitutes. The price of inputs, P_I, can be represented by

$$P_I = (PRM \cdot S)^{1 - \gamma} ULC^\gamma.$$

Then $\frac{P_Q}{P_I} = (\frac{PRM \cdot S}{ULC})^{\alpha + \gamma - 1} (\frac{ULC}{ULC^* \cdot S})^{-\beta}$.

[6] In this context, long-term capital flows are transactions in debt or equity instruments with a term to maturity longer than the longest operative forward market (N days). As $N \to \infty$ all capital flows are treated alike.

[7] If Ko is at the end of a quarter, then the change in K over the previous quarter is given by:

$$\Delta_{90} K = - \sum_{j=-89}^{o} \sum_{i=0}^{N} jTj+i - \sum_{j=-89}^{o} \sum_{i=0}^{N} jGj+i.$$

If there is no forward official intervention ($jGj+i=0 \ \forall i>0$) and trade contracts are spread evenly over the course of the next two quarters, then:

$$\Delta_{90} K \approx LTCq_0 - \frac{1}{2}(CAq_0 + CAq_1) - Gq_0,$$

where q_0 represents the quarter from day -89 to day 0 and q_1 is the following quarter, LTC represents net long-term capital inflows, CA represents the current-account balance, and G represents net official monetary movements.

[8] If the wealth variable is money plus bonds plus K_A, then this equation is similar to the equations for net foreign assets found in international portfolio balance models.

References

Arndt, Sven W. (1968) "International Short Term Capital Moveme,zs: A Distributed Lag Model of Speculation in Foreign Exchange." *Econometrica* 36 (January): 59–70.

Bank of Canada. (1980) "Short-Term Interest Rates and the Exchange Rate." *Bank of Canada Review* (January): 3–11.

Beenstock, Michael. (1978) *The Foreign Exchanges: Theory, Modelling and Policy*. London: Macmillan.

Beenstock, Michael. (1979) "Arbitrage, Speculation, and Official Forward Intervention: The Cases of Sterling and the Canadian Dollar." *Review of Economics and Statistics* 61 (February): 135–39.

Beenstock, Michael and Bell, Steven. (1979) "A Quarterly Econometric Model of the Capital Account in the U.K. Balance of Payments." *The Manchester School of Economic and Social Studies* 47 (March): 33–62.

Black, Stanley W. (1968) "Theory and Policy Analysis of Short-Term Movements in the Balance of Payments." *Yale Economic Essays* 8 (Spring): 5–78.

Black, Stanley W. (1972a) "International Monetary Markets and Flexible Exchange Rates." Board of Governors of the Federal Reserve System, Staff Economic Studies, No. 70. Washington, D.C.

Black, Stanley W. (1972b) "The Use of Rational Expectations in Models of Speculation." *Review of Economics and Statistics* 54 (May): 161–65.

Branson, William H. (1968) *Financial Capital Flows in the U.S. Balance of Payments*. Amsterdam: North-Holland.

Branson, William H. and Hill, Raymond D., Jr. (1971) *Capital Movements in the OECD Area: An Econometric Analysis*. OECD Occasional Studies. Paris: OECD.

Bryant, Ralph C. (1975) "Empirical Research on Financial Capital Flows." In *International Trade and Finance: Frontiers for Research*, edited by Peter B. Kenen, pp. 321–62. Cambridge: Cambridge University Press.

Bryant, Ralph C. and Hendershott, Patric H. (1970) *Financial Capital Flows in the Balance of Payments of the United States: An Exploratory Empirical Study*. Princeton Studies in International Finance No. 25. Princeton, N.J.: Princeton University, Dept. of Economics, International Finance Section.

Buiter, Willem H. (1980) "Implications for the Adjustment Process of International Asset Risks: Exchange Controls, Intervention and Policy Risks, and Sovereign Risk." NBER Working Paper No. 516. Cambridge, Mass.: National Bureau of Economic Research.

Caves, Richard E. and Reuber, Grant L. (1971) *Capital Transfers and Economic Policy: Canada, 1951–1962*. Cambridge, Mass.: Harvard University Press.

Choudhry, Nanda K.; Kotowitz, Yehuda; Sawyer, John A.; and Winder, John W.L. (1972) *The TRACE Econometric Model of the Canadian Economy*. Toronto: University of Toronto Press.

Dooley, Michael P. (1974) "A Model of Arbitrage and Short-Term Capital Flows." International Finance Discussion Paper No. 14. Washington, D.C.: Federal Reserve Board.

Dornbusch, Rudiger. (1976) "Expectations and Exchange Rate Dynamics." *Journal of Political Economy* 84 (December): 1161–76.

Dornbusch, Rudiger. (1978) "Monetary Policy Under Exchange-Rate Flexibility." In *Managed Exchange-Rate Flexibility: The Recent Experience*. FRB Boston Conference Series No. 20. Boston: Federal Reserve Bank of Boston.

Dornbusch, Rudiger. (1980a) "Exchange Rate Economics: Where Do We Stand?" *Brookings Papers on Economic Activity* 1: 143–205.

Dornbusch, Rudiger. (1980b) "Exchange Risk and the Macroeconomics of Exchange Rate Determination." NBER Working Paper No. 493. Cambridge, Mass.: National Bureau of Economic Research.

Dornbusch, Rudiger and Fischer, Stanley. (1980) "Exchange Rates and the Current Account." *American Economic Review* 70 (December): 960–71.

Frankel, Jeffrey A. (1979) "The Diversifiability of Exchange Risk." *Journal of International Economics* 9 (August): 379–93.

Frankel, Jeffrey A. (1980) "Tests of Rational Expectations in the Forward Exchange Market." *Southern Economic Journal* 46 (April): 1083–1101.

Freedman, Charles. (1973) "Components vs. Aggregates: An Aspect of the Aggregation Problem." Mimeo. Bank of Canada.

Freedman, Charles. (1974) *The Foreign Currency Business of the Canadian Banks: An Econometric Study*. Bank of Canada Staff Study No. 10. Ottawa: Bank of Canada.

Freedman, Charles. (1979) "The Canadian Dollar, 1971–76: An Exploratory Investigation of Short-Run Movements." NBER Working Paper No. 380. Cambridge, Mass.: National Bureau of Economic Research.

Freedman, Charles and Longworth, David. (1980) "Some Aspects of the Canadian Experience With Flexible Exchange Rates in the 1970s." Bank of Canada Technical Report No. 20. Ottawa: Bank of Canada. See also NBER Working Paper No. 535.

Freedman, Charles; Longworth, David; and Masson, Paul. (1977) "The Role of U.S. Interest Rates in Canadian Interest-Rate Equations: An Exploratory Analysis." Bank of Canada Technical Report No. 9. Ottawa: Bank of Canada.

Frenkel, Jacob A. (1980) "Flexible Exchange Rates in the 1970s." NBER Working Paper No. 450. Cambridge, Mass.: National Bureau of Economic Research.

Gaab, Werner. (1980) "On the Role of Interest Arbitrage, Speculation, and Commercial Hedging in the Determination of the Forward Exchange Rate: The Case of the Flexible German Mark, 1974–1977." In *The Economics of Flexible Exchange Rates*, edited by Helmut Frisch and Gerhard Schwödiauer, pp. 345–77. Proceedings of a Conference at the Institute for Advanced Studies, Vienna, 29–31 March 1978. Berlin: Duncker & Humblot.

Girton, Lance and Roper, Don. (1977) "A Monetary Model of Exchange Market Pressure Applied to the Postwar Canadian Experience." *American Economic Review* 67 (September): 537–48.

Haas, Richard D. (1974) "More Evidence on the Role of Speculation in the Canadian Forward Exchange Markets." *Canadian Journal of Economics* 7 (August): 496–501.

Haas, Richard D. and Alexander, William E. (1979) "A Model of Exchange Rates and Capital Flows: The Canadian Floating Rate Experience." *Journal of Money, Credit and Banking* 11 (November): 467–82.

Hakkio, Craig. (1980) "Exchange Rates and the Balance of Trade." Mimeo. Chicago: Northwestern University.

Hawkins, Robert G. (1968) "Stabilizing Forces and Canadian Exchange-Rate Fluctuations." *The Bulletin* (New York University Institute of Finance) No. 50–51 (July): 28–65.

Helliwell, John. (1969) "A Structural Model of the Foreign Exchange Market." *Canadian Journal of Economics* 2 (February): 90–105.

Helliwell, John and Maxwell, Tom. (1972) "Short-Term Capital Flows and the Foreign Exchange Market." *Canadian Journal of Economics* 5 (May): 199–214.

Hodgson, John S. and Holmes, Alexander B. (1977) "Structural Stability of International Capital Mobility: An Analysis of Short-Term U.S.–Canadian Bank Claims." *Review of Economics and Statistics* 59 (November): 465–73.

Hodjera, Zoran. (1973) "International Short-Term Capital Movements: A Survey of Theory and Empirical Analysis." *International Monetary Fund Staff Papers* 20 (November): 683–740.

Hodjera, Zoran. (1976) "Alternative Approaches in the Analysis of International Capital Movements: A Case Study of Austria and France." *International Monetary Fund Staff Papers* 23 (November): 598–623.

Hutton, John P. (1977) "A Model of Short-Term Capital Movements, the Foreign Exchange Market and Official Intervention in the UK, 1963–1970." *Review of Economic Studies* 44 (February): 31–42.

Kenen, Peter B. (1978) *A Model of the U.S. Balance of Payments*. Lexington, Mass: D.C. Heath.

Kesselman, Jonathan. (1971) "The Role of Speculation in Forward-Rate Determination: The Canadian Flexible Dollar 1953–1960." *Canadian Journal of Economics* 4 (August): 279–98.

Knight, Malcolm. (1976) "A Monetary Approach to the Determination of the Floating Canadian Dollar: Some Empirical Results." Paper presented at the Canadian Economics Association meetings, Laval University.

Kohlhagen, Steven W. (1977) "The Stability of Exchange Rate Expectations and Canadian Capital Flows." *Journal of Finance* 32 (December): 1657–69.

Kohlhagen, Steven W. (1978) "The Behavior of Foreign Exchange Markets — A Critical Survey of the Empirical Literature." Salomon Brothers Center for the Study of Financial Institutions, Monograph Series in Finance and Economics 1978–3. New York: New York University, Graduate School of Business Administration.

Kohlhagen, Steven W. (1979) "Testing for the Role of Speculation in the Forward Exchange Market: Some Problems If There Are Fisherian Expectations." *Review of Economics and Statistics* 61 (November): 608–10.

Kouri, Pentti J.K. and Porter, Michael G. (1974) "International Capital Flows and Portfolio Equilibrium." *Journal of Political Economy* 82 (May/June): 443–67.

Lee, Chung H. (1977) "A Survey of the Literature on the Determinants of Foreign Portfolio Investments in the United States." *Weltwirtschaftliches Archiv* 113 (Heft 3): 552–69.

Levi, Maurice D. (1978) "The Weekend Game: Clearing House vs. Federal Funds." *Canadian Journal of Economics* 11 (November): 750–57.

Levich, Richard M. (1979) "On the Efficiency of Markets for Foreign Exchange." In *International Economic Policy: Theory and Evidence*, edited by Rudiger Dornbusch and Jacob A. Frenkel, pp. 246–67. Baltimore: Johns Hopkins University Press.

Longworth, David. (1979) "Floating Exchange Rates: The Canadian Experience." Ph.D. dissertation, Massachusetts Institute of Technology.

Longworth, David. (1980a) "Canadian Intervention in the Foreign Exchange Market: A Note." *Review of Economics and Statistics* 62 (May): 284–87.

Longworth, David. (1980b) "An Empirical Efficient Markets Model of Exchange Rate Determination." Mimeo. Bank of Canada.

Longworth, David. (1981) "Testing the Efficiency of the Canadian-U.S. Exchange Market Under the Assumption of No Risk Premium." *Journal of Finance* 36 (March): 43–49.

Martin, John P. and Masson, Paul. (1979) "Exchange Rates and Portfolio Balance." NBER Working Paper No. 377. Cambridge, Mass.: National Bureau of Economic Research.

Masson, Paul. (1980) "Dynamic Stability of Portfolio Balance Models of the Exchange Rate." Mimeo. Bank of Canada.

McCallum, Bennett T. (1977) "The Role of Speculation in the Canadian Forward Exchange Market: Some Estimates Assuming Rational Expectations." *Review of Economics and Statistics* 59 (May): 145–51.

McCallum, Bennett T. (1979) "Testing for the Role of Speculation in the Forward Exchange Market: A Reply." *Review of Economics and Statistics* 61 (November): 611–12.

McCormick, Frank. (1977) "A Multiperiod Theory of Forward Exchange." *Journal of International Economics* 7 (August): 269–82.

Ormerod, Paul A. (1980) "The Forward Exchange Rate for Sterling and the Efficiency of Expectations." *Weltwirtschaftliches Archiv* 116 (Heft 2): 205–24.

Pippenger, John. (1978) "Interest Arbitrage Between Canada and the United States: A New Perspective." *Canadian Journal of Economics* 11 (May): 183–93.

Powrie, T.L. (1964) "Short-Term Capital Movements and the Flexible Canadian Exchange Rate, 1953–1961." *Canadian Journal of Economics and Political Science* 30 (February): 76–94.

Rhomberg, Rudolf R. (1960) "Canada's Foreign Exchange Market: A Quarterly Model." *International Monetary Fund Staff Papers* 7 (April): 439–56.

Rhomberg, Rudolf R. (1964) "A Model of the Canadian Economy Under Fixed and Fluctuating Exchange Rates." *Journal of Political Economy* 72 (February): 1–31.

Sargen, Nicholas P. (1977) "Exchange Rate Flexibility and Demand for Money." *Journal of Finance* 32 (May): 531–44.

Spraos, John. (1959) "Speculation, Arbitrage and Sterling." *Economic Journal* 69 (March): 1–21.

Stoll, Hans R. (1968) "An Empirical Study of the Forward Exchange Market Under Fixed and Flexible Exchange Rate Systems." *Canadian Journal of Economics* 1 (February): 55–78.

Tryon, Ralph. (1979) "Testing for Rational Expectations in Foreign Exchange Markets." International Finance Discussion Paper No. 139. Washington, D.C.: Federal Reserve Board.

Tsiang, S.C. (1959) "The Theory of Forward Exchange and Effects of Government Intervention on the Forward Exchange Market." *International Monetary Fund Staff Papers* 7 (April): 75–106.

Comment

by
Pierre Fortin

David Longworth's paper nicely summarizes and extends the empirical evidence he and Freedman have been generating in the last two years on Canada–United States exchange rates. The seventy-reference bibliography and the wealth of subscripts, superscripts, prescripts, and postscripts testify that it is a good academic paper. At the same time, the rather skimpy section on the policy implications is typical of the kind of papers Bank of Canada staff are constrained to write by their very functions. This has come to me as a slight disappointment given that we are holding a round table on *economic policy* and given Longworth's competence in this subject area.

I shall therefore first examine the credibility of the empirical evidence adduced by Longworth on purchasing-power parity, interest-rate parity, and efficiency in the Canada–United States exchange markets. Secondly, I shall attempt to make up for the paper's modesty in the policy area and concentrate on some of its implications for intervention policy and for the conduct of monetary policy in Canada. Let me emphasize that I am no exchange market freak and that I shall rather speak as a potential user of Longworth's results.

The paper is strongest in its short demonstration that the purchasing-power-parity hypothesis is not useful as the sole short-run predictor of the exchange rates, but that (covered) interest-rate parity holds up to a (macro-economically) small magnitude of about twenty-five basis points (equation (1)). However, I have less confidence in his econometric evidence on the high elasticity of the arbitrage schedule (equation (2)), because it is hard to know if the right-hand variable (short-term capital) is adequately measured, and because the regression essentially fits a straight line in a scatter diagram of prices and quantities, so that the result cannot be interpreted properly.

Nevertheless, the verdict in favour of interest-rate parity is clear. This is particularly helpful for Canadian macro-economists who can now more or less take for granted that:

$$s = f + r^* - r, \tag{1}$$

and use this information in conjunction with aggregate demand and supply equations that depend so crucially on the spot exchange rate.

However, a complete model of the Canadian macro economy requires a further piece of information, namely how the forward exchange rate (f) is determined. That is precisely where Longworth's problems begin.

It is customary to *assume* in this context that the speculative schedule is highly elastic so that the forward exchange rate approximately measures the expected exchange rate ($\hat{s}$):

$$f = \hat{s}. \tag{2}$$

As a result, the problem is transformed into discovering how exchange-rate expectations are formed. One option, then, is to model expectations formation explicitly. This is what Freedman did in his paper presented at last year's Conference on Issues in Canadian Public Policy.[1] His model naturally assumed an adaptive expectations mechanism in which the long-run expected exchange rate was a function of variables such as relative GNE deflators, net long-term capital inflow, the terms of trade, relative unemployment rates, relative potential GNPs, and surprises in the current-account position. The problem with Freedman's approach, however, is that the weights attributed by market participants to these various influences do not seem to be stable over time. I take this as indirect evidence that the market is uncertain about the true model of short-run exchange-rate determination (just as Bank of Canada and other economists are) and/or uncertain about the values and lag structures that should be attributed to each determinant of the exchange rate.

The rational expectations hypothesis makes *precisely the opposite* assumption that market participants know the true reduced form for the exchange rate and the true values of the parameters involved. If they use that information efficiently, then their forecasts of the future value of the exchange rate (s_1) will be unbiased, that is:

$$s_1 = \hat{s} + \epsilon, \tag{3}$$

where ϵ, the unanticipated depreciation, is pure white noise. Hence, *if* (2) and (3) hold together, the forward exchange rate will also be an unbiased predictor of next month's exchange rate:

$$s_1 = f + \epsilon, \tag{4}$$

which is precisely the form under which Longworth tests market 'efficiency'. If (2) and (3), and hence (4) held simultaneously, then substitution of (4) into (1) would at once yield:

$$s_1 = s + r - r^* + \epsilon. \tag{5}$$

This would serve as the basic exchange-rate equation in Canadian macro models.

The stumbling block, of course, is that the evidence gathered by Longworth does *not* support the proposition that the spot exchange rate is just the forward rate up to white noise as implied by (4) (see particularly his equation 3.4). I find this evidence pretty convincing. It is then only a matter of logic to infer that either one of the two following propositions is wrong:

A. The speculative schedule is not infinitely elastic, so that the forward rate is not the market's expected future spot rate (equation 2 is wrong).

B. The rational expectations hypothesis does not describe market behaviour accurately, so that the unanticipated change in the spot rate is not pure white noise (equation 3 is wrong).

Longworth seems ready to maintain that for short maturities (less than six months) the speculative schedule is very elastic, given the volatility of the exchange rate. But he obviously has no direct test that $f=\hat{s}$ to offer (his equation 4.1 would suggest it holds, albeit with substantial imprecision).

Hence, he implicitly argues that the strict rational expectations hypothesis does not hold and he concludes that "the Canadian-U.S. exchange market has been inefficient" (p. 74). It is important to emphasize here that the concept of efficiency adopted by Longworth is extremely strong: it requires (1) that market participants make the best use of the available information, and (2) that they have full knowledge of the true model of the exchange rate and of the numerical values of the relevant exogenous variables (some of which are future values) and of their parameters. Market 'inefficiency' here may mean that knowledge on such a scale is simply out of reach for a variety of understandable reasons, and not necessarily that economic agents do not make the best use of a (less than ideal) situation. They may still be efficient in the classical sense of the word.

Contrary to what Freedman and Longworth assert in a previous paper,[2] I do not find Longworth's results puzzling or surprising. The incomplete and uncertain nature of the market's knowledge of the true numerical model of the exchange rate, which is reinforced by the central role played by the future and by shifts in the objectives of Bank of Canada intervention, is quite sufficient to explain the stickiness of the exchange rate observed by Freedman and confirmed by Longworth. In fact, Benjamin Friedman[3] has recently shown that if *efficient* economic agents are assumed to *learn* an evolving economic structure over time, instead of knowing it perfectly and instantaneously, their optimal course of action would closely resemble adaptive expectations. This should provide comfort to those market participants who might be shocked to hear Bank of Canada staff accuse them of inefficiency.

I would therefore summarize the Canadian evidence as providing pragmatic support for (covered) interest parity at the macro level and being consistent with the equality between the expected spot exchange rate and the forward exchange rate for short maturities, although in this last case direct evidence is harder to come by. Carrying equation 2 into 1, therefore, would yield the most believable exchange rate equation for Canada:

$$s = \hat{s} + r^* - r. \tag{6}$$

The loose end in this equation is the lack of a reliable and stable equation for the expected spot rate $\hat{s}$. The reason for this loose end is not the dearth of competence among students of the market's behaviour, but the elusive nature of the expectations formation process itself.

This is the appropriate juncture to begin discussion of the policy implications of Longworth's findings. I must say at the outset that I have found his section on the implications of exchange-market inefficiency for resource allocation not very useful as it stands. First, the econometric evidence on the effects of various factors on the composition of output is rather suspect in view of the clear signal of serious misspecification that autocorrelation coefficients greater than .5 or .6 give in equations based on quarterly data. The problem may be left-out biases of sorts, in particular the absence of the lagged values of the explanatory variables on the right-hand side. Secondly, even if his estimates of the real-exchange-rate elasticity of the composition of output were believable, there is a strong presumption that output would adjust with *smaller* short-run intensity and speed to nominal exchange-rate variations than to international differentials in cost trends if only, as is most likely, firms take more time to consider permanent exchange-rate changes than developing cost differentials. Thirdly, even if my first two criticisms are ignored and Longworth's elasticity estimates are taken at face value, his warning that the misallocation consequences of exchange-market 'inefficiency' could be significant remains void of any content until we are given an indication of the actual magnitude of the extent of such inefficiency. This is an impossible task, however, since one would have to know what values the nominal exchange rate and all the other variables in the macro model would have taken if profit-maximizing market participants had been fully knowledgeable of the true economic relationships involved. At any rate this exercise would be pointless since it would only tell the difference between an out-of-reach ideal world where perfect information would prevail and the actual, less than ideal, and often painful, realities of our world where imperfect information is the rule. The outcome of such a calculation would provide *no* indication of inefficiency in the customary sense of this word, except to the extent that part of it came from the detrimental impact of changing Bank of Canada intervention policy on the way the market forms its exchange-rate expectations.

This brings me to discuss the role of the central bank in the exchange market. I must emphasize with Longworth and many others that the exchange rate is a central variable in the determination of Canadian aggregate demand, prices, income distribution, and the allocation of resources, and that the Bank of Canada cannot and should not tolerate excessive short-run gyrations in this key price. The high volatility of the Canadian-U.S. exchange rate has been a fact of life since 1973, and equation 6 makes clear that part of the volatility must have stemmed from the volatility of exchange-rate expectations. At the centre of my remarks on the incomplete and uncertain knowledge with which the market has operated is the possibility that the shifting mode of Bank of Canada intervention did puzzle market participants. In this respect, one can identify three distinct periods after the decision to float in 1970. In the first period, 1970–1974, the Canadian dollar continued to be quasi-fixed relative to the U.S. dollar and received the full backing of the Bank. In the second period, 1974–1977, the exchange rate began to fall into benign neglect in policy formulation, especially after the Bank turned officially monetarist in 1975. Since 1977, the Bank has become concerned over the value of the Canadian dollar again and has prevented further depreciation. As a result, monetary growth in Canada is now bounded above by the upper limit of the declared target band, and bounded below by the need to set interest rates high enough to maintain the value of the Canadian dollar above $0.83 U.S. I argue that a more consistent, open, and understood exchange-rate strategy on the part of the Bank in the 1980s could only make the expected and actual exchange rate more stable, and that we would all be better off as a result. It would, of course, serve no purpose to criticize the Bank for its changing exchange-rate policy and for its monetarist affair in the 1970s. These have been difficult times and everybody, including the Bank, has had to *learn* how to cope wih the new floating environment. Hopefully, in the 1980s, the avoidance of excessive exchange-rate stability, as opposed to money-supply stability, will remain as important a policy preoccupation of the Bank as it has been in the last three years. Despite its shortcomings, Longworth's equation for the impact of the real exchange rate on the composition of output clearly suggests that excessive exchange-rate instability will exacerbate the problems of our primary-sector producers who already have to cope with unstable international prices for their staples, not to mention the vulnerability of our manufacturing producers to foreign competition.

The summary of Longworth's findings embedded in the exchange-rate equation 6 further implies a swift and predictable effect of monetary policy on the exchange rate. Faster monetary expansion decreases interest rates and depreciates the Canadian dollar. Hence, easier money fosters expansion both through the interest-sensitive components of aggregate demand and through the direct stimulative impact of the depreciation on net exports. However, the latter effect arises only with a substantial average lag, as the events following the 1977–1978 depreciation have demonstrated. On the other hand, the depreciation raises the prices of imports and exports and therefore shifts the Phillips curve upward quickly and long before higher employment moves the economy up *along* the curve. In other words, the more open the economy the more inflationary expansionary monetary policy is in the very short run, the more rapidly the LM curve tends to return to its initial position, and the less stimulative monetary policy is in terms of output and employment. It follows that in an open economy monetary policy loses some of its punch in the short run as an expansionary instrument and gains in relative efficiency as an anti-inflationary instrument.

That much is very well known, but the important question here is: How significant is this shift in relative efficiency in practice? The answer, of course, depends crucially on the weight of foreign prices in the Canadian producer and consumer price indices and on the responsiveness of current wage inflation to lagged wage inflation, lagged producer price inflation, and lagged consumer price inflation. The upward shift in the Phillips curve is largest if the consumer price-wage feedback dominates the wage bargain, and it is smallest if the wage-wage feedback is the main driving force. I am happy to report that in a paper that Keith Newton and I have just finished writing, we have been able to find that consumer prices play no significant role in wage determination and that lagged wages and lagged producer prices account respectively for about two thirds and one third of the inflation inertia factor.[4] If the exchange-rate elasticity of producer price inflation is as high as 0.15 in the short run, then one can infer immediately that after one year the exchange-rate elasticity of wage inflation would be only 0.05 (=.33 × .15), so that a 5 per cent exchange-rate depreciation would have wages inflate only 0.25 per cent faster. Depreciation generates an upward shift in the Phillips curve, but its magnitude is small.

The basic conclusion that emerges from these considerations is that despite the greater openness of the Canadian economy compared to that of the United States, monetary policy remains a powerful tool of short-run employment stabilization. The fear frequently expressed by Bank of Canada and Department of Finance officials, that the stimulative potential of exchange-rate depreciation vanish into inflationary smoke, would seem to borrow too much from European experience and would not reflect the true behaviour of the Canadian labour market. Unfortunately, the same observation that the wage-wage feedback dominates the wage determination process in Canada lends credence to the efficiency of wage-reducing measures like

outright wage controls, of which I can only forecast that we shall see
more in the 1980s.

Notes

[1] Charles Freedman, (1979) "The Canadian Dollar, 1971–76: An Exploratory Investiga-
tion of Short-Run Movements," in *Issues in Canadian Public Policy (II)*, edited by
Ronald G. Wirick and Douglas D. Purvis, proceedings of a conference held at the
Institute for Economic Research, Queen's University, Kingston, pp. 64–104.

[2] Charles Freedman and David Longworth, (1980) "Some Aspects of the Canadian
Experience with Flexible Exchange Rates in the 1970s," Bank of Canada Technical
Report No. 20 (Ottawa: Bank of Canada).

[3] Benjamin M. Friedman, (1979) "Optimal Expectations and the Extreme Information
Assumptions of 'Rational Expectations' Macromodels," *Journal of Monetary Economics*
5 (January): 23–41.

[4] Pierre Fortin and Keith Newton, (1980) "Labour Market Tightness and Wage Inflation
in Canada," paper prepared for presentation at a Brookings Conference, Washington,
D.C., 6–7 November.

Comment

by
Paul Krugman

David Longworth's very valuable paper is part of a recent and very encouraging trend in exchange-rate economics: the appearance of serious critical testing of exchange-rate theories. In the first few years after floating exchange rates began, most empirical work was an attempt to find support for the theories coming out of Chicago, Cambridge, or Princeton, and what we had were results showing that each theory looked right over some limited subset of the data. Now, however, we are getting more comprehensive tests, by Hansen and Hodrick (1980), Bilson (n.d.), and Frankel (1980), for instance. Longworth's paper appears to be an addition to the literature, and his essentially negative conclusions are in line with what others are now finding.

One criticism I have of Longworth's paper is the decision to organize it around the 'modern theory' of forward exchange. This theory is far from being widely accepted; its association of different types of investment with distinct classes of arbitrageurs, speculators, and so on is out of keeping with the more modern (as distinct from 'modern') emphasis on portfolio choice. And the key element, the upward-sloping arbitrage schedule, is hard to explain in terms of either portfolio choice or transaction costs.

A much better way to read Longworth's results, I would argue, is as a verdict on four, simple 'proportionality' propositions, which many have argued do or should hold in foreign exchange markets. These propositions, using familiar notation, are the following:

$$\Delta s = \Delta p - \Delta p^* \text{ (purchasing-power parity).} \tag{1}$$

That is, depreciation in the exchange rate equals the difference between domestic and foreign inflation rates.

$$f - s = i = i^* \text{ (covered-interest parity).} \tag{2}$$

The forward premium equals the interest differential.

$$f = \hat{s} \text{ (risk neutrality).} \tag{3}$$

The forward rate is the market's expectation of the future spot rate.

$$\hat{s} = E[S/I] \text{ (rational expectations).} \tag{4}$$

The market's expectation of the spot rate is the best forecast possible using information available at the time.

An acceptance of all four of these propositions is the characteristic feature of many Chicago-style models; but many authors have used some of the assumptions without the others. For example, Dornbusch's (1976) famous 'overshooting' model accepts (2) to (4) but not (1); Freedman has estimated exchange-rate equations in which (4) is replaced by an *ad hoc* expectations equation but (2) and (3) are retained.

What does this paper find? Longworth rejects purchasing-power parity out of hand, which is not surprising, but it does not hurt to give the expiring horse another kick. In a technical sense Longworth rejects covered interest parity, but the deviations are very small and unlikely to matter for most purposes.

The surprising result, but one which conforms with other recent findings, is that the joint hypothesis (3) and (4) fails; that is, the forward rate is not an unbiased predictor of the future spot rate. In fact, the current spot rate is a better predictor, and when both are put in the equation the forward rate comes out with a negative sign.

What are we to make of this result? One answer might be to hang on to market efficiency while rejecting risk neutrality and to ascribe the bias to shifting risk premia. However, the shifts in these premia would have to be very large to make the forward rate actually be negatively related to the future spot rate. There is also other evidence on this: Frankel has shown that asset supplies do not seem to affect exchange rates in a way consistent with a risk premium story, and Bilson has shown that the expected profits to be had by exploiting the forward rate's bias are very large.

My own preferred explanation of this result is that, in fact, our equation (4) does not hold. And it does not hold for an important reason. Rational expectations assumes that market participants are able to act as if they know the structure of the economy, so that in our theoretical models agents' predictions correspond to the model's predictions. It is usually argued that this is a reasonable model even if people do not explicitly know the economy's structure, because in equilibrium they will arrive at a forecasting procedure that implicitly takes the necessary information into account. The problem, I would argue, is that the market *is not* in equilibrium: the foreign exchange market is a market still in the process of learning about itself. The result is that when we look back at past experience, we find the market persistently wrong, which does not mean that we could have done better.

If we accept this view, it has some important consequences. For example, rational expectations theorists have convinced us that we need not worry about destabilizing speculation; speculative bubbles are inconsistent with market efficiency. But in a market engaged in a learning process, we can no longer be confident that the market will 'work'; we know almost nothing about how markets converge to a rational expectations equilibrium, and actually have no assurance that they will converge. Since Longworth shows that exchange-rate fluctuations have real resource-allocation effects, this is a serious worry.

The point that needs emphasizing is not that the market may be unstable. It is that we just do not know how to evaluate or predict the behaviour of a market in expectational disequilibrium. It is even far from clear that stabilizing the market is the right policy. In some control models where parameters are uncertain, the optimal policy is to throw the economy from side to side for a while to learn more about how it works. For all we know, the best exchange-rate policy might be to induce large swings in the rate for several years to give the market a chance to learn more about itself. This sounds absurd, and I am not proposing it seriously, but it is just as well- or as ill-grounded in theory as the suggestion that central banks should smooth out exchange-rate fluctuations.

In summary, Longworth's paper is very useful in helping confirm something that we were already beginning to suspect: we do not know very much about exchange-rate determination.

References

Bilson, J. (n.d.) "The 'Speculative Efficiency' Hypothesis." Mimeo. Chicago: University of Chicago.

Dornbusch, Rudiger. (1976) "Expectations and Exchange Rate Dynamics." *Journal of Political Economy* 84 (December): 1161–76.

Frankel, Jeffrey. (1980) "Monetary and Portfolio-Balance Models of Exchange Rate Determination." NBER Summer Institute Paper No. 80–7. Cambridge, Mass.: National Bureau of Economic Research.

Hansen, Lars Peter and Hodrick, Robert J. (1980) "Forward Exchange Rates as Optimal Predictors of Future Spot Rates: An Econometric Analysis." *Journal of Political Economy* 88 (October): 829–53.

Summary
of
Discussion

Ron Wirick opened the discussion by commenting on the alternative tests of efficiency in the Longworth paper. He was unsure, given the lack of knowledge about transactions costs, if any given model of efficiency would yield results systematically different than some other kind of model. Should such consistent patterns not be attainable, Wirick felt that one could not claim that Longworth's evidence disproved the efficiency argument.

The larger issue of the effect of intervention by the central bank on interest and exchange rates, and hence on the structure of the model as developed and tested by Longworth, dominated much of the ensuing discussion. Wirick, supported by *Jack Galbraith*, thought that an intervention rule, or some kind of clear signal concerning policy by the central bank, was very important. This provision of extra information would simplify private-sector decision making, particularly where risk is such an important factor. Wirick added that one of the reasons for potential error is that the private sector might guess incorrectly what the policy response is. Incorrect judgements clearly had ramifications for the economy.

Russ Boyer, commenting on the argument that government intervention is synonymous with inefficiency in the exchange market, noted that such inefficiency might be expected if the intervention is undertaken by a big participant such as the Bank of Canada or one or more of the provinces. *Paul Krugman* and *Charles Freedman* disagreed, Krugman arguing that while variability might be expected and indeed aggravated if government intervention were erratic, there was no reason to presume inefficiency assuming risk neutrality and rational expectations. Freedman added that the many sources of uncertainty should not be confused with bias. He stated that there seemed to be agreement that the market was in expectational disequilibrium of some sort because traders were still learning. The relevant standard errors were thus large but this should not affect the tests.

Pierre Fortin spoke to Boyer's comments concerning the role of the Bank of Canada and of the provinces in the exchange market. He agreed with the view that just because the Bank of Canada was a big participant in the market, the rational expectations hypothesis as such was not undermined. He felt rather that the problem was one of frequent shifts in Bank of Canada policy causing both inefficiency and higher variances for the following periods. With respect to the provinces, Fortin agreed that they were indeed large borrowers. In the present political environment, however, Fortin argued that effective consultation, rather than federal government or central bank directives, was all that was necessary.

Fortin also disagreed with a suggestion, put forward in passing by Krugman, that perhaps the optimal policy of a central bank was to swing the economy from one side to the other in order to provide information to the private sector and public policy makers concerning the parameters of the system. He felt that while an important lesson of the 1970s had been that swings actually exist, it was important to recognize that they emanated from changes in the international primary sectors, not from government. Short-run monetarism had thus been decisively rejected, although longer-term monetarism had simultaneously been confirmed. Fortin thought that the broad strategy of the Bank of Canada should be made clear, and that excessive fluctuations in the exchange rate should be avoided. These latter changes led to serious feedbacks on the real sector of the economy although not, according to Fortin's results, on wages.

Freedman led off the final theme of the discussion by raising the issue as to whether efficiency involved an either/or question concerning the setting of monetary and exchange-rate targets. He suggested that any reading of Bank of Canada policy to date showed that it had not been an either/or situation. What had been occurring, Freedman suggested, was a focus on exchange rates in the short run and on monetary policy in the intermediate run. By keeping monetary targets where they ought to be, Freedman continued, the exchange rate became an endogenous variable. In the longer run, nevertheless, the exchange rate would return to where it ought to be in the context of differential movements of monetary policies in different countries and of certain kinds of real shocks such as those experienced during the 1970s. If adhering to an exchange-rate target range clearly became wrong, Freedman concluded, the monetary aggregate would dominate, especially in the longer run.

Galbraith asked Freedman how the monetary target might best be selected, particularly if the exchange rate were changing rapidly. Freedman replied that the answer would depend on the direction of causation. Intervention in the exchange market would be consistent with monetary targeting, for example, if there were to be a sharp downward movement in the dollar and it were expected that the drop would be reversed relatively quickly.

Tom Courchene at this point added a note of concern. Courchene thought it dangerous that the Bank of Canada might hold to a certain interest rate in the short run because it had taken a particular view of the exchange-rate level. He felt that this would lead to a conflict because, in effect, the exchange rate would be a function of the money supply which, in turn, is a function of the exchange rate. Freedman replied that Courchene was overstating the Bank's commitment to a fixed interest rate. There was much volatility of both interest and exchange rates, and in the long run sharp movements were offset. With respect to the manner in which the Bank of Canada intervenes in the market, Freedman asserted that the technique was such that exchange-rate intervention had no effect on base.

Krugman, in conclusion, wondered if the symptoms being described were an accurate description of the policy problem at hand. Given inflation differentials and the volatility of exchange rates, Krugman asked if the remedy to be prescribed for the symptoms was perhaps the crawling peg. Longworth indirectly supported this view by pointing out that there is an important distinction to be made between changes in interest-rate differentials and changes in other factors affecting the exchange rate. In fact, one of the reasons in favour of floating the exchange rate was the occurrence of large permanent real shocks that led, of necessity, in the long run to changes in real exchange rates.

Long-Term Capital Flows and Foreign Investment

3

by
Robert M. Dunn Jr.

The preparation of a paper on the behaviour of the long-term capital account of the Canadian balance of payments under current conditions presents some problems. If Canada were operating a fixed exchange-rate system, it could reasonably be assumed that movements of foreign exchange reserves were the sole or dominant accommodating item in the balance of payments, and, therefore, that the current and capital accounts were entirely autonomous. This assumption would make it possible to view the long-term capital account in isolation; that is, without allowing for the possibility that it responds or adjusts to shifts in other items in the payments accounts.

A regime of floating or flexible exchange rates, even if managed or 'dirty', complicates matters considerably. If the float were clean, the long-term capital account would simply be the current account plus the short-term capital account with the sign reversed. The behaviour of the long-term capital account would then reflect both its autonomous response to external factors such as changing interest or profit rates and its adjustment to shifts in other items in the balance of payments through exchange-rate changes. An analysis of the long-term capital account would appear possible only as part of a simultaneous consideration of all major items in the balance of payments and of changes in the exchange rate.

A managed or 'dirty' float adds an adjusting or accommodating item in the form of discretionary central bank intervention under the assumption that such intervention is stabilizing and is thus arranged to slow what otherwise might be rapid exchange-rate movements. As long as central bank intervention does not produce the equivalent of a fixed exchange rate, the previous problem remains. Analysis of shifts in the long-term capital account would then appear to depend both on the external factors such as relative yields that normally appear in such discussions, and on all of the factors that determine other major items in the balance of payments (including central bank intervention) and that, hence, cause or affect exchange-rate changes. A conference paper that is intended to discuss the long-term capital account while other papers at the same conference deal with other items in the balance of payments would appear to have some inherent problems.

It may be possible, however, to defend viewing the long-term capital account as relatively isolated despite these difficulties. The defence is based on the argument that the current and short-term capital accounts carry the vast majority of the adjustment burden in a regime of flexible exchange rates, and that although the long-term capital account is not purely autonomous, it is at least far closer to being autonomous than the other major items in the payments accounts. Despite arguments by Laffer and Miles to the contrary, there is a fairly strong consensus in the empirical literature that the trade account does respond in a stabilizing way to changes in the exchange rate.[1] The response may be lagged, but a shock to another item in the accounts that causes the exchange rate to move will eventually produce an adjusting or accommodating movement in the trade balance. The historically discussed transfer problem is solved through the exchange rate as, for example, a large flow of capital into Canada causes an appreciation of the Canadian dollar, which in turn produces a trade and current-account deficit that moves real capital into the country. This transfer of financial into real capital may require some time, since the relevant elasticities are generally thought to be considerably lower in the short than the long run, but eventually the trade account will adjust or accommodate to shifts elsewhere in the payments account as the exchange rate moves.

The short-run adjustment of the balance of payments to the exchange rate is likely to occur primarily in the short-term capital account. That reaction will hopefully be stabilizing (it typically has been in the Canadian case) and represents a combination of speculative reactions and the restoration of real balances. If the Canadian dollar depreciates, stabilizing expectations will lead speculators to move funds into Canada, and vice versa. The depreciation of the Canadian dollar will also reduce the real value of Canadian dollar cash balances held by both foreigners and Canadians and lead to short-term capital inflows as such balances are restored. Both of these reactions depend on the assumption that a depreciation does not lead speculators and others to expect a further exchange-rate movement in the same direction.

Since stabilizing speculative flows are likely to be short term, the long-term capital account might be viewed as relatively autonomous; that is, as largely dominated by external factors rather than by shifts in other payments items operating through the exchange rate.

A monetarist analysis of payments adjustment, however, would not allow such a distinction among payments items with regard to whether they react to the exchange rate. A depreciation of the Canadian dollar, caused by an external shock to one payments item, would cause an increase in the Canadian price level, which would reduce the real money supply in Canada. The resulting excess demand for money would cause a parallel excess supply of goods and of all financial assets as people tried to restore real holdings of money. The long-term capital account would be expected to respond along with other items in the balance of payments. Monetarists often resist suggesting which items they expect to carry most of the adjustment process, although it is sometimes suggested that goods markets respond more slowly to the exchange rate or other forces than do markets for financial assets and, consequently, that the primary response to an exchange-rate change would be found in the capital account. There would be no strong reason, however, to believe that the long-term capital flows would be less responsive than short-term funds, so the long-term capital account could not be viewed as autonomous. To the extent that any item in the balance of payments shifted and produced an exchange-rate change, the long-term capital account would bear some of the adjustment burden as people tried to restore real cash balances after the price level responded to the exchange rate.

Despite this argument that the long-term capital account should not be viewed in isolation but, instead, as part of an adjustment process to other items in the payments accounts, most of what follows will view it as autonomous and, consequently, as not part of an adjustment process when other payments items shift. This will be done in part to avoid an excessive invasion of the topics of the other papers and in part to make the topic of this paper manageable.

Long-Term Capital Flows and Canadian Dependence

The dominant role of the Canadian capital account has been to finance large and growing current-account deficits, and the majority of this financing has typically been provided by long-term inflows.

As can be seen from Table 1, Canada's current-account deficit, whether measured with or without net retained earnings, has been large and has grown about as fast as the economy. The improvement in the current-account balance that began in the late 1960s and early 1970s was reversed in the middle of the decade, and Canadian current-account deficits in the late 1970s and early 1980s have been almost as large a percentage of GNP as was the case in the early 1960s (although still not as large as in the late 1950s). Canada's dependence on external (primarily U.S.) sources for funds and resources to maintain investment levels has not declined. Hopes that this dependence was coming to an end in the early 1970s were disappointed in the second half of the decade as earlier levels of dependence returned.

Table 1
CANADIAN CURRENT-ACCOUNT DEFICITS AS
A PROPORTION OF GNP: 1960–1981
(percentage)

1960	3.2	1971	−0.5
1961	2.3	1972	0.4
1962	1.9	1973	−0.1
1963	1.1	1974	1.0
1964	0.8	1975	2.9
1965	2.0	1976	2.0
1966	1.9	1977	2.1
1967	0.8	1978	2.1
1968	0.1	1979	1.9
1969	1.1	1980	0.7
1970	−1.3	1981	1.6

Source: Calculated from data in the *Bank of Canada Review* (April 1982), Tables 68 and 52.

Note: If net retained earnings were included in the Canadian current-account deficit, the percentages above would be increased by about 1 per cent. Net retained earnings were about 0.8 per cent of Canadian GNP in the early 1960s, but this figure increased to about 1.4 per cent by the mid-1970s, suggesting that the recent upward trend in the data above would be even stronger with retained earnings included. They are not included because no data are available for the late 1970s. For earlier data, see T.L. Powrie, *The Contribution of Foreign Capital to Canadian Economic Growth* (Edmonton: Mel Hurtig, 1977), Table A.15.

The effect of expected inflation on interest payments partially offsets this impact. Since interest rates presumably reflect expected inflation, part of Canada's interest-payments outflows actually reflect a return of capital. Put another way, Canada's real indebtedness obviously falls as a result of inflation. For estimates of the size of this effect, see David Longworth, "International Indebtedness in a Long-Run Context: Implications for Canada," mimeo, p. 9. It appears that Canada's current-account deficit as a percentage of GNP is reduced by about 1 per cent as a result of this factor during recent years.

Table 2 indicates the nature of the necessary funds that financed the current-account deficits. Short-term capital flows have been unstable and often small; the average short-term inflow during the 1960–1980 period was only $603 million, and the flow was negative during eight of the twenty-one years. Long-term capital inflows, in contrast, have been large and relatively stable. The average inflow during the last twenty-one years was $1856 million, and the net inflow never fell below $600 million. In 1979, and again in 1981, short-term inflows played a dominant role in financing the current-account deficit, but this was not the case typically. The basic structure of Canada's balance-of-payments account has usually been that sizeable and chronic current-account deficits have been financed by equally large and stable long-term capital inflows while short-term funds some-times flowed in, but often moved in the opposite direction, and seldom represented a major source of current-account financing. The huge short-term inflows in 1979 and 1981 were highly unusual and can probably be attributed to temporary factors. A discussion of the behaviour of the Canadian long-term capital account, therefore, might reasonably begin with the question of why Canada's current account has produced such large and chronic deficits that have required financing and thus maintained Canada's dependence on foreign capital.

The typical historical view of dependence on foreign capital is that it is common, if not universal, in the early stages of a country's development and that it automatically declines as development proceeds.[2] A combination of higher domestic savings rates, which result from higher per capita incomes, and lower returns to capital caused by higher capital/labour (and capital/land) ratios reduces both the need and the attractions for foreign capital as an economy develops, and eventually reverses the previous flow as highly developed or mature economies typically become capital exporters.

Table 2
THE CANADIAN CAPITAL ACCOUNT:
SHORT AND LONG-TERM FLOWS 1960–1981
(millions of Canadian dollars)

	Short-Term Capital	Long-Term Capital	Net Capital Movements
1960	164	929	1 093
1961	133	930	1 063
1962	441	688	1 129
1963	− 3	637	634
1964	− 75	750	675
1965	694	833	1 527
1966	− 243	1 228	985
1967	− 395	1 415	1 020
1968	− 439	1 669	1 230
1969	−1 136	2 337	1 201
1970	− 196	1 007	811
1971	1 030	664	1 694
1972	472	1 588	2 060
1973	− 553	628	75
1974	1 310	1 041	2 351
1975	1 620	3 935	5 555
1976	69	8 007	8 076
1977	668	4 217	4 885
1978	1 237	3 081	4 318
1979	6 752	2 099	8 851
1980	1 113	1 305	2 418
1981	14 203	1 340	15 543

Source: Bank of Canada Review (December 1981), Table 68, and *Quarterly Estimates of the Canadian Balance of Payments* (First Quarter 1982).

Note: The Canadian capital account does not include the errors and omissions item, which consists both of unrecorded capital transactions and a variety of other transactions such as illegal imports. This item used to be included in the American capital account on the basis of the argument that most such errors and omissions were actually capital flows.

In Canada's case, however, rapid increases in GNP per capita have not eliminated or greatly reduced the country's dependence on foreign capital. The continuation of large current-account deficits, which necessitates a large volume of foreign financing, understandably frustrates many Canadians. Nationalists do not like a situation of dependence on foreign capital, particularly when the inflows often take the form of direct investment from the United States. While some are tempted to imply that it is somehow the fault of the United States that Canada remains dependent on foreign capital, this temptation does not address the real reasons for Canada's continuing need for external resources. As a result, it may be useful to mention a few reasons for this situation and to suggest some changes in the Canadian economy that might be expected to reduce or eliminate this dependence.[3]

The first important factor in Canada's continuing need for foreign capital has nothing to do with policy decisions in Ottawa and is consequently not readily subject to change. Canada's comparative advantages have tended to lie in resource-based industries, which are inherently capital intensive. Minerals, hydro-power, petroleum, forestry, and even farming require more capital per dollar of output than do the rapidly growing sectors of the economy of the United States' and Canada's other major trading partners. It might be argued that Canadian policy should then be designed to encourage the growth of less capital-intensive sectors of the economy at the expense of growth in resource-based industries, thus reducing Canada's need for external capital to maintain a desired growth rate. However, this would not appear to be a wise policy in a world in which the terms of trade of resource-based economies are almost certain to improve significantly during the next few years. This would seem to be a particularly inappropriate time to attempt to move the Canadian economy away from its past pattern of resource-based exports in order to reduce the country's need for capital.

The second reason for the large capital requirements of the Canadian economy has been the unusually rapid growth of the Canadian labour force.

As can be seen from Table 3, the Canadian labour force has grown much more rapidly than that of Canada's major industrial competitors. This means that Canada must invest a higher percentage of GNP than other countries in order to avoid excessive unemployment and to maintain capital/labour ratios to sustain output per worker. The rapid growth of the Canadian labour force is not a new or temporary phenomenon, but has continued since at least the late 1950s.

For many years this growth resulted primarily from the arrival of large numbers of working-age immigrants. This heavy immigration

Table 3
CIVILIAN LABOUR FORCE, EMPLOYMENT,
AND UNEMPLOYMENT
(Average Annual Percentage Changes, 1958–1968 and 1969–1980)

	Labour Force	Employment	Unemployment
United States			
1958–68	1.5	1.9	−4.8
1969–80	2.4	2.0	9.4
Canada			
1958–68	2.6	2.8	−1.4
1969–80	3.2	2.9	7.8
France			
1958–68	0.6	0.5	8.8
1969–80	0.9	0.3	14.1
Italy			
1958–68	−1.0	−0.7	−6.4
1969–80	1.4	0.9	10.0
Japan			
1958–68	1.4	1.5	−4.1
1969–80	0.9	0.8	9.0
United Kingdom			
1958–68	0.4	0.3	2.9
1969–80	0.4	0.1	12.0
West Germany			
1958–68	0.1	0.1	−8.4
1969–80	−0.1	−0.5	21.0

Source: OECD, *Labour Force Statistics*, various issues through November 1981. Data are from individual country tables.

occurred during a period in which the internal growth of the Canadian labour force was relatively slow. In recent years, however, immigration has slowed substantially, but the combination of the arrival of the post-war baby boom at working age and the changing work patterns of women has produced rapid internal labour-force growth.

In a few years, the baby boom will have finished entering the labour force; it will be followed by considerably smaller age cohorts reaching working age. If working patterns among women stabilize, the natural rate of growth of the labour force will decline significantly in Canada. If the Canadian government retains the somewhat more restrictive immigration policies of recent years as these changes occur in the internal population, the overall rate of growth of the labour force will decline. This will reduce Canadian needs for investment, in that considerably lower percentages of GNP invested in new plant and equipment will be consistent with unchanged unemployment rates and past trends in the capital/labour ratio. If the Canadian economy can operate successfully with a somewhat lower investment level, domestic savings rates will obviously come far closer to providing the necessary resources. Reliance on current-account deficits, and hence on long-term capital inflows, could then decline.

Table 4
ROLE OF IMMIGRATION IN CANADIAN
LABOUR-FORCE GROWTH, 1955–1981

Year	(1) Civilian Labour Force (annual averages)	(2) Change in Labour Force	(3) Immigrants Entering Labour Force	(4) Immigrants Entering Labour Force as Percentage of Change in Labour Force
	(thousands)	(thousands)	(thousands)	$(3) \div (2) \times 100$
1955	5 610	—	—	—
1956	5 782	172	91	52.9
1957	6 008	226	151	66.8
1958	6 137	129	63	48.8
1959	6 242	105	54	51.4
1960	6 411	169	54	32.0
1961	6 521	110	35	31.8
1962	6 615	94	37	39.4
1963	6 748	133	46	34.6
1964	6 933	195	56	28.7
1965	7 141	208	74	35.6
1966	7 420	279	99	35.5
1967	7 694	274	120	43.8
1968	7 919	225	95	42.2
1969	8 162	243	84	34.6
1970	8 374	212	78	36.8
1971	8 631	257	61	23.7
1972	8 920	289	59	20.4
1973	9 276	356	92	25.8
1974	9 639	363	106	29.2
1975	9 974	335	81	24.2
1976	10 206	232	61	26.3
1977	10 498	292	48	16.4
1978	10 882	384	35	9.1
1979	11 207	325	48	14.8
1980	11 522	315	63	20.0
1981	11 830	308	57	18.5

Sources: Statistics Canada, *The Labour Force* (various issues), and Immigration Canada, *Immigration Statistics* (various issues). Data for 1973 through 1981 are from the *Bank of Canada Review* (May 1982), Tables 51 and 57. Labour-force data from 1973 on are based on the *Revised Labour Force Survey* and are therefore not strictly comparable with earlier years.

This scenario for reduced Canadian reliance on external capital requires, however, the maintenance of a decidedly restrictive immigration policy as internal labour-force growth slows. Strong political pressures from domestic employers and from foreign residents seeking entry into Canada will undoubtedly develop against such a policy. If, however, the Canadian government really wants to reduce the dependence of the country on foreign capital, the continuation of a restrictive immigration policy that significantly reduces the rate of growth of the labour force would make a sizeable contribution to the desired goal.

The other reasons for Canadian dependence on foreign capital are on the other side of the investment/savings identity. Not only is the Canadian economy capital intensive, it also has maintained insufficient savings rates for past levels of investment. Although private savings rates in Canada have been about twice as high as have been typical in the United States, they have not been as high as those prevailing in Europe and Japan, as shown on Figure 1. Moreover, the public sector in Canada has run large continuing deficits that tend to crowd out private borrowers. Often those financing private investments in Canada are crowded out of Canada and into the United States. A great deal of Canadian private saving is used to finance public-sector deficits rather than productive private investment.

As can be seen in Table 5, Canada has had public-sector deficits since 1977 that have represented a considerably larger percentage of GNP than those prevailing in the United States. The other countries that have had large public-sector deficits such as Italy, Germany, and Japan have also had much higher household savings rates than either Canada or the United States. This suggests that the Canadian private savings rate has not been high enough to finance both large public-sector deficits and a level of domestic investment that is sufficient to avoid excessive unemployment and maintain labour productivity growth.

If the public sector is viewed as including enterprises such as the hydro authorities, Canadian government deficits become an even larger share of GNP.

Much of this borrowing was used to finance projects such as James Bay, so it cannot all be viewed as a net drain of funds from financing investment. The borrowing levels implied in Table 5, which do not include government enterprises, suggest this drain more accurately. Total public-sector borrowing in Table 6 is so large, however, that it does indicate why Canadian private financing needs are often crowded into foreign capital markets such as the United States.

The second element in a Canadian program to reduce dependence on foreign capital should be based on a significant increase in the economy's savings rate through a reduction in public-sector dis-

Figure 1
HOUSEHOLD SAVING RATIOS[a]
Quarterly, Seasonally Adjusted

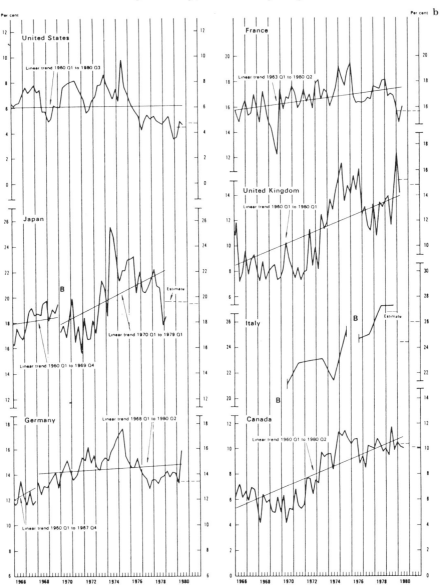

a Source: OECD, *Economic Outlook* (December 1980), p. 134.
b Net savings as percentage of disposable income.

Table 5
PUBLIC-SECTOR SURPLUS OR DEFICIT (−) AS A
PERCENTAGE OF GNP*

	1963– 1969	1970– 1973	1974	1975	1976	1977	1978	1979	1980
United States	0.0	−0.2	−0.3	− 4.5	−2.1	−1.0	0.0	0.5	−1.2
Canada	0.8	0.6	0.4	− 2.9	−1.8	−2.6	−3.1	−1.9	−2.1
France	0.4	0.8	0.6	− 2.2	−0.5	−0.8	−1.8	−0.7	0.3
Italy	−2.8	−5.4	−5.4	−11.1	−9.1	−7.9	−9.7	−9.3	−8.4
Japan	−2.7	0.9	0.2	− 4.3	−3.6	−3.8	−5.5	−4.8	−4.2
United Kingdom	−0.9	−0.7	−5.3	− 5.7	−5.0	−3.4	−4.3	−3.1	−3.1
West Germany	−0.2	0.3	−1.2	− 6.3	−3.6	−2.4	−2.6	−2.9	−3.4

* The 1964–1973 data appear to be based on slightly different definitions and are not directly comparable with the 1974–1980 data.
Sources: 1963–73: OECD, *Economic Outlook* (September 1979), p. 143.
      1974–75: OECD, *Economic Outlook* (July 1976), p. 25.
      1976: OECD, *Economic Outlook* (December 1979), p. 34.
      1977: OECD, *Economic Outlook* (July 1981), p. 33.
      1978–80: OECD, *Economic Outlook* (July 1982), p. 29.

saving. If the Canadian public sector ran considerably smaller operating deficits over the average business cycle, the result would be a higher savings rate for the economy as a whole and a reduced need for foreign capital to maintain desired investment levels.

The linkage between smaller public-sector deficits and reduced current-account deficits (requiring smaller long-term capital inflows) could be expected to operate through interest rates and the exchange rate. Reduced public-sector borrowing would produce more buoyant capital markets (lower interest rates and higher price/earnings ratios for equities) if the Bank of Canada maintained an unchanged rate of money-supply growth. Nominal interest rates would probably fall more than real yields due to reduced inflationary expectations resulting from a decline in public-sector deficits. The reduction in real (and nominal) interest rates would discourage financial capital inflows or encourage outflows, putting downward pressure on the Canadian dollar in the exchange market. The resulting depreciation of the Canadian dollar would produce a lagged improvement in the current account, which would represent a reduction in the flow of real capital into the economy.[4]

This linkage may seem excessively simple, and it is almost certain that some expectations process could be thought of that would complicate it greatly, but the underlying problem seems clear. The Canadian economy as a whole (including government) has not saved enough to finance levels of investment that are consistent with acceptable unemployment levels and desired rates of growth of labour productivity during a period of very rapid labour-force growth. As

Table 6

CANADIAN PUBLIC-SECTOR BORROWING 1960–1981
(millions of dollars)

	Federal	Provincial	Municipal	Total	Total as a Percentage of GNP
1960	$ 612	$ 480	$ 370	$ 1 462	3.8
1961	890	946	333	2 169	5.5
1962	801	687	244	1 732	4.0
1963	827	898	374	2 099	4.6
1964	457	938	401	1 796	3.6
1965	−52	762	248	958	1.7
1966	430	1 566	349	2 345	3.8
1967	900	2 049	466	3 415	5.1
1968	1 545	1 927	288	3 760	5.2
1969	339	1 952	239	2 530	3.2
1970	1 844	2 078	176	4 098	4.8
1971	2 547	2 599	257	5 403	5.8
1972	1 599	2 911	445	4 955	4.7
1973	−147	2 674	398	2 925	2.4
1974	4 212	3 765	542	8 519	5.8
1975	3 967	6 794	1 098	11 859	7.2
1976	4 233	9 268	1 237	14 738	7.7
1977	8 006	7 463	1 205	16 674	8.0
1978	10 490	7 240	649	18 379	8.0
1979	8 284	6 464	587	15 335	5.9
1980	11 388	8 710	439	20 537	7.1
1981	12 782	11 508	361	24 651	7.5

Source: Bank of Canada Review (April 1982), Tables 28 and 52.

increases in the labour force slow with the completion of the arrival of the baby boom at working age and with the maintenance of a relatively restrictive immigration policy, less investment will be needed by the economy. If savings rates can then be increased, primarily through a sizeable reduction in public-sector deficits, Canadian savings should become sufficient to finance the country's investment needs. Once capital and exchange markets have adjusted to these new circumstances, a combination of somewhat lower real interest rates and a modest depreciation of the Canadian dollar should eliminate the flow of both financial and real capital into the economy.

Canadians may decide, however, that the required tightening of public-sector budgets is too painful and that they would rather continue to absorb more than the economy produces by depending on foreign funds and resources. Large and continuing public-sector deficits, and the resulting low savings rate for the economy as a whole, can be reconciled with the economy's investment needs if current-account deficits continue to provide a net flow of resources into the economy. This will require a continuing reliance on capital inflows, however, the majority of which will be in long-term forms and part of which will probably be in the form of equity. This will not please Canadian nationalists who want to reduce or eliminate the foreign ownership of Canadian industry and resources.

New York as a Canadian Financial Intermediary

Another major element in explaining the behaviour of the Canadian long-term capital account is the past tendency of Canada to use New York as a financial intermediary between savers who want relatively liquid assets and borrowers who want long-term funds and who may be viewed as less than perfect credit risks. Canada has often had sizeable outflows of short-term capital and simultaneous inflows of long-term funds. When New York borrows short-term funds from Canada and lends long-term funds back, Canada is effectively importing inter-mediation services from the United States. The cost of this import is the difference between long-term and short-term interest rates in New York, which is usually, but not always, positive.

It was seen in Table 2 that although this pattern of capital flows is not constant, it is certainly quite common. In eight of the fourteen years from 1960 through 1973, Canada had net capital outflows on short-term account and simultaneous inflows of long-term funds. During the latter half of the 1970s, for reasons that will be discussed later, this pattern changed. Short-term capital flowed into Canada during every year from 1974 through 1981, and during three of those years (1974, 1979, and 1981) short-term inflows were larger than long-term inflows. The relationship in which the United States imported short-term money from Canada and lent long-term funds back, thereby acting as an intermediary between Canadian savers and borrowers, operated during much of the 1960s and early 1970s, but not after 1973.[5]

A discussion of the past pattern of intermediation must begin with the yield curves prevailing in the two countries. If the differential between long-term and short-term yields in Canada is typically greater than the same yield differential in the United States, an incentive exists for two directional capital flows in which the United States attracts short-term funds and lends long-term funds, thus exporting intermediation services. Figure 2 illustrates such a situation.

If U.S. and Canadian rates followed the pattern indicated on Figure 2, the previously described pattern of two directional capital flows could be expected. This assumes, of course, that the differing yield curves do not represent merely differing inflationary expectations that

Figure 2
HYPOTHETICAL YIELD CURVES

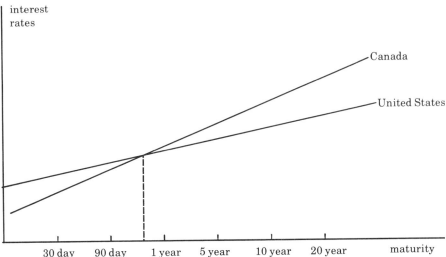

are, in turn, reflected in exchange-rate expectations in a purchasing-power-parity world.

As can be seen in Table 7, the differential between Canadian and U.S. long-term yields was typically considerably greater than the differential between Canadian and U.S. short-term interest rates. Although the yield curves did not actually cross often (1970, 1971, and 1973 were exceptions), the Canadian yield curve was quite consisently steeper than that prevailing in the United States between 1960 and 1974.

Steeper yield curves are typically viewed as resulting from expectations of accelerating inflation, higher interest rates, and a depreciating currency. It is difficult, however, to accept this explanation in the Canadian case since the steeper yield curve existed over a rather extended period in which Canadian interest rates did not rise relative to those in the United States, Canadian inflation did not accelerate relative to U.S. inflation, and the Canadian dollar did not depreciate. If expectations were the basis of a relatively steep Canadian yield curve, those expectations were certainly disappointed rather consistently. Between 1962 and 1974, both Canadian and U.S. inflation, measured by the Consumer Price Index (C.P.I.), averaged 4 per cent. During this same period the Canadian yield curve was steeper than that prevailing in the United States for twelve of thirteen years. In the latter half of the 1970s, Canadian inflation did accelerate relative to the United States, but this was a period in which the Canadian yield curve was often less steep than the U.S. curve. Expectations with

Table 7
CANADA-UNITED STATES INTEREST-RATE DIFFERENTIALS:
LONG-TERM AND SHORT-TERM ASSETS 1960−1981
(annual averages of monthly data)

	(1) Canada Minus U.S. Short-Term Yields	(2) Canada Minus U.S. Long-Term Yields	Column 2 Minus Column 1
1960	0.17	1.17	1.00
1961	0.43	0.99	0.56
1962	1.13	1.05	−0.08
1963	0.45	1.04	0.59
1964	0.20	1.03	0.83
1965	0.57	1.06	0.49
1966	0.63	1.10	0.47
1967	0.65	1.18	0.53
1968	0.91	1.36	0.45
1969	0.03	1.41	1.38
1970	−0.36	0.98	1.34
1971	−0.60	0.72	1.32
1972	0.27	0.93	0.66
1973	−0.71	0.88	1.59
1974	0.56	1.35	0.79
1975	1.67	1.35	−0.32
1976	3.93	1.51	−2.42
1977	1.75	1.24	−0.51
1978	0.49	0.94	0.45
1979	0.64	0.59	−0.05
1980	0.12	0.63	0.51
1981	2.45	1.41	−1.04

Sources: Long-term data for 1960−1976 are from the Data Resources Inc. data bank. Short-term yields for 1960−1976 are from various issues of the *Federal Reserve Bulletin* (Table A−35) and from various issues of the *Bank of Canada Review* (Table 19). U.S. short-term data are for commercial paper and Canadian data are for finance paper. Long-term yields are for Canadian provincial bonds and U.S. corporate bonds. All 1977 through mid-1980 figures are from pp. S-52−53 of the *Bank of Canada Review* (July 1980). Data after mid-1980 are from pp. S-58−59 of the *Bank of Canada Review* (February 1982).

regard to future interest rates and inflation undoubtedly affected the relationship between Canadian and U.S. yield curves in particular instances, but it is hard to believe that this was a dominant force over a long period in which Canadian interest rates did not show a sharp upward trend relative to U.S. interest rates and Canadian inflation did not accelerate relative to U.S. inflation. Some other reason for the fairly consistent pattern of steeper Canadian yield curves seems necessary.

As part of another study, an attempt was made to explain the pattern of a steeper Canadian yield curve by asking a number of

Canadian financial market participants in Canada and the United States why they thought this pattern had been so prevalent.[6] While responses to such a questionnaire can hardly be viewed as authoritative, they do come from the people who were closest to the markets and also provide a number of interesting insights that might justify further investigation. The following answers appeared relatively often:

1. The most commonly cited cause was the belief that Canadian savers and portfolio managers are more risk averse and consequently desired a more liquid mix of assets than those in the United States. The result was a stronger demand for short-term paper and a weaker demand for long-term bonds than would be found in the United States. Market yields adjusted to these differing patterns of asset demands, producing a steeper yield curve. This argument was commonly made by Canadian as well as U.S. financial market participants.

2. It was also suggested that the rapidly growing sectors of the Canadian economy are inherently more long-term capital intensive than are the growing sectors of the U.S. economy. Natural resources and energy projects need long-term funds while the rapidly growing services sector of the U.S. economy can operate with shorter-term financing. Differing patterns of asset supply in the two markets then produce differing yield structures. Canadian borrowers want to sell relatively more long-term debt, pushing prices down and yields up, and vice versa in the United States.

3. Some market participants argued that relatively thin or narrow capital markets, such as those existing in Canada when compared to the United States, will automatically tend to produce a steeper yield curve. To the extent that secondary markets for outstanding securities are thin and somewhat unstable, lenders are encouraged to operate at rather short maturities in order to reduce the likelihood that they will have to sell assets before maturity in uncertain markets. If borrowers share this view of domestic capital markets, they will try to borrow for the full period for which funds will be needed in order to avoid having to roll over debt under what may be difficult circumstances. If a country's capital markets are broad and relatively stable, however, lenders are more willing to purchase long-term assets with confidence that they can be sold at less risk if funds are needed before maturity, and borrowers are more willing to sell short-term paper, expecting that such loans can be rolled over relatively easily later on. If this argument is accurate, borrowers in relatively thin or illiquid markets will try to sell relatively more long-term paper, producing higher bond yields, and lenders will try to purchase relatively more short-term paper,

producing lower interest rates for those maturities. The result is a steeper yield curve in Canada than in the United States.

4. Finally, it was suggested that debt-management policies in the two countries differ, with the U.S. Treasury selling more short-term paper, while the Government of Canada tends to borrow at longer maturities, producing a steeper yield curve in Canada.

A Shift in Yield Curve Patterns: 1975–1981

Since the middle of the 1970s, a major shift in the Canada-United States pattern of relative yield curves and of capital flows has occurred. As was seen in Table 7, the Canadian/U.S. short-term yield differential widened sharply, but there was no such increase in the spread between Canadian and U.S. bond yields. The result was that during the 1975–1977 period, the Canadian yield curve was less steep than that prevailing in the United States. During 1978 the previous patterns returned briefly in that the Canadian yield curve was steeper, but the difference was very small. During 1979 and the first half of 1980, yield curves in *both* countries were downward sloping, but the differential between Canadian and U.S. bond yields was smaller than the difference between short-term interest rates. Both yield curves sloped downwards, but the Canadian yield curve sloped downward more steeply. During all of this period except 1978, the differential between Canadian and U.S. long-term interest rates was smaller than the difference between short-term yields, meaning that the incentive for Canadian use of New York as a financial intermediary no longer existed. Canadian interest rates remained higher than U.S. yields at both maturities, but the long-term differential narrowed considerably late in the decade while the short-term differential remained quite wide.[7] During 1981 both yield curves had negative slopes, but the spread between Canadian short- and long-term yields was far wider than that prevailing in the United States.

This shift in the pattern of yields produced some predictable changes in the pattern of capital flows. Short-term capital flows were positive throughout the 1974–1981 period, so the earlier pattern of frequent short-term outflows and long-term inflows ended. During 1979 and 1981, short-term inflows were far higher than long-term inflows so the pattern in which Canada depended primarily on long-term funds to finance current-account deficits did not operate.[8] It is far from clear, however, that the 1979 and 1981 patterns of yields and capital flows are more than the temporary results of highly unusual circumstances in financial markets in both countries.

The Behaviour of the Long-Term Capital Account and Some of Its Subcategories

During the 1960–1974 period, there was no clear trend in total long-term capital inflows. Net inflows averaged $1.2 billion per year, rising in the latter half of the 1960s and falling slightly in the early 1970s. Canada's net debtor position in long-term forms increased by about $17.5 billion during this fifteen-year period, but after allowance for inflation, Canada's real indebtedness to the world may not have increased very much.[9] In the latter half of the 1970s, however, net long-term capital inflows became much larger. The average inflow was about $4.3 billion in long-term forms during the 1975–1979 period, meaning that Canada's long-term indebtedness increased by over $22 billion in five years. Since inflation was more rapid in this period, the increase in Canada's real indebtedness was considerably smaller, but $22 billion is still a sizeable increase in nominal long-term indebtedness for a five-year period, particularly for a country that is not a large net importer of oil. During 1980 and 1981, net inflows of long-term capital declined to about $1.3 billion per year, which probably represents no increase in real long-term indebtedness.

The increase in net long-term indebtedness did not result from direct investment flows. Net direct investment showed no trend during the 1960s, declined sharply after 1971, and has been negative during every year since 1974. The net outflow during 1978–1979 totalled over $3.7 billion and $2.2 billion in 1980 alone. This recent decline in net direct investment flows was caused in part by a decline in inflows from abroad (which were actually negative in 1976), which began in the mid-1970s, but to a greater degree by a sharp increase in Canadian direct investment abroad, most of which has been in the United States. During 1981, repatriation of foreign-owned assets by Canadians, largely because of the Canadianization feature of the National Energy Program, gave rise to substantial outflows of direct investment funds from Canada.

Direct investment flows cannot easily be attributed to average profit rates since such investments are for individual projects that may earn more or less than the typical return on equity in a country. In any event, there was, until 1981, no evidence of declining profit rates in Canada; the share of Canadian GNP going to corporate profits increased slightly during the latter half of the 1970s after having shown no apparent trend during the previous fifteen years. The decline that occurred in 1980 and 1981, and continued into 1982, was probably a result of cyclical factors rather than any permanent change in the economy.

The decline in inflows of foreign (mainly American) direct investment was instead probably caused by a combination of tightened liquidity conditions within most U.S. corporations, a widespread suspicion among investors that they were not quite as welcome in Canada as they had been in the past, and the effects of the difficulties in Quebec. A combination of high interest rates, a depressed stock market (which made it unattractive to sell more stock), and severe inflation in the cost of capital equipment meant that most U.S. firms faced difficulties in financing domestic plant and equipment investment needs during the latter half of the 1970s. One result of such a financial situation is that firms become considerably less interested in sending funds abroad to finance direct investments. When this financial constraint is combined with the common feeling that additional U.S. direct investments were not wanted by many influential Canadians and with considerable uncertainty as to the ultimate effects of the 1976 Quebec provincial election, it is hardly surprising that flows of direct investment into Canada declined.

The sharp increase in Canadian direct investment in foreign countries in general and the United States in particular may have come as something of a surprise. These investments averaged only $132 million per year in the 1960s, rose to $505 million in the first half of the 1970s, and then increased further to an average annual rate of $1350 million during the latter half of the decade. About $4.5 billion flowed out of Canada during 1978–1979, $2.8 billion in 1980, and $4.9 billion in 1981 alone.

There are a number of possible reasons for this increase, beginning with a depressed U.S. equities market that offered obvious bargains for those able to finance acquisitions. The Canadian stock market had risen sharply in the late 1970s, meaning that similar investments in existing firms would have been far more expensive in Canada. A sizeable part of the Canadian money, however, apparently went into a

Table 8

CANADIAN CORPORATE PROFITS AS A PROPORTION OF GNP: 1960–1981
(percentage)

1960	10.1	1971	9.2
1961	10.3	1972	10.3
1962	10.4	1973	12.5
1963	10.7	1974	13.6
1964	11.6	1975	11.9
1965	11.4	1976	10.5
1966	10.9	1977	10.0
1967	10.3	1978	11.1
1968	10.7	1979	13.3
1969	10.4	1980	12.8
1970	9.0	1981	10.3

Source: Calculated from data in the *Bank of Canada Review* (April 1982), Table 52.

few industries, with real estate and oil drilling being the most widely discussed. The oil industry investments probably resulted from the continuation of domestic oil price controls in Canada and the rapid easing of such controls in the United States. The result is that a driller's net return per barrel of newly discovered oil is reportedly considerably higher in the United States, and that Canadian oil firms have been moving drilling operations south. Canadian firms are reported to be important participants in the increase in drilling in the U.S. Rocky Mountains area. The sharp increase in Canadian investments in U.S. urban real estate may be the result of bargain hunting. The U.S. market became quite depressed in the late 1970s, as a result of earlier civil disturbances, considerable overbuilding of commercial office buildings in some markets, and distress sales by over-extended real estate investment trusts (REIT) or banks that had foreclosed on such trusts. Pessimism about urban real estate markets was widespread among U.S. investors, and banks that had lost large sums in the REIT debacle were not interested in becoming heavily involved again. The result was unrealistically low prices, which a few well-financed Canadian firms were apparently among the first to discover. A few Canadian firms have reportedly moved very large sums into the United States to finance purchases of urban properties. Finally, uncertainties about the future of Quebec apparently encouraged a number of Canadian firms to reduce their exposure there, and a few of these firms probably moved south rather than west. General uncertainties about Canadian economic policies during 1981 may have produced both the sharp decline in common stock prices and the huge flow of direct investment funds to the United States. Whatever the various reasons, Canadian direct investments have recently become much more important in the U.S. economy.

Net New Issues

In recent years the Canadian long-term capital account has been virtually dominated by net new issues, that is, by Canadian sales of new bonds abroad minus out-payments for bonds reaching maturity. The vast majority of these bonds have typically been sold in the United States.

The sale of new bonds was a fairly stable source of capital inflows at $1 billion to $2 billion per year during the late 1960s and the first half of the 1970s. This source of capital inflows rose sharply after 1973 and reached almost $9 billion in 1976, the dominant borrowers being provincial governments (including enterprises such as hydro authorities) and private corporations. These borrowings declined somewhat in the late 1970s, but this decline was partially offset by a sharp increase in federal government borrowing abroad in 1978, 1979, and 1980. Sales of new issues remained at $5 billion or more through the

Table 9
NEW ISSUES AS A PERCENTAGE OF TOTAL CANADIAN
LONG-TERM CAPITAL INFLOWS: 1960–1980

	New Issues as a % of the Long-Term Capital Account	New Issues Minus Redemptions as a % of the Long-Term Capital Account
1960	45	18
1961	54	28
1962	103	61
1963	152	101
1964	144	101
1965	146	100
1966	115	74
1967	90	65
1968	111	85
1969	80	62
1970	115	61
1971	176	50
1972	106	68
1973	204	87
1974	231	175
1975	126	104
1976	112	101
1977	139	118
1978	208	165
1979	242	138
1980	381	222
average 1960–69	104	70
average 1970–80	185	117

Source: Calculated from data in the *Bank of Canada Review* (December 1981), Tables 68 and 71.

latter half of the decade. Net new issues peaked at about $8 billion in 1976 and declined to just under $3 billion in 1979 and 1980 due to a steady increase in capital outflows to retire maturing bonds. The level of capital inflows from net new issues was, however, strikingly higher during the latter half of the 1970s than it had been earlier and increased further in 1980–1981. It is interesting that this increase occurred despite the fact that long-term interest rates were extremely high in both countries during this period. Real yields, however, may not have been particularly high if rapid inflation was expected in both countries.

The difference between Canadian and U.S. long-term interest rates widened somewhat in the mid-1970s, but this may also have represented only the expectation of more rapid inflation in Canada than in the United States, an expectation that was fulfilled during much of the latter half of the decade. In 1978–1979, however, this interest-rate differential narrowed sharply, but flows of funds from net new issues were $5.2 billion and $3.2 billion during these two years, a far higher level than prevailed in the 1960s and early 1970s when the differential was at similar levels. Again, however, it is difficult to know what real interest rates Canadian borrowers thought they were paying since it is not clear how much inflation or what exchange-rate changes bond issuers expected at maturity. If borrowers always view the long-term interest-rate differential as the likely difference in rates of inflation, so that real bond yields are always equal, and if they expect purchasing-power parity to prevail over the long run, interest rates alone never provide an incentive to borrow in the United States rather than Canada.[10] If, however, Canadians expected rapid inflation in the United States and the recovery of the Canadian dollar from its 1976–1977 depreciation, interest rates prevailing in the United States in the late 1970s would seem to be bargains.

Freedman and Longworth found that the difference between Canadian and U.S. bond yields does not explain at all well changes in the proportion of Canadian provincial bonds sold abroad, but that when the ratio of total Canadian bond issues to GNP is added as a variable, the explanatory power of the equation is improved considerably.[11] For corporate bonds, however, the interest-rate differential is more successful in explaining the proportion of capital that is raised abroad, and the ratio of total issues to GNP adds very little explanatory power. It appears that Canadian provincial borrowers went to New York when the Canadian bond schedule was relatively crowded, but that corporate borrowers responded more to relative interest rates. If one puts aside the problem of inflationary expectations for a moment, this result might be explained by the argument that provincial governments or hydro authorities are not under great pressure to minimize costs. A public utility such as a hydro authority is a monopoly, and it can relatively easily pass on additional costs to its customers. The managers of such enterprises may not have any personal financial incentive to minimize costs, but they do have an incentive to avoid embarrassing construction delays or other publicly noticeable problems arising from difficulties in scheduling financing. As a result such managers may simply go to New York whenever the Canadian bond schedule looks crowded in order to guarantee that they will get their funds when needed to meet construction schedules. Modest differences in real or nominal interest rates may seem to be a minor consideration to such borrowers.

Financial managers of private corporations, however, face a quite different competitive climate and probably have different incentives. They are under considerable pressures to minimize costs and, consequently, are likely to be much more responsive to interest rates.

They may be more willing to use short-term funds while waiting for an appropriate time to borrow long term and, consequently, may be less likely to go to New York merely because the Canadian bond schedule is crowded.

The size of individual borrowers relative to the Canadian capital market is another important factor in understanding the behaviour of flows of capital from new issues. Econometric models of capital flows are implicitly based on the assumption that the market is made up of large numbers of borrowers and lenders, and that therefore flows are not likely to be significantly affected by the behaviour of one or a few large borrowers who have particular financing problems or construction schedules. Canadian capital markets do not fit this assumption at all well. There are a few hydro authorities and other provincial enterprises that are very large borrowers by the standards of any capital market and that are absolutely enormous relative to Canadian markets. Although corporate borrowing is probably less concentrated, even in this market there are a few firms such as Canadian Pacific and the large oil companies that would be major borrowers in any market and that are huge relative to Canadian capital markets. This means that the borrowing behaviour of one enterprise, which may be based on the construction schedule for a project such as James Bay, can almost dominate new issues in the Canadian long-term capital account. It also means that some of the most important Canadian borrowers do not have the option of operating solely in the Canadian market. The maximum size of an issue that can be placed in Canada is considerably smaller than the requirements of some borrowers, and the concentration of major borrowers means that prudent bank officers and other portfolio managers reach their lending limits to single borrowers long before the needs of enterprises such as Ontario Hydro or Hydro Québec are met.

There is an important industrial organization aspect to Canadian long-term capital inflows that is caused by the fact that major Canadian borrowers are far larger relative to the local capital market than is the case in the United States. As long as managers of financial intermediaries follow the normal rules of prudent lending, which limit the percentage of an institution's capital that may be extended to a single borrower, a number of major Canadian borrowers will have to operate in New York or elsewhere outside Canada irrespective of relative interest rates. Hydro Québec borrowed well over $1 billion in a single offering in New York a few years ago as part of a financing program for James Bay that required many billions of dollars. For a single institution that needs that much money for a single project, it is not interest rates alone that determine where it borrows. If Hydro Québec had been eight or ten separate enterprises financing a number of individual projects totalling the cost of James Bay, the money might have been found in Canada, but not for a single enterprise and a single project.

Studies of Canada's long-term capital account might produce improved explanations of recent flows if they explicitly and separately dealt with the needs of a few large borrowers that cannot reasonably expect to find the funds they need in Canadian capital markets.

Policy Questions

The short-term question facing the Canadian government relating to capital flows is what is the least disruptive way to finance a large and ongoing current-account deficit. Until the middle of the 1970s, virtually all of the financing was in long-term forms, but this changed during the last few years. From 1974 through 1981, short-term capital inflows occurred every year and totalled over $27 billion. In 1979, and again in 1981, the short-term capital account dominated total capital inflows. Such continued dependence on short-term capital for current-account financing would appear to present some risks. Short-term capital flows tend to be unstable and to include a sizeable speculative element, which means that continued reliance on them might be expected to produce a Canadian exchange market that is less stable than experienced in the past. Long-term capital flows have been more stable and predictable, but have the disadvantage of having often come in the form of direct investment that caused unpopular levels of foreign control of the economy. In recent years, however, these direct investment inflows have slowed, and outflows of Canadian funds for direct investment abroad have become sizeable. The funds leaving Canada for direct investments abroad might ideally be available for purchases of foreign-owned firms if Canada is seriously pursuing a reduction of the level of foreign control of the economy. The reduction of direct investment inflows into Canada and the 1981 outflows for take-overs of foreign-controlled Canadian companies have advanced this goal, but the large outflows of Canadian funds for direct investment abroad have not. Ottawa might want to consider how to keep more of this money in Canada, but this raises difficult questions with regard to domestic oil prices, tax rates, and other factors affecting investment incentives. Reliance on new bond issues as the dominant means of financing the current-account deficit would appear to have some obvious attractions. The funds thus raised tend to be relatively stable, in that such bonds are not often or quickly sold back to Canada, so such reliance would not encourage exchange-rate instability to the extent that heavy use of short-term funds might. Raising funds through new bond issues also does not involve any politically unpopular increase in foreign ownership or control of the Canadian economy. If Canada decides to encourage primary reliance on bond issues for current-account financing, that would imply an attempt to return to the pre-1975 situation in which the Canadian yield curve was typically steeper than that prevailing in the United States.

The long-term issue facing Canada remains the extent to which the current account should be allowed to produce a large and chronic deficit that requires long-term or other financing. Canada's apparent goal of increased economic independence would appear to imply an end to dependence on foreign capital and consequently a positive balance or surplus on current-account transactions. This could require an increase in domestic savings rates relative to investment, and the most obvious way to move in that direction is to significantly reduce the size of chronic public-sector deficits. Again, however, the apparent balance-of-payments goal conflicts with domestic political considerations. Governments that raise taxes or reduce expenditures sufficiently to produce a sizeable decline in the public-sector deficit are seldom popular or long-lived. Voters favour the abstract principle of fiscal prudence, but not the policy changes that are necessary to bring it about. Policies that would reduce or eliminate Canada's chronic current-account deficits and its resulting need for large, long-term capital inflows are available, but it is far from easy for an elected government to pursue them.

Notes

[1] Marc A. Miles, (1979) "The Effects of Devaluation on the Trade Balance and the Balance of Payments: Some New Results," *Journal of Political Economy* 87 (June): 600−620. This article is based on the author's dissertation, which was directed by Arthur Laffer. It represents a test of Laffer's often expressed views that devaluations have little, if any, effect on the trade balance.

[2] For a useful discussion of Canada's indebtedness, see David Longworth, "International Indebtedness in a Long-Run Context: Implications for Canada," mimeo. The historical stages' approach to the balance of payments has a long history. Recent examples of work in this area are Dragoslav Avramovic *et al.*, (1964) *Economic Growth and External Debt* (Baltimore: Johns Hopkins University Press); Geoffrey Crowther, (1957) *Balances and Imbalances of Payments* (Boston: Harvard University, Graduate School of Business Administration); and Nadav Halevi, (1971) "An Empirical Test of the 'Balance of Payments Stages' Hypothesis," *Journal of International Economics* 1 (February): 103−17.

[3] Gordon Sparks comments that this argument contains an implicit value judgement that Canada 'ought' to become less dependent on foreign capital. He argues instead that if Canadians prefer current over future consumption at world interest rates, it is perfectly rational for the economy to save less than it invests at that interest rate and to import the difference through a current-account deficit that is financed by foreign borrowing. Two responses to this argument are worth noting. First, this pattern has intergenerational effects in that the current generation is deciding to consume more at the expense of future generations consuming less, which at least raises a question of equity. Secondly, and more important, the Canadian voters have elected a government that has clearly and strongly expressed a preference for a more independent Canada, which would seem to imply being less dependent on capital inflows from the United States.

[4] One discussant questioned whether this section of the paper argued that current-account deficits cause long-term capital inflows, or vice versa. The reply would be that levels of investment in excess of domestic savings at world interest rates and at levels

of GNP that demand management policies maintain/cause both current-account deficits and capital inflows. Demand for goods and services in excess of output causes current-account deficits, and demand for borrowed funds in excess of flows of funds into domestic capital markets from savings cause capital inflows.

[5] The Canadian capital account and flows to and from the United States have been used interchangeably here because the bilateral flow has historically dominated the Canadian capital account. This is not quite as true now as it has been in the past, however, as Canadian involvement in Euro-currency markets has increased significantly.

[6] Robert M. Dunn Jr., (1978) *The Canada-U.S. Capital Market: Intermediation, Integration, and Policy Independence* (Montreal: C.D. Howe Research Institute).

[7] Charles Freedman of the Bank of Canada suggests two possible reasons for the recent change in the Canadian yield curve. First, Canadians may have become convinced by the Bank of Canada's commitment to monetarism, and therefore expect considerably less inflation. Secondly, Canadian capital markets may have become more competitive due to the end of the Winnipeg Agreement through which Canadian banks limited interest rates paid on deposits.

[8] One discussant noted that much of the 1978–1979 long-term foreign borrowing was undertaken by the federal government in order to rebuild foreign exchange reserves. Domestic borrowing was obviously not an alternative source of funds in this case, and this borrowing might reasonably be entered in the foreign exchange reserves part of the balance-of-payments accounts rather than in the long-term capital account.

[9] The inclusion of net retained earnings would add about $12.6 billion to the increase in Canada's long-term net debtor position during these fifteen years. See Thomas L. Powrie, *The Contribution of Foreign Capital to Canadian Economic Growth* (Edmonton: Mel Hurtig, 1977), Table A 15 for data on net retained earnings through 1976.

[10] This argument is discussed in Charles Freedman and David Longworth, (1980) "Some Aspects of the Canadian Experience with Flexible Exchange Rates in the 1970s," Bank of Canada Technical Report No. 20 (Ottawa: Bank of Canada).

[11] *Ibid.*, p. 29.

Comment

by
Gordon R. Sparks

We are indebted to Robert Dunn for a comprehensive and well-presented review of the state of Canada's long-term capital account. His analysis focuses on a number of factors that I would agree are the important ones, but I think the paper suffers somewhat from the lack of an explicit theoretical framework. This leads to some unfortunate inconsistencies, in particular with regard to the relation between the current account and the capital account. In spite of the fact that much of the paper focuses on autonomous determinants of capital inflow such as resource investment opportunities and population growth, the author makes a number of misleading statements that suggest that causation runs from the current account to the capital account, thereby encouraging the popular misconception that "Canada's current account has produced such large and chronic deficits that have *required* financing and thus maintained Canada's dependence on foreign capital" (pp. 110–11, emphasis added).

As an appropriate theoretical framework for analysing the determinants of long-term capital flows, I would suggest the Fisherian intertemporal choice model as depicted in the following figure. The production possibilities curve describes the available trade-off between current and future consumption and reflects the autonomous factors mentioned above. The slope of the budget line is one plus the world interest rate and the tangency point determines the current output of consumption goods AB. The tangency with an indifference curve then determines the current-account deficit and the capital-account surplus at the amount BC.

This framework focuses then on the interaction of savings preferences and investment opportunities as determinants of the balance of payments, and it can be used to analyse the effects of public-sector deficits on the balance of payments. A relationship between the public-sector and current-account deficits has been emphasized by the Cambridge Economic Policy Group in the United Kingdom, and there has been a striking correlation between the two in Canada, particularly in the past five years. The familiar Mundell model of an open economy with a flexible exchange rate and perfectly elastic capital

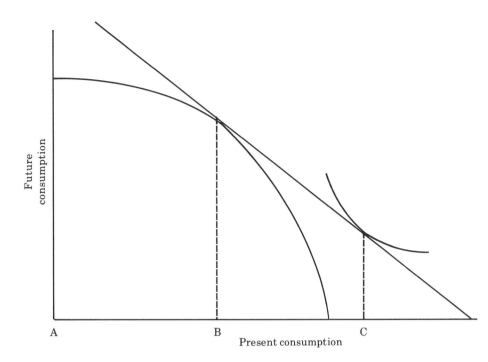

flows provides an explanation of the mechanism connecting the government deficit and capital inflows. In the Fisherian framework, an increase in the government deficit will be matched one-for-one by an increase in the capital-account surplus if the deficit has no effect on the economy's productivity or on private saving. This suggests that a more careful analysis of the effects of government activity on perceived private consumption and wealth is needed to sort out this relationship. It may also be desirable to take account of the effects of inflation on nominal interest payments. As pointed out by Barber and McCallum,[1] both the government deficit and the current-account deficit are exaggerated by the inflation premium component of interest payments.

Note

[1] Clarence L. Barber and John C.P. McCallum, (1980) *Unemployment and Inflation: The Canadian Experience* (Ottawa: Canadian Institute for Economic Policy).

Comment

by
John Cuddington

Writing a paper that not only describes Canadian long-term capital flows and foreign investment but also *explains* them is not an easy task, as Robert Dunn's introductory remarks remind us. Of course, long-term capital flows plus short-term capital flows plus changes in official indebtedness to foreign monetary institutions ('official reserves') must equal the current account, as a matter of accounting. Any economic explanation of the behaviour of individual accounts within the balance of payments must not be inconsistent with this fact!

Being aware of this, Dunn suggests a method of attack: consider long-term capital flows to be autonomous, rather than an accommodating item that responds passively to other external factors. To defend this approach he uses the argument that:

> ...the current and short-term capital accounts carry the vast majority of the adjustment burden in a regime of flexible exchange rates, and . . . although the long-term capital account is not purely autonomous, it is at least far closer to being autonomous than the other major items in the payments accounts (p. 108).

In spite of this alleged autonomous nature of long-term capital flows, Dunn later emphasizes the role of short and long interest-rate differentials *vis-à-vis* the United States, addresses the claim that Canadians lend short and borrow long using the New York capital market as an intermediary, and claims that a depressed U.S. stock market enticed Canadians to invest abroad. All of these factors and many others suggest to me that long-term capital flows are no more or less autonomous than other components of the foreign accounts. It also suggests that the distinction between 'autonomous' and 'accommodating' transactions is not particularly useful. Wisely, many international economists have abandoned the distinction.

What is important for Dunn's purposes is the degree of stability — cyclical and secular — of various components of the balance-of-payments accounts. In the Canadian case, short-term, private capital flows and changes in official reserves have been much less stable from year to year than long-term capital flows. Short-term capital flows have often been small, sometimes positive and sometimes negative. Long-term capital flows in contrast have been persistently large and positive. As Dunn puts it:

> The basic structure of Canada's balance-of-payments account has usually been that sizeable and chronic current-account deficits have been financed by equally large and stable long-term capital inflows while short-term funds sometimes flowed in, but often moved in the opposite direction, and seldom represented a major source of current-account financing (p. 110).

He goes on to ask why Canada has been a persistent importer of long-term capital or, put more provocatively, "why Canada's current account has produced such large and *chronic* deficits that have required financing and thus maintained Canada's dependence on foreign capital" (pp. 110–11, emphasis added).

The explanations Dunn provides are several. They largely revolve around the notion that Canada's domestic saving consistently falls short of domestic capital investment needs: (1) Canada has a comparative advantage in capital-intensive, resource-based industries, (2) unusually rapid growth in the Canadian labour force has necessitated a high level of investment just to maintain the existing capital/labour ratio, (3) Canadian household saving is low by European or Japanese standards (although it is twice the U.S. rate), and (4) large public-sector deficits absorb a large portion of private saving that could otherwise be funnelled into private investment.

I see the above as reasons why Canada's *current-account* deficits have consistently been large, but not necessarily why these deficits have been financed by *long-term* capital inflows. Recall that the current-account balance must always equal national (private plus public sector) saving minus investment; this is an accounting identity. In many situations, however, it provides a useful analytical perspective for examining current-account trends over time once domestic saving and investment behaviour have been satisfactorily modelled. These current-account deficits are mirrored by long-term capital flows only if short-term private and official capital flows tend to be ephemeral and self-reversing over time, or if private short-term capital inflows/outflows are just offset by official reserve gains/losses.

There is a presumption in Dunns' discussion that short-term capital flows offset or finance short-term perturbations of the current account around its long-run path. The long-term capital account reflects the *long-run trend levels* in saving minus investment. Short-run oscillations in net saving, on the other hand, show up predominantly in *short-term* capital flows and changes in official reserves. If this is in fact the case for Canada, which has not been rigorously demonstrated by Dunn, then the time profile of the long-term capital account may indeed look like the smoothed current-account balance (but with the opposite sign). Hence long-term capital flows could be explained by examining long-run trends in domestic saving and investment. Furthermore, the long-term capital account would appear to be relatively stable — throughout the business cycle and in spite of short-term interest-rate gyrations and exchange-rate volatility.

I believe that further empirical work is necessary to substantiate the validity of this interesting working hypothesis. One might, for example, examine the correlation between *short-term* capital flows and movements in the current-account balance around its long-term trend. The correlations between each of these time series and long-term capital flows could also be investigated. If long-term capital flows *are* "relatively autonomous" (to use Dunn's description), they should not be found to be highly correlated with (past or present) short-term movements in these other accounts. If, on the other hand, Canadians are consistently lending short term and borrowing long term as Dunn's discussion of "New York as a Canadian Financial Intermediary" suggests, one might expect to find a negative contemporaneous correlation between movements in the short- and long-term capital accounts. It is certainly not sufficient evidence of the existence of this international financial intermediation phenomenon merely to note that: "In eight of the fourteen years from 1960 through 1973, Canada had net capital outflows on short-term account and simultaneous inflows of long-term funds" (p. 119). After all, long-term capital flows were positive *every* year from 1960 to 1980. And short-term capital *inflows* rather than outflows accompanied these long-term inflows in the remaining six of the fourteen years.

Dunn's paper also addresses the important question about whether persistent long-term capital inflows and the 'chronic' current-account deficits that presumably accompany these capital flows are in Canada's best interest. Before the welfare implications of sustained inflows of long-term capital can be determined, it is important to examine their *composition*. Do they take the form of long-term loans that may involve little threat to Canadian economic sovereignty, or do they involve direct foreign investment with a concomitant loss of domestic control over Canadian resources? In the latter case, policy makers would presumably want to know the extent to which the rate of domestic capital accumulation would be reduced if direct foreign investment was limited and the ultimate cost in terms of slower economic growth. If investment by domestic residents can be increased to fill the void left by restricting foreign investment, the cost in terms of a lower level of current consumption would have to be assessed.

It is desirable to analyse the net saving of various sectors — household, business, and the public sector — within the economy and to compare the importance of these sectors in total national saving and investment to their importance in total international asset transactions that show up in the capital account. In recent years, for example, there have been large government fiscal deficits that have absorbed a considerable portion of total domestic saving. Since the mid-1970s, federal as well as provincial and municipal governments have also become much more active borrowers in the New York capital market. In fact, external public-sector borrowing has recently become much more important than U.S. direct investment in Canada as a source of long-term capital inflows. Any discussion about the alleged costs of dependence on foreign capital and what might be done about it must certainly take into consideration this shift in the composition of long-term capital flows.

When the private sector borrows abroad in the process of carrying out profit-maximizing investment decisions in Canada, there is a presumption that Canadian GNP, and with it economic welfare, will be increased. When the government borrows abroad (or domestically for that matter), one must ask whether this presumption is equally valid. What are the relative merits of the government borrowing abroad rather than domestically, thereby easing the tightness of the domestic credit markets, compared to *domestic* financing of fiscal deficits, which forces more private firms undertaking capital investment to seek (apparently) cheaper external financing? There may be a tendency for total external borrowing by a country to increase when the government finances its deficits externally. The reduced crowding-out effect in domestic credit markets and the lower domestic interest rates this may entail may well reduce voter resistance to large public-sector deficits.

These are merely conjectures at this point. The important conclusion for investigation of the question, "Is Canadian reliance on foreign capital excessive?" is that one must first take a disaggregated look at the domestic saving-investment process and the social worth of increased capital investment (with the higher labour productivity it would imply). The 'window' that we get on this process just by examining the balance-of-payments accounts will certainly not provide much guidance for policy-making purposes.

Summary
of
Discussion

Discussion following presentation of the paper by Robert Dunn picked up the themes raised by the commentators, principally the issue of Canada's dependence on foreign capital, the significance of the changing nature of long-term capital flows, and the question of whether long-term capital flows have been autonomous or were required to finance the large deficit on current-account transactions. In addition, a number of participants commented on the statistical treatment of some of the items in the balance-of-payments accounting framework.

Robert Dunn led off on the dependency issue by noting that, despite the questions raised by the commentators, the impression one receives from vocal individuals and groups in Canada is that the country's dependence on foreign capital has been excessive. *Pierre Fortin* observed that by some measures we were not doing too badly, since the ratio of Canada's international indebtedness to GNP had fallen from about 40 to 50 per cent in the 1960s to just 25 per cent more recently. In the view of *Paul Krugman*, in order to deal with the question of dependency as measured by changes in the proportion of the capital stock owned by foreigners, it is important to know what information is wanted; if set up properly, the balance-of-payments data will provide the information.

A number of points related to Canada's dependency on foreign capital were made by *Don Daly*. He noted that the capital stock per person employed is higher in Canada than in the United States, making Canada the most capital-intensive country in the world while, as shown in Dunn's paper, household savings ratios are lower in Canada than in most other countries except the United States. He added, however, that depreciation allowances and capital consumption are larger in relation to GNP in some other countries; this difference reflects, in part, the higher capital-to-output ratio in Canada than in any other country. Daly thought that considerable scope exists in Canada for achieving a more efficient use of both labour and capital, especially in the manufacturing sector and that such changes, together with the expected slower rate of growth in the 1980s, could lead to lower investment ratios in Canada in the future and would imply less pressure for long-term capital than suggested in Dunn's paper. In this connection, Fortin observed that Dunn had not looked closely enough at Canada's savings rates, which have risen sharply. Part of this rise had been spuriously related to inflation, but part was due to the savings-enhancing programs of the federal government. The question he raised was what would be the long-term effects of these programs after they had become mature. He went on to observe that demographic factors may also be having important effects on the rate of saving in Canada.

The changing nature of inflows of foreign capital was of concern to some, including *Fergus Chambers* who observed that Canada has been shifting from equity to debt financing over time, a situation that is building greater rigidity into our debt-service obligations. Dunn's response was that the move from equity to debt would at least reduce the problem of dependency.

Mac Urquhart suggested that one of the reasons for the changing nature of capital flows in recent years was that both U.S. and Canadian corporations have been investing increasingly in other parts of the world; consequently, direct inflows of capital to Canadian subsidiaries have suffered from a relative shift in perceived opportunities by their parents. Dunn responded that he did not think it was a matter of U.S. direct investment leaving Canada to go somewhere else but rather that U.S. investment abroad had declined almost everywhere since 1975.

No real consensus was reached on the question of whether capital flows induced the deficit or the deficit necessitated an inflow of capital. Dunn defended his early emphasis on the current account as the driving force by reiterating that Canada has historically incurred a large gap between investment and saving that has produced both a current-account deficit and, through its capital markets effects, high interest rates, which in turn induced large capital inflows; these were two sides of the same coin. In Canada's case, the major part of the capital inflows have been of a long-term nature.

Charles Freedman wondered if a distinction in the time horizon being discussed would influence the nature and direction of causation. He felt that in the short run, for example, as a first approximation one could view the current account and long-term capital account as being determined independently by different factors and then the whole thing equilibrated by short-term flows on the capital side. He went on to note that in the long run, however, all these must be viewed as determined simultaneously and that it is not fruitful to talk about one driving the other in any simple way. He suggested that for long-run analysis it would be necessary to model the behaviour of the major long-term borrowers, for example, corporations and the federal, provincial, and local governments. In their decisions on borrowing in domestic versus foreign capital markets, interest-rate differentials and the problems of access to particular financial markets play a major role. Freedman concluded that the current account cannot in any simple way be considered to be a determinant of long-term capital movements.

The other major topic of discussion related to the statistical treatment of some balance-of-payments items, particularly interest payments to non-residents and retained earnings. Dunn agreed with the point made by *Gordon Sparks* that proper inflation adjustment, by treating the inflationary component of interest payments abroad as a capital outflow rather than an import of services, would reduce the current-account deficit in relation to GNP, probably by about 1 per cent. He went on to add that Canada, like a number of other countries, does not properly account for net retained earnings in its payments accounts either. If they were more appropriately treated as a dividend outflow (i.e., an import of a service) on the current account and simultaneously repatriated as a direct investment inflow, then the current-account deficit would be about 1.25 per cent higher, in relation to GNP, than it is currently. The point on treatment of retained earnings was reiterated by Krugman. Both Freedman and *Kevin Clinton* raised the point that errors and omissions have bedevilled the measurement of the capital flows and that, in their view, it was not clear whether the greatest measurement errors were in the capital account, particularly in the form of unreported flows of short-term funds, or in the current account in such items, for example, as imports of marijuana into Canada.

Structural Changes in the Canadian Trade Balance During the 1970s

4

by
Neil Bruce* with Hossein Rostami

1. Introduction

Except for the years 1970, 1971, and 1973, the Canadian current account has been in deficit for the past thirty years. During the 1970s this current-account deficit increased sharply both in nominal terms and as a percentage of GNP, initiating a flurry of concern about a chronic and potentially acute current-account deficit. Moreover, in 1975 the merchandise-trade balance slipped into deficit for the first time since 1960 despite the fact that the terms of trade had substantially improved since 1971. The merchandise-trade deficit, calculated using 1971 prices, would have been much greater and longer lasting in the mid-1970s had it not been for this 'fortuitous' improvement in the terms of trade. [1]

Concern about the current deficit was mitigated somewhat by the subsequent improvement in the merchandise-trade balance and the recognition that part of the increased current-account deficit during the 1970s was due to higher interest rates that increased the service-account deficit. These higher interest payments reflect inflation premia and properly belong in the capital account. When adjusted, the current-account deficit expressed as a percentage of GNP was only marginally above historic levels in the late 1970s. [2]

One result of this heightened concern about the current account is that the role played by the structure of Canadian trade in the determination of the merchandise-trade balance has become an issue. Robinson asserts that the structure of merchandise trade, specifically the concentration of exports in primary and semi-processed goods (staples) and the concentration of imports in manufactured goods has made it "impossible . . . to achieve a trade surplus . . . equal [to] the growing deficit in services, interest and dividends."[3] Wilkinson argues that the low income elasticities of demand for primary goods and the high income elasticities of demand for manufactured goods implies that as the world economy grows, "Canada's merchandise trade balance will deteriorate, not improve, over the longer run."[4] To the proponents of this point of view, the improvement in the merchandise-trade balance after 1975 does not invalidate their contention that there exists a serious structural problem in the balance of trade because the deficit in manufactured goods has grown. This increased deficit in manufactured goods has been offset by a still larger increase in the surplus in staples. Therefore, the current-account balance has been reduced but at the cost of worsening the structural imbalance in merchandise trade. According to this view, the situation requires 'structural remedies'. These remedies are, effectively, restrictive commercial policies that comprise part of an industrial strategy designed to foster growth in manufacturing industries in Canada.

Apart from the 'structuralist' controversy, the composition of the trade account may be of considerable interest for other reasons. For example, there has been recent concern about identifying 'competitive sensitive items' in the trade balance, that is, commodities in which the trade balance is particularly responsive to changes in factor costs and relative prices. It is argued that the effects of domestic cost inflation, currency depreciation, and other developments influencing costs and prices will affect the trade balance largely through these items. Another concern is the relative importance of domestic and foreign variables in the determination of traded-goods prices and quantities traded. For some commodities, domestic variables might be relatively important in the determination of the trade balance whereas for others, the state of the foreign economy is the main determining factor.

The outline of the rest of this paper is as follows. Section 2 considers the difference between structural and conventional macro-economic theories of the current account and merchandise-trade balance. Section 3 presents an informal empirical examination of developments in the merchandise-trade balance during the 1970s. Section 4 provides a theoretical framework for examining the causal influences on trade quantities and prices by commodity group. Section 5 presents a preliminary econometric analysis of these causal influences.

2. Conventional and Unconventional Theories of Current-Account Balance Determination

A useful starting point in any discussion about the current account is the following identity:

$$CAB \equiv Y - A, \tag{1}$$

where CAB is the measured current-account balance (a positive value being a surplus), Y is gross national product at current prices, and A is 'absorption' or gross domestic expenditure on consumption, investment, and government goods and services. This identity makes it clear that a current-account deficit $(CAB < 0)$ represents a collective attempt to absorb more goods and services than the economy is producing by dis-hoarding financial wealth or acquiring foreign liabilities.

At the most aggregate level, the economy is treated as if production and expenditure consist of a single composite commodity, output/expenditure plans are undertaken by a single representative individual, and the rest of the world consists of a single country. Thus, the current-account balance depends on the determination of aggregate output and expenditure levels and not on the composition of trade. Some macro-economic theories can be expressed entirely in this single commodity framework, such as the simple monetary theories that emphasize the choice between consuming the single commodity and hoarding the single, monetary asset. Other macro-economic theories require some commodity structure to be specified. For example, the simple Mundell-Fleming model assumes that domestic products are distinct from those imported from world markets. In this case, total absorption must be disaggregated into expenditure on domestic and foreign goods and a foreign demand schedule for domestic goods must be specified. In addition, domestic output may be disaggregated into 'sheltered' (domestic) goods and those that are produced domestically but are identical to goods being traded in world markets. In these models, the elasticities of substitution between domestic and world goods in demand and supply can now play a role in current-account determination. Nevertheless, the macro-economic view continues to stress the role of aggregate, economy-wide influences in the determination of the current-account balance.

The 'structuralist' approach argues that the explanation of current-account deficits is found in those sectors in which the deficits occur. Therefore, to understand the current account, one examines the industry and commodity groups in which the domestic economy has a trade deficit, the trading partners with whom we have a bilateral trade deficit, or even which decision-making groups absorb goods by dis-hoarding (for example, the public versus the private sector, low-income households versus high-income households). While this strategy of looking for an immediate link between sectoral deficits and overall deficits cannot be dismissed on an a priori basis, it may be seriously misleading to associate sectoral trade deficits with overall trade deficits. In another regard, Arthur Okun commented to the effect that we may learn little about the cause of a flat tire by observing that it is flat only on the bottom. Similarly we may learn little about the current-account deficit by observing in which commodities the deficits occur, or with which trading partners we have bilateral deficits.

Structuralists posit the following recursive model. Structural factors, specifically the commodity composition of Canadian trade in which exports are concentrated in resource-intensive, semi-processed goods (staples) and imports are concentrated in manufactured goods with high labour value added, impose a chronic current-account deficit on the Canadian economy as well as a higher unemployment rate. This deficit must be financed by capital inflows that, in the past, have made Canada an international debtor of impressive proportions and will cause even larger deficits in the future because of the flow of interest and dividend payments to foreigners that will result from the increased external debt. In addition, the structure of Canadian trade is inimical to growth and development since Canada does not share in the more rapidly expanding world trade in manufactured goods, except as an importer. Thus, the structuralist view of the current-account deficit is intimately connected with the view that foreign investment in the Canadian economy is largely unwanted and socially undesirable.

In contrast, the 'conventional' view treats the structure of the trade account and the level of the current-account balance as separate issues for the most part. The composition of Canadian trade reflects a comparative cost advantage in resource and land-intensive commodities, while the current-account deficit reflects greater intended expenditure on consumption and investment goods than the economy is producing. An increase in the current-account deficit occurs because of a rise in absorption (which may be caused by expansionary fiscal or monetary policy and/or increased investment opportunities) or because of a fall in domestic output. This in turn may be caused by supply-side developments such as reduced productivity and profitability in production, or demand-side developments such as a fall in demand for Canadian goods induced by domestic cost inflation, over-valuation of the exchange rate, or a recession in the economies of our major trading partners.

From the macro-economic point of view, the appropriate policy response to a current-account deficit that is felt to be too large is expenditure reduction and switching, accomplished with contractionary monetary and fiscal policies and/or depreciation. Structuralists argue that expenditure-reducing policies are undesirable because they create domestic unemployment while depreciation will be inadequate because of low price elasticities of import and export demand.[5] On this basis they argue that depreciation should be augmented by policies involving direct and indirect subsidies to import-competing industries, especially manufacturing, further government incentives to research and development, the continued subsidization of energy expenditures in order to give Canadian industry a 'competitive' edge over foreign firms, increased trade restrictions, particularly of manufactured imports and preferably in the form of quotas, and further constraints on foreign investment.[6] Those of a conventional viewpoint do not favour such policies, in general, since they would reduce the volume of trade and therefore reduce productivity and efficiency in the economy. Thus, trade restrictions might reduce output and thereby increase the current-account deficit.[7]

3. Developments in Canadian Merchandise Trade During the 1970s

We now turn to the commodity structure of the merchandise-trade account and the trade balance. Ignoring the service account we can express the trade balance by the identity:

$$T \equiv \sum_{i=1}^{N} P_i (Q_i - D_i), \tag{2}$$

where Q_i is the quantity of good i produced domestically and D_i is the quantity demanded. In Table 1, the merchandise-trade balance for the years $1970-1979$ is divided into two broad components: manufactures and staples.[8] While the total merchandise balance fell between 1970 and 1975 and rose thereafter, it is clear that over the decade there has been a steadily increasing deficit in manufactured goods offset by an increasing surplus in staples. A few minutes' reflection should convince the reader that Table 1 actually contains very little useful information about the role of the commodity structure despite frequent references to such a table.[9] Given a deficit in manufactures and surplus in staples in 1970, the mere rise in the money prices of traded goods and the increase in trade volume would cause the observed trends with little change in the overall trade balance or in the commodity composition of merchandise trade itself. Four factors contributing to the change in the trade balance in each item and the total can be identified using equation (3) below.[10]

$$\Delta T_i \equiv (V_i^x - V_i^I)\frac{\Delta Q^T}{Q^T} + (V_i^x - V_i^I)\frac{\Delta P^T}{P^T}$$

$$+ [V_i^x (\frac{\Delta Q_i^x}{Q_i^x} - \frac{\Delta Q^T}{Q^T}) - V_i^I (\frac{\Delta Q_i^I}{Q_i^I} - \frac{\Delta Q^T}{Q^T})] \tag{3}$$

$$+ [V_i^x (\frac{\Delta P_i^x}{P_i^x} - \frac{\Delta P^T}{P^T}) - V_i^I (\frac{\Delta P_i^I}{P_i^I} - \frac{\Delta P^T}{P^T})]$$

In equation (3) the subscript i denotes commodity group (M = manufactures, S = staples); the superscripts X, I, and T denote exports, imports, and traded goods respectively; V is value in current dollars; Q is value at 1971 prices (or 'quantity'); and P is price. The first term on the right-hand side of equation (3) is the change in the trade balance in component i attributable to growth in the quantity of trade; the second term is the change attributable to the increase in the price level of traded goods; the next term gives the change in the balance due to relative changes in the quantity of exports and imports of commodity i; and the final term gives the change in the balance due to changes in the terms of trade, that is, changes in the relative prices of exports and imports of the commodity as compared to traded goods as a whole.

In Table 2 the year-to-year changes in the merchandise-trade balance in manufactured goods, staples, and total goods are decomposed into these four components for the years 1971–1979. Also shown are the changes for the period 1971–1975, 1975–1979, and the total period 1971–1979. Over the total period 1971–1979, the total trade balance changed very little while the deficit in manufactured goods and the surplus in staples increased by over $10 billion each. Table 2 shows that the changes in the merchandise and staples balances are more than accounted for by the rise over the decade in both the quantity of goods traded and the prices at which they are traded. Relative changes in the quantities of exports and imports had little effect on the increased deficit in manufactured goods, while relative changes in the quantities of staples exported and imported actually reduced the increase in the staples surplus. During the sub-period 1971–1975, the total trade balance declined by approximately $3.5 billion. Table 2 indicates that this occurred mainly because of the relative change in the quantities of exports relative to imports. This relative change in quantities was greater in staples than in manufactured goods and in both cases was offset somewhat by terms-of-trade changes. During the period 1975–1979, the total trade balance increased by over $4 billion. As a result, by 1978 and 1979 the trade surplus reached levels that exceeded the exceptional years of the early 1970s. Table 2 indicates that this improvement came about mainly because of a large change in the quantity of exports relative to imports. Moreover, this improvement as a result of changes in relative quantities was totally concentrated in manufactured goods with the staples sector actually reducing the increase in the trade surplus. On a year-to-year basis, Table 2 reveals some interesting facts. The largest deterioration in the trade balance due to changes in relative quantities of exports and imports occurred between 1973 and 1974 (during which the United States entered a sharp recession), although the greatest deterioration in the trade balance itself occurred between 1974 and 1975. During 1973–1974, changes in the terms of trade increased the trade surplus while they decreased it between 1974 and 1975. Finally, between 1978 and 1979, the relative change in the quantities of exports and imports reduced the trade balance by the largest amount since 1973–1974. This relative change in quantities occurred in both manufactured goods and staples but was larger in the latter. A sharp improvement in the terms of trade resulted in a small improvement in the overall trade balance between 1978 and 1979.

Table 1
MERCHANDISE TRADE BALANCE IN MANUFACTURES AND STAPLES, CANADA, 1970–1979
(millions of dollars)

Year	Manufactures	Staples	Merchandise Trade Balance
1970	− 2 589	5 457	2 868
1971	− 3 200	5 401	2 201
1972	− 4 034	5 515	1 481
1973	− 5 551	7 645	2 094
1974	− 8 209	8 926	717
1975	− 9 350	7 962	−1 388
1976	− 9 150	10 132	982
1977	− 9 663	11 854	2 191
1978	−10 673	13 413	2 740
1979	−13 366	16 148	2 782

Source: Calculated from data in the *Bank of Canada Review* (1970–1980), Tables 74 and 75.
Note: Staples and manufacturing aggregations were obtained as follows:
Staples imports = fuels and lubricants + industrial materials + food.
Manufacturing imports = all other merchandise imports.
Staples exports = farm and fish products + forest products + metals and minerals + chemicals and fertilizers.

A summary view of the composition of exports and imports by commodity group (and changes thereof) over the 1970s is shown in Tables 3 and 4. The figures shown above those in parentheses are the value shares of each commodity group while the figures in parentheses are the 'quantity' shares. These quantity shares are the value shares calculated on the basis of the counter factual assumption that relative prices remain at 1971 levels.

The value shares in both exports and imports remained remarkably constant over the decade with the only obvious trend being the rise in the import share of fuel and lubricants. Grouping the commodities together into manufactures and staples indicates that there was little change in the value share of manufactured goods trade over the decade. However, the relative price of staples to manufactures increased substantially over the decade and this is true whether or not petroleum prices are included in the staples price index. Consequently, when we observe the quantity shares shown in parentheses, it is clear that there were some notable trends during the 1970s, particularly in exports, which were obscured by the relative price changes. The most obvious trend is the increase in the quantity share of manufactured goods in exports from 38 per cent in 1971 to nearly 50 per cent in 1979; that is, if relative prices were at 1971 levels, the quantities of manufactured goods exported in 1979 would account for half of the value of all exports. Correspondingly, the quantity share of

Table 2

FACTORS CONTRIBUTING TO CHANGES IN CANADA'S MERCHANDISE TRADE BALANCE IN MANUFACTURES AND STAPLES 1971–1979

(millions of dollars)

Year	Commodity	Change in Trade Balance	Due to			
			Growth in Trade Quantity	Increase in Trade Prices	Relative Quantities of Exports & Imports	Terms of Trade
1971–72	M	– 837	– 444	– 105	– 226	– 62
	S	115	675	160	– 990	270
	T	– 722	231	55	– 1 216	208
1972–73	M	– 1 517	– 597	– 487	– 773	341
	S	2 130	825	674	– 266	897
	T	613	228	187	– 1 039	1 238
1973–74	M	– 2 658	– 218	– 1 646	– 2 134	1 340
	S	1 282	309	2 335	– 1 948	586
	T	– 1 376	91	689	– 4 082	1 926
1974–75	M	– 1 141	604	– 1 134	163	– 773
	S	– 964	– 532	1 000	– 931	– 501
	T	– 2 105	72	– 134	– 768	– 1 274

Period	Type					
1975–76	M	200	− 887	− 139	1 177	49
	S	2 170	857	134	371	808
	T	2 370	− 30	− 5	1 548	857
1976–77	M	− 513	− 428	− 856	1 440	− 669
	S	1 722	463	926	1 612	−1 279
	T	1 209	35	70	3 052	−1 948
1977–78	M	− 1 010	− 644	−1 084	1 888	−1 170
	S	1 559	759	1 276	− 32	− 444
	T	549	115	192	1 856	−1 614
1978–79	M	− 2 693	− 745	−1 910	−1 499	1 461
	S	2 735	894	2 328	−2 232	1 746
	T	42	149	418	−3 731	3 207
1971–75	M	− 6 153	− 655	−3 372	−2 970	846
	S	2 563	1 277	4 169	−4 135	1 252
	T	− 3 590	622	797	−7 105	2 098
1975–79	M	− 4 016	−2 704	−3 989	3 006	− 329
	S	8 186	2 973	4 664	− 281	831
	T	4 170	269	675	2 725	502
1971–79	M	−10 169	−3 359	−7 361	36	517
	S	10 749	4 250	8 833	−4 416	2 083
	T	580	891	1 472	−4 380	2 600

Source: Calculated by the author, using equation 3, from information in Tables 74–77 of the *Bank of Canada Review*.
Note: M = Manufactures; S = Staples; T = Total.

Table 3
CANADIAN EXPORT SHARES BY COMMODITY (%), 1970–1979
(figures in brackets are constant 1971 dollar shares)

Year	Farm & Fish	Forest	Metals & Minerals	Chemicals & Fertilizers	Manufactures Less Automobiles	Manufactures Including Automobiles
1970	11.1	17.4	28.6	3.2	16.3	37.2
	(11.4)	(17.8)	(27.3)	(3.2)	(16.6)	(37.7)
1971	12.5	17.3	25.9	3.1	15.2	38.8
	(12.5)	(17.3)	(25.9)	(3.1)	(15.2)	(38.8)
1972	11.6	17.9	24.5	2.9	17.4	40.8
	(11.1)	(17.1)	(25.1)	(3.0)	(17.6)	(41.3)
1973	13.1	17.7	26.0	2.8	17.0	38.1
	(10.0)	(16.1)	(26.3)	(3.1)	(18.5)	(42.6)
1974	12.7	17.2	31.0	3.1	15.8	33.7
	(8.6)	(16.9)	(26.0)	(3.4)	(18.2)	(43.0)
1975	12.7	15.3	30.0	3.2	16.9	36.4
	(9.9)	(14.2)	(24.0)	(3.2)	(19.2)	(46.5)
1976	11.5	17.0	28.2	3.7	15.6	37.5
	(10.0)	(15.7)	(21.7)	(3.5)	(17.6)	(47.3)
1977	10.9	17.7	26.3	4.0	15.4	39.2
	(10.3)	(15.9)	(19.6)	(3.7)	(16.8)	(48.4)
1978	10.7	18.1	24.2	4.5	16.7	40.7
	(9.9)	(16.0)	(18.0)	(4.3)	(18.5)	(50.1)
1979	10.7	18.0	25.5	5.1	20.3	38.7
	(9.5)	(16.0)	(17.3)	(4.9)	(23.5)	(49.7)

Source: Calculated from data in the *Bank of Canada Review* (1970–1980), Tables 74 and 76. Rows do not add to 100% because of exclusion of exports of foreign products.

staples has declined — most sharply in metals and minerals. It is also true that the quantity share of manufactured imports, particularly motor vehicles and producers' equipment, has risen, but this increase is smaller in magnitude than that which occurred in exports.

In the above discussion it was noted that during the 1970s, changes in the terms of trade offset the change in the trade balance resulting from changes in the relative quantities of exports and imports, while changes in the relative price of staples to manufactures obscured the changes in relative importance of manufactured goods to staples in the composition of merchandise exports. Table 5 presents a closer examination of the changes in the total terms of trade and the terms of trade in manufactured goods and staples that have occurred during the decade. The overall terms of trade improved rapidly between 1971 and 1974, declined slowly between 1974 and 1976, and more rapidly thereafter. By 1978, the overall terms of trade had almost declined to

Table 4

CANADIAN IMPORT SHARES BY END USE (%), 1970–1979

(figures in brackets are constant 1971 dollar shares)

Year	Lubricants & Fuel	Industrial Materials	Food	Construction Materials	Motor Vehicles	Manufactures			
						Other Transportation Equipment	Producers' Equipment	Other Consumer Goods	Total Manu-factures*
1970	5.5 (6.1)	22.8 (21.8)	7.0 (7.0)	2.3 (2.3)	24.6 (24.8)	3.4 (3.5)	22.5 (22.2)	10.6 (10.8)	63.4 (65.1)
1971	5.8 (5.8)	21.8 (21.8)	6.4 (6.4)	2.3 (2.3)	27.6 (27.6)	2.5 (2.5)	22.5 (22.5)	10.9 (10.9)	65.8 (65.8)
1972	5.7 (5.5)	20.8 (21.3)	6.6 (6.5)	2.5 (2.5)	27.5 (27.6)	2.3 (2.3)	21.4 (21.8)	11.9 (11.5)	65.6 (65.7)
1973	5.7 (4.9)	20.9 (20.3)	7.0 (6.0)	2.7 (2.6)	26.9 (28.3)	3.0 (3.2)	21.0 (22.1)	11.7 (10.9)	65.3 (67.1)
1974	10.5 (3.8)	21.4 (19.9)	6.9 (5.6)	3.1 (3.3)	23.6 (28.0)	2.9 (3.5)	20.0 (23.3)	10.9 (10.7)	60.5 (68.8)
1975	11.9 (4.0)	18.4 (17.8)	6.7 (5.9)	2.4 (2.9)	24.8 (29.2)	2.9 (3.4)	21.3 (24.2)	10.6 (11.1)	62.0 (70.8)
1976	10.8 (3.4)	18.5 (17.9)	6.6 (6.4)	2.5 (2.9)	26.1 (29.7)	1.7 (1.9)	20.4 (23.0)	12.1 (12.9)	62.8 (70.4)
1977	9.7 (3.1)	18.5 (17.7)	6.9 (6.2)	2.4 (2.5)	28.3 (32.1)	1.7 (1.9)	20.0 (22.5)	11.7 (12.1)	64.1 (71.1)
1978	8.9 (2.8)	19.7 (18.7)	6.5 (5.9)	2.2 (2.3)	27.7 (31.2)	2.2 (2.5)	20.6 (23.3)	11.5 (11.7)	64.2 (71.0)
1979	9.1 (2.6)	22.1 (19.6)	5.9 (5.5)	2.2 (2.3)	25.0 (29.1)	3.0 (3.5)	21.2 (24.7)	10.4 (12.0)	61.8 (71.8)

Source: Calculated from data in the Bank of Canada Review (1970–1980), Tables 75 and 77.

* Total of Columns (1), (2), (3), and (9) does not equal 100% because of exclusion of 'Special Items' category.

1971 levels but then rose sharply between 1978 and 1979. Table 5 indicates that the terms of trade in manufactured goods and staples display different patterns than the overall terms of trade. In general, the terms of trade for each group change by much less than the total. For example, in 1974 the total terms of trade were over 15 per cent higher than in 1971, while the manufacturing and staples terms of trade were only 3 and 2 per cent higher respectively. However, during the 1974−1975 period in which the total terms of trade declined, the manufacturing terms of trade declined by a similar order of magnitude and the staples terms of trade also declined but by a smaller amount. During the same period there was a large depreciation of the Canadian dollar.

The relationship between the terms of trade and the relative price of staples and manufactures is clarified by using equation (4).[11]

$$\frac{\Delta P^X}{P^X} - \frac{\Delta P^I}{P^I} = (\sigma_S^X - \sigma_S^I)\,(\frac{\Delta P_S}{P_S} - \frac{\Delta P_M}{P_M})$$

$$+ [\sigma_S^X (\frac{\Delta P_S^X}{P_S^X} - \frac{\Delta P_S}{P_S}) - \sigma_S^I\,(\frac{\Delta P_S^I}{P_S^I} - \frac{\Delta P_S}{P_S})]$$

$$+ [\sigma_M^X (\frac{\Delta P_M^X}{P_M^X} - \frac{\Delta P_M}{P_M}) - \sigma_M^I (\frac{\Delta P_M^I}{P_M^I} - \frac{\Delta P_M}{P_M})]. \tag{4}$$

In equation (4) the subscripts S and M denote staples and manufactures; the superscripts X and I denote exports and imports; and σ denotes the value share. The right hand side of (4) breaks down the proportional

Table 5
TERMS OF TRADE, CANADA, 1970−1979
(ratio of export prices to import prices)

Year	P^X/P^I (Total)	P_M^X/P_M^I (Manufactures)	P_S^X/P_S^I (Staples)	Inverse Exchange Rate
1970	101.8	100.1	102.1	.958
1971	100	100.0	100	.990
1972	101.2	98.8	102.4	1.010
1973	107.1	99.2	107.1	.999
1974	115.3	103.1	102.2	1.022
1975	110.2	98.2	98.3	.983
1976	112.3	99.2	103.6	1.014
1977	106.8	96.5	97.0	.940
1978	102.2	92.4	95.6	.877
1979	108.3	95.5	99.6	.854

Source: Calculated from data in the Bank of Canada Review (1970−1980), Tables 76 and 77.
Legend
P^X = Index of Export Prices
P^I = Index of Import Prices

change in the total terms of trade into three factors. The first term is the proportional change attributable to changes in the relative price of staples to manufactured goods; the second term is the proportional change attributable to changes in the staples terms of trade; and the final term is the amount attributable to changes in the manufactured goods terms of trade.

In Table 6 we have evaluated these components for the annual percentage changes in the terms of trade between 1971 and 1979 and for the sub-periods 1971–1974 and 1974–1978. The table indicates that between 1971 and 1974 the substantial improvement in the Canadian terms of trade is almost totally attributable to the rise in the relative price of staples to manufactured goods. Thus, the structure of Canadian trade (that is, the relative importance of staples in exports as compared to imports) was instrumental in the terms-of-trade improvement during this period, which mitigated the decline in the trade balance. It should be recognized that this increase in the terms of trade substantially increased real income in Canada, since a larger quantity of imports could be obtained for the same quantity of exports. A detailed discussion of how terms-of-trade improvements increase Canadian real income is given by Longworth (1980, p. 16).

Table 6
FACTORS CONTRIBUTING TO CHANGES IN THE TERMS OF TRADE
(percentage changes)

Year	Total	Contributing Factor		
		Change in Relative Price of Staples & Manufactures	Change in Staples Terms of Trade	Change in Manufactures Terms of Trade
1971–72	1.2	.7	1.1	− .6
1972–73	5.8	3.6	2.0	.2
1973–74	7.7	8.0	−2.3	2.0
1974–75	− 4.4	.2	−1.6	−3.0
1975–76	1.9	− .6	1.9	.6
1976–77	− 5.0	− .6	−2.6	−1.8
1977–78	− 4.3	− .7	− .6	−3.0
1978–79	6.0	2.2	1.7	2.1
1971–74	14.7	12.3	.8	1.6
1974–78	−11.8	−1.7	−2.9	−7.2

Source: Calculated by author, using equation (4), from information given in Tables 74–77 of the *Bank of Canada Review*. Aggregate indexes are weighted averages of their components.

Between 1974 and 1978, the terms of trade fell. Table 6 indicates that this fall is attributable to declines in the terms of trade in staples and manufactured goods, particularly the latter. The decline would have been worse (thus the rise in the trade balance less and the reduction in real Canadian income greater) had manufactures been dominant in Canadian exports. In view of this it is difficult to argue that the Canadian trade structure played a detrimental role in the 1970s. Finally, the evidence that the terms of trade fell in staples and manufactures over the period in which the Canadian dollar underwent a major depreciation suggests a link between the exchange rate and the terms of trade.[12]

In summary, the observed changes in the trade balance in manufactured goods and staples between 1970 and 1979 can be attributed to the increases in the volume of trade and the prices of traded goods that have occurred over the decade. The deterioration in the total trade balance between 1970 and 1975 can be attributed to slow growth in the quantities of exports relative to imports, but this slow growth was more concentrated in staples. The improvement in the trade balance after 1975 involved rapid growth in the quantities of manufactured exports relative to imports with relative growth in export and import quantities of staples actually reducing the trade balance. In most cases, terms of trade changes offset movements in quantities. During the decade, there was a material shift towards exports of manufactured goods despite the observed constancy in the value shares.

4. Causal Influences on Merchandise Trade by Commodity Group: A Theoretical Analysis

In this section we undertake a theoretical examination of the determinants of trade prices and quantities by commodity group. In general, we expect that relative prices, factor costs, and income variables in both Canada and the economies of Canada's trading partners are important in the determination of the price and quantity traded of a commodity. This is because Canada's excess supply of a commodity must equal our trading partner's excess demand, while the price of a traded commodity in Canada is likely to be linked to the foreign currency price times the exchange rate. We now discuss the role of domestic and foreign variables in the determination of trade quantities and prices.

Two polar cases can be identified, both of which have played important roles in the well-known international macro-economic models. In the first polar case, the domestic economy is a price taker for commodities; that is, foreign excess supply is indeterminate at exogenous world prices. As a result, domestic excess supply solely determines quantities traded and, given the law of one price,[13] the exchange rate, and world prices determine domestic prices. The other polar case assumes that Canada has price-making power for traded commodities and that producers adjust output to meet demand at domestically set prices. Then the level of quantities demanded is determined solely by foreign excess demands and prices are determined by domestic factors.

Both of these polar cases appear in common macro-economic models of an open economy. The monetary models usually assume that the first polar case, the price-taker model, describes the markets for all traded goods, while the Mundell-Fleming model assumes that the first polar case describes only the market for imports and that the second polar case describes the market for exports. This bifurcation restricts the structural detail that must be considered in the model to two commodity groups — exports and imports, and identifies the exchange rate with the single relative price in the output market — the terms of trade. Recently, Appelbaum and Kohli (1979) have provided some evidence that Canada is not a price taker for export goods in aggregate while the price-taking hypothesis cannot be rejected for imports. While this implies that foreign excess demand is not indeterminate for exported goods in aggregate, it need not imply that the domestic excess supply of such goods is irrelevant as is assumed in the Mundell-Fleming model.

The general case is shown in Figure 1, which is drawn for the case where i is an exported good. On the vertical axis is measured the domestic money price P_i of good i, and on the horizontal axis is measured the domestic excess supply and foreign excess demand in quantity units of good i. Q_i and Q_i^* denote domestic and foreign output of good i and D_i and D_i^* denote domestic and foreign demand for good i. The upward-sloping schedule $X_i^s(Z)$ represents the domestic excess supply schedule of good i and Z is a vector of domestic variables. The downward-sloping schedule $X_i^q(Z^*)$ is the foreign excess demand schedule and Z^* is a vector that includes the foreign counterparts to Z and the exchange rate, changes in which shift the $X_i^q(Z^*)$ schedule proportionately if the exchange rate is normalized to unity initially. The equilibrium prices and quantities traded are found by the intersection of the two schedules as shown. In this general case, these equilibrium values depend on both domestic and foreign variables, Z and Z^*.[14] In the first polar case, the $X_i^q(Z^*)$ schedule becomes flat so that P_i is fixed and the $X_i^s(Z)$ schedule determines quantities. In the second polar case, $X_i^q(Z)$ is flat, fixing domestic prices, while the $X_i^q(Z^*)$ schedule determines quantities.

The effect of various domestic and foreign variables on prices and quantities traded of good i can now be examined.

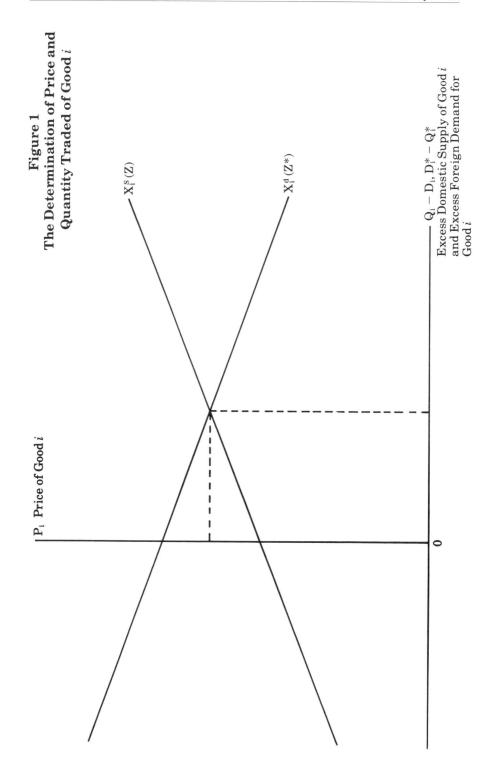

Figure 1
The Determination of Price and
Quantity Traded of Good i

P_i Price of Good i

$X_i^s (Z)$

$X_i^d (Z^*)$

0

$Q_i - D_i, D_i^* - Q_i^*$
Excess Domestic Supply of Good i
and Excess Foreign Demand for
Good i

Foreign Income Changes

An increase in foreign income shifts the $X_i^d(Z^*)$ schedule to the right (assuming good i is normal), thereby raising the quantity of net exports and the price of good i. In the price-taking economy case, $X_i^d(Z^*)$ is flat so foreign income changes are irrelevant. The recorded effect of U.S. income changes on Canadian merchandise trade requires that Canada not be a price taker for some broad category of traded goods.

Domestic Income Changes

A rise in Canadian income may shift the $X_i^s(Z)$ schedule to the right or left since domestic output and absorption of good i will both rise. If $X_i^s(Z)$ shifts to the right, the quantity of net exports of good i would rise, and P_i could fall if $X_i^d(Z^*)$ is downward sloping. In general, the effect would depend on whether output changes were biased for or against the commodity and whether the income elasticity of the commodity was high or low. While manufactured goods generally have high income elasticities, it is also the case that growth was biased towards manufactures during the 1970s. The annual real growth rate in non-agricultural manufactured goods was 4.1 per cent between 1971 and 1979 as compared to 2.1 per cent for forestry and mining. Consequently, the higher income elasticities of manufactured goods do not necessarily imply that rapid domestic growth will cause a secular deterioration in the trade balance in manufactured goods. Also, from an aggregative viewpoint, it can be argued that the marginal propensity to absorb is less than unity. Thus for most commodities, the $X_i^s(Z)$ schedule should shift to the right when domestic income rises thereby raising the quantity of net exports.[15] For these reasons there is no a priori reason that growth will cause the Canadian trade balance to deteriorate in the long run, nor has there been any empirical reason to believe it.

Domestic Cost Inflation

Between 1970 and 1975, unit labour costs in Canadian manufacturing rose at a rate in excess of labour costs in the United States while the exchange rate remained constant. If Canadian producers are price takers, they would find output prices rising less rapidly than labour costs, thus reducing profitability and inducing firms to cut back production or cease operating; that is, the $X_i^s(Z)$ schedule would shift left thus reducing net exports. If P_i is domestically determined in part or whole (that is, $X_i^d(Z^*)$ is not flat), then the price elasticity of foreign demand would be important in determining the effect of domestic cost inflation. In the second polar case it would be the only channel through which domestic cost inflation would influence the trade balance.

The Rise in Resource Prices

During the first half of the decade, the price of staples rose rapidly relative to manufactured goods both for exported and imported commodities. The relative price of staples reached a peak in 1975, declined slowly, and then again rose sharply in 1978.

The rise in the relative price of staples was due to the world-wide explosion in raw material prices and the fact that raw materials comprise a larger fraction of the costs of staples than of manufactures. Since the increase was common to Canada and its trading partners, the foreign and domestic excess demand/supply schedules would shift upwards for a given commodity. However, since staples constitute a larger fraction of Canadian exports than imports, the terms of trade improved and increased Canadian income during the first half of the decade as discussed above. This would raise absorption of the average commodity and shift the X_i^S schedule to the left thereby reducing the quantity of net exports. If, as seems likely, the marginal propensity to absorb manufactured goods is greater than staples, then one would expect the rise in the relative price of staples to depress net exports of manufactures. Thus the structural shift toward increased quantities of manufactured exports observed above is all the more impressive in light of the rise in staples' prices.

The Depreciation of the Canadian Dollar

In the fourth quarter of 1976, the value of the Canadian dollar in units of U.S. currency began a sharp decline, stabilizing around $0.85 U.S. by 1979. This increase in the exchange rate shifts the $X_i^q(Z^*)$ schedule upwards by the amount of the depreciation. The $X_i^S(Z)$ schedule may also be shifted upwards if domestic production costs of good i are increased by the depreciation. This may occur if good i uses inputs for which prices are set in world markets or if the prices of domestic inputs such as labour rise because the depreciation raises the cost of living. If factor costs rise in the same proportion as the depreciation, the $X_i^S(Z)$ schedule would rise by the same amount as the $X_i^q(Z^*)$ schedule and trade quantities would be unchanged. However, wages did not rise enough in Canada after 1975 to offset the depreciation so the $X_i^S(Z)$ schedule shifted up only partially. Thus depreciation can be expected to increase the quantity of net exports and the prices of traded goods as illustrated in Figure 2.

The increase in the quantity of net exports will be greater the smaller the upward shift in $X_i^S(Z)$, the flatter is $X_i^S(Z)$, and the flatter is $X_i^q(Z^*)$. Thus commodities with high elasticities of foreign and domestic excess demand/supply and for which factor costs are insensitive to depreciation are most likely to be the ones for which quantities of net exports will rise most as a result of depreciation. There are some

Figure 2

Effect of Depreciation on Trade in Good *i*

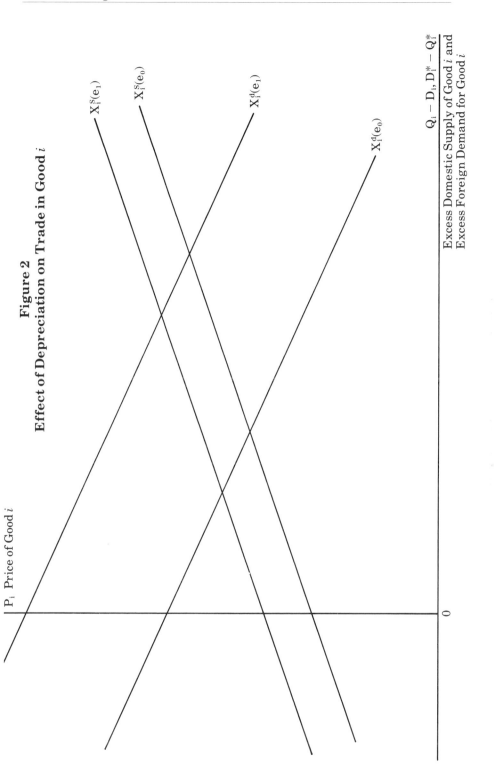

P_i Price of Good *i*

$X_i^s(e_1)$

$X_i^s(e_0)$

$X_i^d(e_1)$

$X_i^d(e_0)$

$Q_i - D_i, D_i^* - Q_i^*$

Excess Domestic Supply of Good *i* and
Excess Foreign Demand for Good *i*

0

a priori reasons for believing manufactured commodities are more likely to fulfil these conditions.

5. Causal Influences on Commodity Trade: An Econometric Evaluation

In this section we report preliminary results from an econometric evaluation of the causal influences on merchandise trade by commodity group. This investigation is based on the theoretical framework described above. We used the broad commodity groups classified in the *Bank of Canada Review*. There are seven import groups:

1. Fuels and Lubricants
2. Industrial Materials
3. Construction Materials
4. Producers' Equipment
5. Transportation Equipment and Parts (excluding motor vehicles)
6. Motor Vehicles and Parts
7. Consumer Goods

For exports we use five commodity groups:

X1. Fish and Fish Products
X2. Forest Products
X3. Metals and Minerals
X4. Chemicals
X5. Manufactures and Miscellaneous

For each category of exports we specify a domestic excess supply equation and a foreign excess demand equation. The excess demand equation is of the form:

$$X_i^d = \beta_{0i} + \beta_{1i} RP_i^* + \beta_{2i}Y^* + \beta_{3i}RW_i^*, \tag{5}$$

plus a time trend, seasonal dummies, and an error term. In equation (5), X_i^d is the quantity of foreign excess demand for good i; RP_i^* is domestic selling price divided by the product of the exchange rate and the U.S. consumer price index; Y^* is real U.S. gross national product; and RW_i^* is the ratio of the U.S. selling price of good i divided by per unit factor costs in the U.S. production of good i. The presumed signs are $\beta_{1i}, \beta_{3i} < 0$, and $\beta_{2i} > 0$.

Since there are likely to be time and cost constraints on the adjustment of actual quantities to desired levels, we also estimate a partial adjustment model of the form $X_t - X_{t-1} = \lambda(\bar{X}_t - X_{t-1}) + \epsilon_t$ where $\bar{X}_t$ is the desired level of the dependent variable and λ is the adjustment coefficient. In such equations the dependent variable lagged by one quarter is entered as an independent variable. The coefficient on the lagged dependent variable is one minus λ so the long-run coefficients are found by dividing through by one minus this coefficient. It might be noted that the long-run coefficients may be significant where the short-run coefficients were not. We did not carry out such tests, however.

The domestic excess supply equations for exported commodities are specified

$$X_i^s = \gamma_{0i} + \gamma_{1i} RP_i + \gamma_{2i} Y + \gamma_{3i} RW_i + \gamma_{4i} C_i, \tag{6}$$

plus time trend, seasonal dummies, and the error term. RP_i is the domestic selling price of good i divided by the domestic C.P.I. This variable is intended to capture substitution effects in domestic absorption of exported goods. RW_i is the ratio of the selling price of export i divided by unit factor costs in the production of good i; Y is domestic real GNP; and C_i is capacity utilization in domestic production of good i. The presumed signs are $\gamma_{1i}, \gamma_{3i} > 0$ and $\gamma_{2i}, \gamma_{4i} < 0$. This equation is also specified in partial adjustment form.

In the event that the first polar case describes the situation for Canadian exports, then the export supply equation (6) should determine export quantities. If the second polar case describes the export market, then the export demand equation (5) will determine export quantities. More generally, both the export demand and supply equations can determine the export quantities.

For imported commodities, only the domestic excess demand equation is specified and estimated since it seems probable that Canada is a price taker for imported commodities. The equation is specified as:

$$I_i^d = \alpha_{0i} + \alpha_{1i} RP_i + \alpha_{2i} Y + \alpha_{3i} RW_i + \alpha_{4i} C_i, \tag{7}$$

plus time trend, and so on. The presumed signs are $\alpha_{1i}, \alpha_{3i} < 0$ and $\alpha_{2i}, \alpha_{4i} > 0$. The equations are also specified in partial adjustment form.

Because of time constraints, among other things, we were faced with severe data limitations. Unit factor costs by commodity group in U.S. production were unavailable so RW_i^* was dropped in the estimation of equation (5). For equations (6) and (7), unit wage costs were used as a proxy for domestic unit factor costs. This is inadequate since labour content varies considerably by commodity group. We estimated all equations in log-linear form so all coefficients can be interpreted as elasticities. We used the Cansim mini-base as our data source and constructed some variables for the commodity groups from the Standard International Trade Classification (S.I.T.C.) level data.

In Table 7 we present the results for import demand by end use classification. Using the Ordinary Least Squares (O.L.S.) method, a time trend variable was included in linear form. Where this linear time trend coefficient was negative, we used a quadratic time trend. The lagged dependent variable is included for a commodity group when the coefficient on such a variable was significant. Iterative methods of estimation (Beach-MacKinnon) were used when the $D.W.$ or h statistic indicated auto-regression. Significant negative price

Table 7
ESTIMATED DEMAND FUNCTION FOR IMPORTS BY END USE
(Ordinary Least Squares Method)

End Use	Constant	RP	Y	RW	C	I_{-1}	ρ	$\bar{R}^2$	D.W.	h	S.E.E.	Comments
Fuel & Lubricants	-11.62 (-1.34)	.062 (.89)	1.62 (1.78)	-.516 (-2.52)	.47 (1.45)		.11 (.74)	.765	1.91		.0789	OLS with linear time trend and correction for auto-regression using Beach-MacKinnon
Industrial Materials	-5.73 (-1.66)	-.24 (-.9)	.51 (1.31)	.019 (.07)	.73 (4.13)	.40 (3.78)		.96	1.90	.43	.04	OLS with lagged dependent variable (partial adjustment model) and linear time trend
Construction Materials	-33.4 (-3.7)	-.05 (-.15)	2.63 (2.94)	.65 (2.44)	1.59 (3.09)	.49 (5.03)		.94	2.20	-.90	.071	As above
Producers' Equipment	-7.23 (-1.50)	.15 (1.36)	.56 (3.18)	-.35 (-1.24)	.69 (1.31)	.38 (2.93)		.98	2.15	-1.17	.037	As above
Transportation Equip. (excl. motor vehicles)	-15.50 (-4.00)	-1.03 (-2.92)	1.74 (4.22)	.123 (.87)	.034 (.032)	.43 (4.23)		.99	2.01	-.07	.043	OLS with lagged dependent variable, linear time trend and correction for auto-regression using Beach-MacKinnon
Motor Vehicles & Parts	-.168 (-.02)	-.32 (-.79)	-.063 (.08)	.20 (1.00)	.67 (4.43)		.14 (.83)	.97	1.86		.0506	OLS with quadratic time trend and corrected for auto-regression using Beach-MacKinnon
Consumer Goods	-16.34 (-5.26)	-.50 (-2.89)	1.83 (5.07)	.38 (1.77)	-.36 (-1.52)	.58 (6.51)	-.54 (-3.67)	.99	1.91	.37	.046	OLS with lagged dependent variable, linear time trend and correction for auto-regression

Note: Author's estimate.

elasticities were found only for imports of transportation equipment and consumer goods. All imports had positive income elasticities (although some were insignificant) with construction materials, transportation equipment, and consumer goods having the highest income elasticities. Thus not all manufactured imports have high income elasticities since motor vehicles, which constitute a significant fraction of manufactured imports, have a low income elasticity. The relative factor cost variable was only significant and of the expected sign for fuel and lubricants. On a priori grounds this seems most unlikely. The capacity utilization variable in the domestic import-competing industries has the expected positive sign for all groups except consumer goods. This could indicate that high utilization in domestic import-competing industries raises the price of domestically produced commodities, causing substitution towards foreign-made goods, or may reflect non-price rationing in domestic markets causing spill-over into import demand. The latter interpretation is that of Yadav (1977). Finally, lagged adjustment is indicated for all commodity groups except fuel and lubricants and motor vehicles.

Since the error terms for the commodity groups may be correlated, the efficiency of the estimated coefficients may be improved by applying Zellner's Seemingly Unrelated Regressions (S.U.R.) estimation as compared to when the equations are estimated separately, whether or not the coefficients are of the expected sign (Table 8). Technical problems prevented us from using iterative procedures for auto-regression, but note that the $D.W.$ values shown do not necessarily indicate auto-regression under S.U.R.

In Table 9, the results of estimating the demand for exports by commodity group, O.L.S. method, are presented. Again, the lagged dependent variable is included where significant and Beach-MacKinnon procedures are used if auto-regression is indicated. The relative price variable is negative for all export commodity groups but significant for none. Manufactured exports have the highest elasticity with respect to U.S. income with chemicals and fish having income elasticities in the order of unity. Slow adjustment to desired levels of exports is indicated for all commodity groups except manufactures. The results for using the S.U.R. method are shown in Table 10. Significant and negative relative price coefficients are found for fish, metals and minerals, and chemicals, while income elasticities are reduced for all goods except fish. However, no procedures have been used to account for possible auto-regression.

In Table 11 we present the results of the O.L.S. estimation of export supply equations. The relative price variable is insignificant while the relative unit factor cost and capacity constraints variables are significant but do not have the expected signs. This could indicate that real wages and capacity utilization rates are raised by high export

Table 8
ESTIMATED DEMAND FUNCTION FOR IMPORTS BY END USE
(Seemingly Unrelated Regression Method)

End Use	Constant	RP	Y	RW	C	D.W.	S.E.E.	Comments
Fuel & Lubricants	− 5.64 (−.74)	.14 (2.54)	1.00 (1.25)	−.67 (−3.98)	.65 (2.35)	1.71	.073	Seemingly unrelated regression with linear time trend
Industrial Materials	− 9.14 (−2.97)	−.66 (−3.03)	.688 (1.99)	.35 (1.65)	1.167 (8.26)	1.25	.041	As above
Construction Materials	−61.01 (−9.38)	−.067 (−.30)	5.02 (7.49)	1.217 (7.30)	2.48 (7.65)	1.37	.083	As above
Producers' Equipment	−19.14 (−4.59)	.017 (.085)	2.06 (4.69)	.176 (3.13)	.519 (4.29)	1.28	.043	As above
Transportation Equip. (excl. motor vehicles)	−23.37 (−7.02)	−.88 (−6.42)	2.78 (8.31)	−.005 (−.07)	.04 (.87)	1.56	.048	As above
Motor Vehicles & Parts	− 9.57 (−1.57)	.28 (.95)	1.198 (1.9)	−.34 (−2.33)	.79 (7.00)	1.53	.053*	As above
Consumer Goods	−24.56 (−6.99)	−.62 (−5.81)	3.00 (8.16)	.37 (2.80)	−.53 (−3.09)	1.56	.054	As above

Note: Author's estimate.

Table 9

ESTIMATED DEMAND FUNCTION FOR EXPORTS BY COMMODITY
(Ordinary Least Squares Method)

Commodity	Constant	RP^*	Y^*	X_{-1}	ρ	$\bar{R}_2$	D.W.	h	S.E.E.	Comments
Fish & Fish Products	-.8 (-.79)	-.17 (-1.05)	1.23 (2.59)	.55 (4.736)		.76	1.736	1.43	.072	OLS, lagged dependent variable, linear time trend
Forest Products	-.16 (-.147)	-.035 (-.36)	.46 (1.01)	.8 (8.85)		.71	2.11	-.48	.061	As above
Metals & Minerals	-.33 (-.24)	-.11 (-.53)	.89 (1.65)	.60 (4.68)	-.28 (-1.78)	.96	2.04		.087	OLS, lagged dependent variable, linear time trend, corrected for auto-regression
Chemicals	.45 (.66)	-.112 (-.59)	1.22 (4.03)	.278 (2.25)		.98	1.904	.57	.042	OLS, lagged variable, linear time trend
Manufactures	-.8198 (-.473)	-.054 (-.079)	2.246 (2.969)		.538 (3.64)	.96	1.86		.0727	OLS, linear time trend, corrected for auto-regression using Beach-MacKinnon

Note: Author's estimate.

Table 10
ESTIMATED DEMAND FUNCTION FOR EXPORTS BY
COMMODITY
(Seemingly Unrelated Regression Method)

Commodity	Constant	RP*	Y*	D.W.	S.E.E.
Fish &	−.195	−.414	2.036	.89	.316
Fish Products	(−.169)	(−2.57)	(4.02)		
Forest	3.299	−.147	.55	.358	.45
Products	(2.157)	(−1.28)	(.819)		
Metals &	2.236	−.49	.87	1.22	.35
Minerals	(1.55)	(−2.51)	(1.38)		
Chemicals	1.564	−.527	1.24	1.11	.087
	(2.45)	(−3.53)	(4.46)		
Manufactures	1.06	.218	1.42	1.10	.25
	(1.05)	(.62)	(3.218)		

Note: Author's estimate.

demand in accordance with Keynesian demand-determined output assumptions. For most commodities the domestic income variable has the expected negative sign but is insignificant for all commodities except forest products, where it is significant and has the wrong sign. Slow adjustment is only indicated in fish and manufactures. These results cast considerable doubt on the specification and/or the importance of export supply in the determination of export quantities. Table 12 presents estimates of export supply equations using the S.U.R. method. The results are not much different than those obtained by O.L.S. estimation, although the expected negative effect of domestic income on exports (through increased domestic absorption) is now significant in fish and manufactures.

In order to allow for simultaneity between the demand and supply for exports, we also estimated the export demand and supply equations using the two-stage least squares approach (2SLS).[16] The results are presented in Tables 13 and 14. In general, 2SLS estimation increases the magnitude and significance of the relative price and U.S. income variables in the demand for exports. The results for the export supply equations are not changed in a meaningful way. It is not clear why demand should be so important in the determination of Canadian exports, since it is unlikely that Canada has monopoly power in such goods as fish and chemicals.

Table 11
ESTIMATED SUPPLY FUNCTION OF EXPORTS BY COMMODITY
(Ordinary Least Squares Method)

Commodity	Constant	RP	Y	RW	C	X_{-1}	ρ	$\bar{R}_2$	D.W.	h	S.E.E.	Comments
Fish & Fish Products	.41 (.118)	.044 (.248)	−.36 (−.97)	−.46 (−2.98)	1.27 (6.79)	.30 (3.2)		.87	2.22	−.98	.05	OLS, linear two trend, lagged dependent variable
Forest Products	−13.39 (−2.591)	−.0619 (−.376)	1.33 (2.279)	−.837 (−2.394)	.6382 (2.237)		.58 (4.48)	0.95	1.67		.05	OLS, linear time trend, Beach-MacKinnon
Metals & Minerals	7.797 (1.140)	.0006 (.0014)	−.906 (−1.300)	−.1828 (−.77)	1.409 (5.28)			.934	1.82		.078	OLS, linear time trend
Chemicals	.283 (.0771)	−.637 (−1.387)	−.34 (−.982)	−.608 (−2.593)	1.078 (5.095)			.982	1.95		.04	As above
Manufactures	12.99 (2.03)	.92 (1.90)	−1.12 (−1.71)	−.65 (−3.47)	.83 (5.32)	.34 (2.87)		.97	1.71	1.22	.059	OLS, linear time trend, lagged dependent variable

Note: Author's estimate.

Table 12
ESTIMATED SUPPLY FUNCTION OF EXPORTS BY COMMODITY
(Seemingly Unrelated Regression Method)

Commodity	Constant	RP	Y	RW	C	D.W.	S.E.E.
Fish &	2.82	.26	− .69	−.61	1.72	1.4	.052
Fish Products	(.83)	(1.66)	(−1.91)	(−4.74)	(12.54)		
Forest	−9.56	−.04	.85	−1.03	.75	.87	.055
Products	(−2.12)	(−.53)	(1.6)	(−4.86)	(3.81)		
Metals &	5.98	.082	− .75	−.12	1.41	1.78	.071
Minerals	(.99)	(.25)	(−1.23)	(−.60)	(6.03)		
Chemicals	1.30	−.78	− .13	−.17	.8	1.73	.038
	(.43)	(−2.72)	(−.42)	(−.96)	(4.99)		
Manufactures	14.00	.30	−1.08	−.49	.71	1.16	.061
	(2.70)	(.81)	(−2.11)	(−3.57)	(7.34)		

Note: Author's estimate.

Table 13
ESTIMATED DEMAND FUNCTION FOR EXPORTS BY COMMODITY
(Two-Stage Least Squares Method)

Commodity	Constant	RP^*	Y^*	ρ	D.W.	$\bar{R}_2$	S.E.E.
Fish & Fish Products	.462	−.411	1.74	.55	1.60	.91	.074
	(.25)	(−1.40)	(2.21)	(4.21)			
Forest Products	1.11	.136	1.50	.84	2.07	.94	.061
	(.515)	(.611)	(1.58)	(10.24)			
Metals & Minerals	2.57	−.540	.723	.37	2.04	.88	.088
	(1.18)	(−1.61)	(.756)	(2.51)			
Chemicals	.497	−.15	1.71	.42	1.91	.97	.042
	(.496)	(−.48)	(3.89)	(2.80)			
Manufactures	−2.24	−1.69	2.89	.77	1.98	.95	.070
	(−1.07)	(−1.90)	(3.18)	(7.14)			

Note: Author's estimate.

Table 14
ESTIMATED SUPPLY FUNCTION OF EXPORTS BY COMMODITY
(Two-Stage Least Squares Method)

Commodity	Constant	RP	Y	RW	C	ρ	D.W.	$\bar{R}_2$	S.E.E.	Comments
Fish & Fish Products	− 2.72 (−.57)	−.199 (−.65)	.017 (.034)	− .36 (−1.64)	1.46 (6.48)	.31 (2.03)	2.0	.91	.054	Two-stage least squares, linear time trend, Beach-MacKinnon
Forest Products	−13.53 (−2.5)	−.065 (−.4)	1.34 (2.3)	− .83 (−2.41)	.65 (2.28)	.57 (4.40)	1.67	.96	.05	As above
Metals & Minerals	4.69 (.57)	.276 (.5)	−.56 (−.66)	− .32 (−1.04)	1.48 (5.17)		1.83		.078	Two-stage least squares, linear time trend
Chemicals	− 9.538 (−1.40)	1.19 (1.03)	.248 (.50)	−1.15 (−2.92)	1.40 (4.92)		1.88		.040	As above
Manufactures	3.46 (.38)	1.78 (1.94)	−.10 (−.10)	− .51 (−2.32)	.90 (5.40)	.38 (2.53)	1.91	.95	.058	Two-stage least squares, linear time trend, Beach-MacKinnon

Note: Author's estimate.

Notes

* We are indebted to our discussants Tim Hazledine and Tom Maxwell and other participants of the John Deutsch Round Table on Economic Policy for comments and suggestions that improved the paper.

[1] See Freedman and Longworth (1980), p. 60.

[2] For example, Barber and McCallum (1980), pp. 62–63 found that the adjusted current-account deficit was in the order of 1 per cent of GNP, which is comparable to the mid-1960s average. Similar magnitudes were calculated by Longworth (1979).

[3] This assertion was made by Robinson (1980), p. 160.

[4] Wilkinson (1978), p. 5.

[5] I am indebted to my discussant Tim Hazledine for pointing out the connection between the arguments of structuralists and those of the elasticity pessimists of the early Keynesian era.

[6] For example, see Robinson (1980), pp. 165–72.

[7] On these grounds, Daly (1980), who shares some of the concerns of the structuralists about the composition of Canadian merchandise trade, argues that *reduced* trade restrictions are necessary in order to reduce Canada's dependence on slow-growing staples exports and to exploit economies of scale in manufacturing.

[8] The choice of commodities grouped under each category is somewhat arbitrary and dictated by data considerations. For the purposes of this paper we have taken staples to include farm and fish products, forest products, chemicals and fertilizers, fuels and lubricants, and industrial materials. Such categories probably include commodities that should be included in manufactures, and vice versa, but price and quantity indexes were only available for these broad categories so we were constrained to constructing the staples and manufacturing aggregates from them.

[9] The trends displayed in Table 1 were given a prominent role in Robinson's (1980) discussion of the structural problems in Canadian trade. In fact it was on the basis of this evidence that Robinson concluded that the perceived structural problems in Canada's merchandise trade have worsened over the 1970s. These trends were also examined by MacKay and Hannah (1979), pp. 8–9.

[10] We can write $P_i^1 Q_i^1 - P_i^0 Q_i^0$ as $P_i^0 \Delta Q_i + Q_i^0 \Delta P_i + \Delta P_i \Delta Q_i$ or

$P_i^1 \Delta Q_i + Q_i^1 \Delta P_i - \Delta P_i \Delta Q_i$. By adding we obtain $\Delta(P_i - Q_i) \equiv \bar{P}_i \Delta Q_i + \bar{Q}_i \Delta P_i$ where

$\bar{P}_i = (P_i^1 + P_i^0)/2$ and $\bar{Q}_i = (Q_i^1 + Q_i^0)/2$. Then $\Delta(P_i Q_i) \equiv \bar{V}_i \left(\dfrac{\Delta Q_i}{\bar{Q}_i} + \dfrac{\Delta P_i}{\bar{P}_i}\right)$ where $\bar{V}_i = \bar{P}_i \cdot \bar{Q}_i$.

By these steps we obtain $\Delta T_i \equiv \bar{V}_i^X \left(\dfrac{\Delta Q_i^X}{\bar{Q}_i^X} + \dfrac{\Delta P_i^X}{\bar{P}_i^X}\right) - \bar{V}_i^I \left(\dfrac{\Delta Q_i^I}{\bar{Q}_i^I} + \dfrac{\Delta P_i^I}{\bar{P}_i^I}\right)$.

By adding and subtracting $\dfrac{\Delta Q^T}{\bar{Q}^T}$ and $\dfrac{\Delta P^T}{\bar{P}^T}$ we obtain identity (3) in the text.

[11] Since $\dfrac{\Delta P^X}{\bar{P}^X} \equiv \left(\dfrac{\bar{P}_S^X \ \bar{Q}_S^X}{\bar{P}^X \cdot \bar{Q}^X}\right) \dfrac{\Delta P_S^X}{\bar{P}_S^X} + \left(\dfrac{\bar{P}_M^X \ \bar{Q}_M^X}{\bar{P}^X \ \bar{Q}^X}\right) \dfrac{\Delta P_M^X}{\bar{P}_M^X}$ and $\dfrac{\Delta P^I}{\bar{P}_I} \equiv \left(\dfrac{\bar{P}_S^I \cdot \bar{Q}_S^I}{\bar{P}^I \ \bar{Q}^I}\right) \dfrac{\Delta P_S^I}{\bar{P}_S^I}$

$+ \left(\dfrac{\bar{P}_M^I \ \bar{Q}_M^I}{\bar{P}^I \ \bar{Q}^I}\right) \dfrac{\Delta P_M^I}{\bar{P}_M^I}$ we can let $\dfrac{\bar{P}_i^j \ \bar{Q}_i^j}{\bar{P}^j \ \bar{Q}^j} = \sigma_i^j$ and subtract to get (4)

by adding and subtracting $\dfrac{\Delta P_S}{\bar{P}_S} - \dfrac{\Delta P_M}{\bar{P}_M}$. Note $\sigma_S^X + \sigma_M^X = \sigma_S^I + \sigma_S^I = 1$.

[12] If Canada were a price taker for all traded goods, the terms of trade would not be affected by exchange-rate changes. If Canada is a price taker only for imports and has price-making power for exports, depreciation will deteriorate the terms of trade.

[13] We assume the law of one price $P_i = eP_i^*$ holds for the commodity groups discussed despite evidence that this law holds only at the most disaggregated level. In fact, recorded import price indexes are constructed on the assumption of the law of one price.

[14] We can solve for P_i and Q_i as functions of Z and Z^*, which in differential form have the solutions:

$$\Delta P_i = \frac{X_{iZ}^d \; Z^* - X_{iZ}^S \; \Delta Z}{X_{iP}^S \; - X_{iP}^d}$$

$$\Delta X_i = \frac{X_{iP}^S \; X_{iZ}^d \; \Delta Z^* - X_{iP}^d \; X_{iZ}^S \; \Delta Z}{X_{iP}^S \; - X_{iP}^d}.$$

In the price taker case, $X_{iP}^d \to -\infty$ so $\Delta X_i \to X_{iZ}^S \; \Delta Z$ while in the Keynesian price-maker case $X_{iP}^S \to \infty$ and $\Delta X_i \to X_{iZ}^d \; \Delta Z^*$.

[15] The following life-cycle interpretation can be given. A smooth time path of absorption is preferred so variations in output are offset by hoarding and dis-hoarding financial wealth. Collectively this implies a trade surplus when income rises and a trade deficit when income falls.

[16] In order to test the possibility of simultaneity in supply and demand, one can apply a modified version of the test outlined by Hausman (1978) utilizing O.L.S. and 2SLS estimates. The test-statistic relevant for testing the null hypothesis can be written as

$$m = (\hat{b}_{2s} - \hat{b}_0)^1 (Var \; \hat{b}_{2s} - Var \; \hat{b}_0)^{-1} (\hat{b}_{2s} - \hat{b}_0),$$

which in our case is distributed as t with $n(46)$ degrees of freedom. The calculated t-statistics are as follows:

DEMAND (1.93) (0.84) (0.46) (1.48) (0.2).
SUPPLY (1.29) (0.25) (0.69) (1.72) (1.86).

We cannot reject the null hypothesis. However, for fish and fish products, chemical material, and manufactured goods, the value of t-statistics are relatively high to indicate some kind of simultaneity.

References

Appelbaum, Elie and Kohli, Ulrich R. (1979) "Canada–United States Trade: Tests for the Small-Open-Economy Hypothesis." *Canadian Journal of Economics* 12 (February): 1–14.

Barber, Clarence L. and McCallum, John C.P. (1980) *Unemployment and Inflation: The Canadian Experience*. Ottawa: Canadian Institute for Economic Policy.

Daly, D.J. (1980) "Further Improving Manufacturing Productivity in Canada." *Cost and Management* 54 (July/August): 14–20.

Freedman, Charles and Longworth, David. (1980) "Some Aspects of the Canadian Experience with Flexible Exchange Rates in the 1970s." Bank of Canada Technical Report No. 20. Ottawa: Bank of Canada.

Hausman, J.A. (1978) "Specification Tests in Econometrics." *Econometrica* 46 (November): 1251–71.

Longworth, David. (1979) "The Effect of the Inflationary Premium in Interest Rates on the Evolution of the Canadian Balance of Payments." Mimeo. Bank of Canada.

Longworth, David. (1980) "The Terms of Trade: The Canadian Experience in the 1970s." *Bank of Canada Review* (January): 13–25.

MacKay, Ian and Hannah, Robert. (1979) "Canada's Balance of Payments in the 1970s: A Perspective." *Bank of Canada Review* (March): 3–15.

Robinson, H. Lukin. (1980) *Canada's Crippled Dollar: An Analysis of International Trade and Our Troubled Balance of Payments*. Ottawa: Canadian Institute for Economic Policy.

Wilkinson, B. (1978) *Canada's Trade Options*. Ryerson Lecture in Economics. Toronto.

Yadav, Gopal. (1977) "Variable Elasticities and Non-Price Rationing in the Import Demand Function of Canada, 1956:1–1973:4." *Canadian Journal of Economics* 10 (November): 702–12.

Comment

by
Thomas Maxwell

I consider this paper a worthwhile contribution to the literature on the Canadian balance of payments, especially Section 3 where the decomposition and subsequent analysis of the merchandise-trade balance goes a long way towards exploding some of the popular myths. I will direct the bulk of my comments to two areas of the paper: the reasons as to why one should be concerned with the persistence and structure of a current-account deficit, and a conundrum in the empirical results presented in Section 5.

The authors correctly identify the similarities between the structuralists' view and those of the elasticity pessimists (to which one may also add the long-laggers), and they point out some of the problems associated with the structuralist policy prescriptions. However, I believe that the conventional 'macro-economic' view also has to take into account some of the structural aspects of Canadian trade patterns. The first point that needs to be clarified is why one should be concerned about the structure of a consistent current-account deficit when, in macro-economic terms, all it reflects is a nation that has chosen to consume and invest more now than the productive capacity of the domestic economy allows. There are at least three reasons why policy makers are concerned.

1. As debts are usually incurred in a foreign currency, any depreciation of the exchange rate will result in increasing domestic currency debt-service payments. This forces a greater burden of adjustment onto merchandise-trade components. In addition, there may be political problems associated with a high degree of foreign ownership.
2. A persistent deficit, in conjunction with low elasticities and long lags, may prove to be a constraint on economic policy as it diverts attention away from monetary aggregates towards the exchange rate.
3. In a country such as Canada, with exports of both staples and manufactured goods, a strong improvement in the terms of trade in staples will cause an improvement in the merchandise balance. At the same time, if the associated inflationary pressures are not

accommodated by the monetary authorities, the combined effect will be an appreciation in the exchange rate. This will place manufactured exports, which in the case of Canada are not that much more competitive than those of the United States, under increasing competitive pressure. While this may be defended on the basis of comparative advantage, the adjustment costs, especially in view of the regional concentration of staples and manufactured goods, may be very large. While the possibility of favourable terms of trade movements in staples 'crowding out' manufactured goods was discussed briefly in the theoretical analysis of Section 4, it was not, to my mind, given sufficient prominence in the light of Canadian trade patterns.

While part of the difference between the structuralist and macro-economic views can be resolved by empirical evidence (i.e., estimates of elasticities and lags), no policy maker can afford to ignore the structural aspects of Canada's trade — hence the relevance of this paper.

Turning now to the empirical side of the paper, apart from some data problems and a few puzzling results that are fully recognized by the author in the text, the empirical work is missing one aspect. A study dealing with trade balances needs to model both quantities and prices. In the case of imports, where Canada is assumed to be a price taker, import prices prove to be no problem as they are the product of world prices and the exchange rate. In the case of the export volume equations as presented in this paper, foreign excess demand, as opposed to domestic supply factors, is the driving force. Thus, for consistency, the export price equations should be determined by domestic factors. However, if previous empirical work is any guide, estimated export price equations indicate that Canada is principally a price taker! I know of no satisfactory resolution of the conundrum and suggest it could form the basis for future research.

Comment

by
Tim Hazledine

Neil Bruce and Hossein Rostami analyse the recent history of Canada's trade balance in two steps. First, in Section 3, they carry out a *descriptive* accounting decomposition of the changes in the balance in terms of its volume and price components. Then they attempt to *explain* what has happened in a 'price-taking' versus 'price-making' analytical framework, within which recent exogenous events are examined informally (Section 4) and econometrically (Section 5).

I found Section 4 interesting and uncontroversial. I will confine my remarks to the econometric results of Section 5 and to some conjectures on 'structuralism' based on Bruce and Rostami's descriptive findings.

Bruce and Rostami were not very successful at specifying good-looking econometric equations for imports and exports (as they themselves recognize). Their experience is not without precedent; for example, trade flows equations tend to be relatively poorly determined in macro-econometric models. What goes wrong? I have two suggestions:

1. Unlike many other important economic variables (consumption, employment, investment), both imports and exports are largely 'residual' in nature. Imports are the difference between domestic consumption and domestic production for the domestic market; exports are the difference between total domestic production and domestic consumption. When the difference between two variables is small relative to the size of the variables, and when the latter are measured (and modelled) with error, the proportion of 'noise' to explainable variance in the residual can be large.

2. Many imports and exports fluctuate widely (relative to domestic activity) over the short term due to seasonal factors, and even to delays in reporting the data. These fluctuations will be a further source of noise in time-series regressions, such as those shown by Bruce and Rostami, using quarterly data for the sake of maximizing 'degrees of freedom'.

Both of these difficulties might be resolved by modelling long-run changes in export and import behaviour as the direct result of the investment and pricing decisions of firms in industries. Statistics Canada has highly disaggregated data that offer observations on a wide dispersion of magnitudes of changes in the ratios of imports to domestic disappearance and exports to domestic production, and that are numerous enough to obviate the need of using quarterly observations to generate degrees of freedom.

Putting the empirical side on a firmer footing would greatly assist our efforts to resolve important issues associated with the influence of international factors on the domestic economy, such as the validity of 'price-taking' versus 'price-making' assumptions.

Turning briefly to the 'structural' question, Bruce and Rostami's interesting decomposition of changes in the commodity trade structure (Section 3) does seem to show that the fivefold increase between 1970 and 1979 in the current-price manufacturing trade deficit cannot be used by itself to demonstrate a *worsening*, in some sense, of the performance of this sector. However, if by a structural problem we mean a persistent and troublesome 'lumpiness' in the economy (i.e., a situation that does not respond very elastically to available price and aggregate demand policies), then Canada's export staples/import manufactures bias may fit the bill.

For example, consider the complication for exchange-rate policy in an economy exporting staples, of which the supply is rather inelastic, at least in the short run, while importing manufactured goods that are in elastic supply at world prices and that compete with the domestic manufacturing sector. To maintain full and steady employment, one may wish to vary the quantity of manufactured imports; this will entail frequent changes in the exchange rate (and thus in the domestic price of imports) to counteract cyclical shifts in domestic demand conditions. However, a fluctuating exchange rate will have a distributional effect in the staples sector, causing 'boom and bust' cycles that, in turn, may make risk-averse staples' producers less willing to make the investments that, over the long term, would increase the supply of exportables.

Of course, other policies may be able to counteract the mixed effects of exchange-rate fluctuations, but it seems unwise, to me, to be unprepared for the possibility that Canadian economic performance *has* been worsened by certain characteristics that we could call 'structural', in the sense that we would benefit from using unconventional policies to help deal with them.

Comment

by
Donald J. Daly

An important theme in the paper is that there is very little evidence that any important changes in the structure of Canadian trade have taken place during the 1970s. For example, in Table 3 of the Bruce and Rostami paper, the major changes in the value of exports and imports of both manufactures and staples primarily reflect changes in trade volume and trade prices, with limited shifts in the structure of trade.

However, it is widely recognized that the structure of Canadian trade is quite different from that of most other high-income countries, such as the United States, Japan, and the individual countries in Northwest Europe. An important difference is that Canadian exports reflect a much higher share of staples and a much lower share of manufactures, and this is reflected in a large merchandise surplus on staples and a large deficit on manufactures. Exports of manufactures are relatively more important in other high-income countries, and their net exports of manufactures typically pay for their net deficit on staples and primary products. This has given most of these countries an opportunity to share in the rapid growth in trade in manufactured products, a development that has been going on for more than three decades.

In light of this contrast in the position of exports of manufactured products in Canada relative to other high-income countries, it is unfortunate that Bruce and Rostami did not discuss the persisting structural problems of Canadian manufacturing. For example, the levels of output per man-hour in a wide range of individual manufacturing industries are lower in Canada than in the United States, and output per man-hour in total manufacturing was about 25 per cent below that of the United States. This gap is so wide that at recent exchange rates and levels of total compensation, the costs of production of many manufactured products are *higher* in Canada than in the United States. This precludes any general possibility of exporting manufactured products from Canada to the United States or other countries, while imports of manufactured products meet an important part of domestic demand. This is reflected in a continuing net deficit in manufactured products that has been an important feature of the structure of Canadian trade for decades, and this is apparent in the tables in this paper.

This deficit in manufactured products is not necessarily immutable, but reflects to an important degree a logical response by corporate decision makers to the persistence of tariff and non-tariff barriers to trade in manufactured products in both Canada and Canada's major markets. Companies respond by producing a wide range of products and have a high degree of product diversity and short runs in many product varieties. These tendencies are reflected in low productivity and high costs per unit. The current low value of the Canadian dollar only partially offsets the low productivity levels at current wage levels in the two countries.

Only modest changes in the relative position of the net position of staples and manufactures have taken place over the decade, while changes in the price level and quantity level of exports and imports have been large. Any structural problems that have persisted over the whole period or longer would not be apparent in the procedures used in the paper.

Some observers who have expressed concern about the structure of production and trade in manufactured products have recommended the retention of previous tariff barriers, and additional non-tariff measures (such as government purchasing) to encourage domestic producers rather than imports, and a number of the authors referred to in the opening pages of this paper have taken the position. The recommendations of the Science Council staff, for example, have tended to be protectionist and inward looking.

The route that others have recommended to improve the competitive position of Canadian manufacturing in world markets is through a *reduction* (rather than an increase) in tariff and non-tariff barriers, increased specialization, increased productivity, and increased exports of a limited range of products in which Canada has or can easily develop a comparative advantage. This would permit Canada to participate more fully in trade in manufactured products, the most rapidly expanding part of world trade. This is an outward-looking strategy to try to correct the persisting structural problems in productivity and trade in manufactured products that have persisted in Canada for decades and continue to be reflected in the tables in this paper for the 1970s.

By concentrating on the 1970s, the paper does not deal with the concerns about the structure of Canadian trade of those who favour achieving a more efficient and competitive manufacturing sector through reductions in tariff and non-tariff barriers, or the concerns of others who favour more protectionist policies and increased government interventions.

It is to be hoped that future Round Tables on Economic Policy will come back to these important topics again.

Summary
of
Discussion

The general discussion centred on three broad issues. First was the question of how far empirical research could be pushed in the field of external trade, given present deficiencies in disaggregated price and volume data. The discussion then moved on to the topic of industrial strategy in Canada and on how much guidance could be obtained in this area from recent trends in the structure of external trade. Finally, the macro-economic relationship between the trade account, the capital account, and broad economic variables was examined once again.

Charles Freedman mentioned that a considerable amount of work had been done at the Bank of Canada in the area of external trade and supply responses. Yet research efforts so far have been rather disappointing. The results obtained are very disturbing not just because supply responses seem to be insignificant — possibly the result of extremely long response lags — but because coefficients also come in with the wrong sign. *Neil Bruce* pointed out that for certain staples, notably the extractive resource industries, the inconsistencies could reflect intertemporal substitution: in the face of sharply rising prices, producers might be tempted to postpone production in anticipation of even higher prices in the future. However, such a pattern would tend to be very limited in importance and certainly the explanation would not hold for the vast majority of our exports.

Participants were in agreement that econometric estimation at a fine level of disaggregation will remain plagued by the way the price and quantity data are produced presently. Volume estimates are derived by deflating value series by a relevant price index, but Statistics Canada directly compiles only a few such price indices. The remaining price indices are derived on the assumption that Canada is either a price taker on imports or a price setter on exports so that appropriate price measures can be derived directly by adjusting the relevant U.S. index for variations in the exchange rate of the Canadian dollar. This assumption is not always appropriate; as a result, volume estimates are very crude, particularly with regard to trade in manufactures. Given these data problems, it is not surprising that empirical results remain of dubious quality.

The question of Canada's industrial strategy, or lack thereof, then surfaced in the discussion as being a possible source of widening surpluses on staples and deficits on manufactures. However, *Kevin Clinton* pointed out that it can be dangerous to draw inferences on industrial structure from observable trends in particular components of the trade balance. For instance, metals and minerals are an important part of our exports, but their share of total Canadian production has steadily declined over time. Conversely, it would be difficult to draw inferences from the increased deficit in manufactures on the extent to which our industrialization process may, or may not, be falling behind our trading partners. Neil Bruce noted that the Auto Pact has had a major impact on the structure of our external trade since the mid 1960s, but these changes had nothing to do with our evolving industrial structure. Charles Freedman also noted that historical trends in our external trade have been influenced by government controls and regulations so that inferences drawn from trade statistics on the structure of the economy could well be misleading. While the two issues are very much interrelated, it was generally agreed that the question of industrialization and industrial strategy should be addressed directly by looking at the structure of the economy, rather than through the back door with the help of trade statistics.

The discussion then moved on to the links between aggregate volumes, the public-sector deficit, and the trade account. *Guy Glorieux* noted that if there is such a link at the macro level, then it probably has an impact on the structure of our trade balance and it would be interesting to know the direction in which it has worked. One of the more obvious links is the energy sector, with the increasing subsidies paid on foreign crude resulting in both a larger government deficit and a higher level of oil imports. In effect, if it had not been for this subsidy programme, oil imports would have been lower than at present and our trade surplus on staples even higher. Neil Bruce added that similar links could undoubtedly be found on the manufactures side of the trade account. Yet it would be much more difficult to assess the importance of the impact because quantity effects would be influenced by the relative price of domestically produced versus foreign-produced manufactures.

Several participants extended the debate to the capital account of the balance of payments and to the impact of monetary policy on the structure of capital flows. This is particularly important as regards the allocation of foreign capital between equity (involving a change in ownership) and debt (involving only a stream of interest income). The issue raised was how much of a parallel should be drawn between the structure of the trade account and that of the capital account. The former involves a widening surplus on staples, with a depletion of natural resources, more than offsetting a deficit on manufactures, leading to a loss of production income; the latter involves a surplus on debt capital, with a stream of service payments, more than offsetting a deficit on equity capital. While recognizing the importance of monetary and exchange-rate policies in this area, it was felt that the question should really be addressed in the context of portfolio strategy and market efficiency.

Canadian Post-War Balance of Payments and Exchange-Rate Experience

5

by
Russell S. Boyer*

1. Introduction

There now exists an extensive literature on the monetary approach to the balance of payments and the determination of the exchange rate.[1] Such models have had substantial success in explaining the effects of exchange-market pressure upon foreign currency reserve movements and the exchange rate. Most of these models are in reduced forms so that some of the more interesting macro-economic variables are left out; notable among these omitted variables are price levels, interest rates, and the current account.[2]

Girton and Roper (1977) outline one of the most widely cited of such models applied to the Canadian economy. They assume that a variant of purchasing-power parity holds between the U.S. and the Canadian economy, that the money market always clears, and that money demand can be expressed as a simple form dependent on recent values of income. The success of their study comes in spite of the fact that most researchers find it difficult to fit similar models to the Canadian economy.[3]

This paper looks at Canadian post-war data in order to assess whether the mechanisms of the monetary approach appear to be working at a structural level. That is, this paper is concerned with the movements of variables that the monetary models solve out, in order to see whether they reflect the mechanisms that the monetary approach postulates.

In doing this, the paper deals with an area that Freedman and Longworth (1980) have covered in their highly readable paper. However, the time perspective is longer than theirs; this seems appropriate since the present Canadian situation looks more like that of the early 1960s than any period during the 1970s.

Floyd (1977), and Parkin and Bade (1979) also undertake such a longer perspective. Both studies conclude that the monetary independence that a flexible exchange-rate regime affords can be beneficial for Canada if monetary policy is used appropriately. In faulting the Bank of Canada for poor policy, they are following in the tradition of Mundell (1964), Wonnacott (1965), Poole (1967), and Courchene (1976) who see the central bank as failing to allow sufficient movements in interest rates and the exchange rate.

The present paper sees the Bank as doing a good job within the constraints that are imposed upon it, except perhaps during the period 1971 through 1973. The influence of monetary actions upon the economy is far from clear, and the paper suggests instead that budgetary policy, currency substitution, and a few exogenous events had a far bigger impact on post-war developments than did monetary policy. Thus, for example, the parallelism of Canadian nominal interest rates with their U.S. counterparts may well be the result of conditions arising from the demand side rather than any influence on the part of the Bank of Canada.

This paper is organized as follows. First, the influence of the exchange rate on price-level movements in Canada and the United States is considered. Then the discussion turns to the current account and the effects that budgetary policy has had upon it. The analysis of interest-rate behaviour and a discussion of currency substitution follow. This paper incorporates the analysis of the effects of budgetary policy within a more sophisticated monetary model; this perspective undermines the usual argument for flexible exchange rates and a monetary rule. Thus the controversy about deficit financing that is now going on in the United States may have some relevance to Canadian policy discussions.

2. Exchange-Rate Determination and the Monetary Approach

One of the most attractive features of the monetary or asset approach to exchange-rate determination is the simplicity of the models used. A model that is representative of the framework found in a number of recent papers follows:

$$m - p = \alpha \cdot y_d - \eta \cdot r + (1-\alpha) \cdot w \tag{1}$$

$$r = r^* + f^{t+1} - s \tag{2}$$

$$f^{t+1} = \mathrm{E}[s_{t+1}/\Phi_t] \tag{3}$$

(A) $$p = p^* + s \tag{4}$$

$$\dot{w} - \dot{p}w = -\lambda(w - \tilde{w}) \tag{5}$$

$$\tilde{w} = \tilde{w}(y_d) \tag{6}$$

$$TAS = \dot{w} - \dot{p}w. \tag{7}$$

The only variables that appear as level are the domestic and foreign interest rates, r and r^* respectively, and the trade-account surplus, TAS. All others appear as logarithms:

m, the nominal money supply
p, p^*, the domestic and foreign price levels respectively
y_d, real disposable income
w, current real wealth
s, the spot exchange rate
f^{t+1}, the forward exchange rate
$\bar{w}$, target real wealth.

The parameters η and λ are positive. They represent, respectively, the interest-rate semi-elasticity of money demand, and the responsiveness of the trade account to wealth imbalances. The parameter, α, represents the proportion of dependence of money demand upon disposable income rather than wealth, and it should lie between zero and one. Finally, E denotes the mathematical expectations operator, and Φ_t is the information set that conditions these expectations at time t. Explicitly included in this information set is the precise structure of the model that characterizes the economy.

Equation (1) is the equilibrium condition for the money market. The left-hand side of that equation is the real quantity of actual money balances. The right-hand side is the demand for real balances; equality between the two indicates continuous clearing of the money market. The presence of the parameter α in the equation is to capture the fact that disposable income may have an influence on money demand independently of the influence that real wealth has.

The next two equations represent the interest-rate-parity condition. Equation (2) asserts that the difference in interest rates in domestic and foreign currency is matched by the expected change in the spot exchange rate. The current spot rate is known, and, by risk neutrality of speculators, the forward rate must equal the expected future value of the spot rate given the information available at time t, as indicated by equation (3). In this Chicago-style monetary approach, purchasing-power parity is assumed to hold, as equation (4) notes. This can be viewed as a particularly strong specification of the goods market clearing condition.

The last three equations in this model make the connection between desired saving and the accumulation of assets through the trade-account surplus. Thus it is assumed that desired or target wealth is dependent upon disposable income, and that any discrepancy between target wealth and actual wealth causes nominal wealth to increase. This increase in nominal wealth must come about through a trade-account surplus because of the fact that investment at home is assumed to be zero.

The simplicity of this framework makes it useful as a classroom device, especially since it has such strong, clear-cut roles for the exchange rate, the domestic rate of interest, and the forward discount. For example, the exchange rate's function is to make the converted foreign-currency price level equal to the domestic-currency price level, which is determined by domestic monetary conditions alone. Real rates of return are equal in the world since differences in posted interest rates merely match inflation differentials. These, in turn, are equal to the expected change in the exchange rate through the working together of interest-rate parity and purchasing-power parity.

The solution of the system of equations denoted by (A) above is simple in the case where α is equal to one. In that case we can ignore the intertemporal movement of wealth and look entirely at changes in the money supply and in disposable income, both of which are taken to be exogenous. The solution for the exchange rate in this case is as follows:

$$s(t) = \frac{1}{\eta} \int_t^\infty e^{-\frac{1}{\eta}(\tau - t)} [m(\tau) - y_d(\tau)] \, d\tau. \tag{8}$$

This solution assumes that the exchange rate cannot explode to plus or minus infinity without the forcing functions doing the same. It should be noted that this solution says that the current value of the exchange rate is dependent upon all future values of both the money supply and disposable income. Thus, an estimating equation that includes only current values of these variables, and not future expected values, would not be an accurate representation of the model denoted by (A) above.

A competing model to that presented above is the M.I.T.-style asset market exchange-rate determination model. This model assumes that asset markets always clear and that the future value of the exchange rate is determined rationally. Thus we can accept equations (1) through (3) of the model above, but probably with the assumption again that α is equal to one. Equation (4) must be modified to read

$$\tilde{p} = p^* + s, \tag{4a}$$

where $\tilde{p}$ is the price index that will prevail once the system settles down. p itself moves according to equation

(B) $$\dot{p} = \delta \cdot (\tilde{p} - p), \tag{5a}$$

showing that the price moves sluggishly in order to satisfy purchasing-power parity. This equation system denoted by (B) would have a solution much like that given above in equation (8), showing that the current exchange rate depends upon all future values of the exogenous variables. However, there are some important differences between these models (A) and (B) as to their short-run dynamics; in particular, model (B) allows for the possibility of overshooting. It can also be shown that these two models have rather different movements of the price level in response to particular shocks.

It is possible to append to these models a reaction function representing the behaviour of the authorities in the financial markets. One plausible reaction function views the authorities as altering the supply of money in accordance with the value of the exchange rate. Such a reaction function can be designed so that with certain values of the parameters, the economy is on a fixed exchange rate, whereas with other polar values it is on a flexible exchange rate. In-between values for these parameters yield a situation of managed floating.

The valuable contribution of Girton and Roper (1977) is that they note that in equation (1) the money supply and exchange rate are the central variables. We can take their difference and call it *exchange-market pressure* as they do; that difference will be independent of the parameter values for the reaction function. This model presents exchange-market pressure in a particularly trivial fashion since it does not distinguish between domestic credit and foreign exchange reserves. None the less, it does capture the idea that Girton and Roper presented.

There are a number of problems with the idea of exchange-market pressure, especially when domestic credit is introduced directly. In their empirical work, Girton and Roper have not avoided the simultaneity problem arising from the banking system's T accounts; thus their unit coefficient on domestic credit may merely reflect this identity between assets and liabilities rather than capturing the behavioural relationship they claim. Furthermore, as Selody (1979) points out, when exchange-market pressure is introduced in a two-country context, the Girton-Roper measure of exchange-market pressure does not seem appropriate. In particular, it hardly seems likely that a 10 per cent excess demand for money in a large economy like the United States would have the same effect upon the exchange rate as a 10 per cent excess supply of money in a small economy like Canada.

A further problem with the idea of exchange-market pressure is that it fails to take account of the fact that the exchange rate in equations (3), (4), and (5) has quite a different role from the money supply. Future expected values of the exchange rate and the money supply have a very important influence on the current level of the exchange rate. Equating changes in money supply and changes in exchange rates in a simple difference, as exchange-market pressure does, fails to take account of this fact.

3. Purchasing-Power Parity
Between Canada and the United States

During the post-war period, Canada moved away from having Britain as its major trading partner, and by the 1970s approximately 70 per cent of its trade was with the United States. In light of this, it is useful to see how Canadian prices compare with U.S. prices over this time.

Since each country is a major trading partner of the other, it is not surprising that Canadian and U.S. prices move together quite closely. What is surprising is that for most measures of price levels, and especially for the Consumer Price Indices (CPIs), there is a far closer correspondence between the raw price series than there is when an exchange-rate conversion is applied to the U.S. data.

Figure 1 shows the movement of the ratio of the CPIs and the Canadian-U.S. exchange rate. It is clear that the ratio of the CPIs is much more constant than is the exchange rate. This is particularly evident during the periods 1962–1970, and 1970–1975. After 1975 the inflation rates in the two countries diverge somewhat, and the exchange rate displays a minor role in restoring Canada's competitive position. That purchasing-power parity does not hold is a finding that many people have noted, for example, Dornbusch and Krugman (1976). However, because of the persistence of such periods of non-parity, these results in the Canadian case seem particularly dramatic.

This story is repeated for the GNE deflators with only minor variations. After 1976, purchasing-power parity using the exchange-rate conversion was distinctly closer to unity than was the ratio of the raw price indices. In particular, the value of the Canadian dollar was sufficiently low by 1978 to restore the competitive position for Canada that had existed in 1970. It should be quickly noted that the period of the 1960s causes just as much trouble using the GNE deflators as it does using the CPIs. Furthermore, even in the 1970s, there are problems with timing; notably, before 1977 the raw price ratio does better than does that of the converted prices.

This graph is strong evidence that the simple Chicago-style monetary approach is likely to have difficulty in explaining the relative movements of Canadian and U.S. prices. The M.I.T.-style asset market approach can do better, perhaps, because it does not assume that parity holds at all times. However, the movement towards purchasing-power parity that it assumes is hard to discern during much of this period. Similarly, the timing of domestic price movement in the 1970s does not seem to be consistent with a gradual approach to purchasing-power parity. However, such evidence does not mean that we can reject either of these simple models, because so far we have considered only the implications of monetary shocks to the system. It is necessary to include real shocks as well in order to make any sense out of this price index data over the post-war period.

Floyd (1977) has suggested that the exchange rate reflects changes in the equilibrium value of relative prices between U.S. and Canadian goods. On this argument, Canada is seen as producing a set of goods

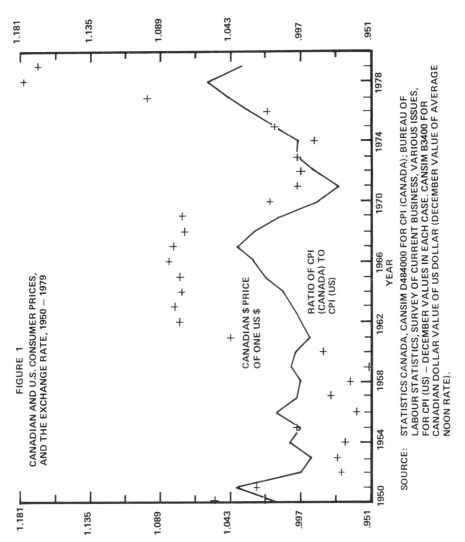

FIGURE 1
CANADIAN AND U.S. CONSUMER PRICES,
AND THE EXCHANGE RATE, 1950 – 1979

SOURCE: STATISTICS CANADA, CANSIM D484000 FOR CPI (CANADA); BUREAU OF
LABOUR STATISTICS, SURVEY OF CURRENT BUSINESS, VARIOUS ISSUES,
FOR CPI (US) – DECEMBER VALUES IN EACH CASE. CANSIM B3400 FOR
CANADIAN DOLLAR VALUE OF US DOLLAR (DECEMBER VALUE OF AVERAGE
NOON RATE).

that is different from that of the United States. Shifts in demand for
Canadian goods relative to U.S. ones cause alterations in the
equilibrium relative prices, or 'terms-of-trade effects'. The emphasis in
the Canadian case is on the movements of relative prices between
natural resources and agricultural products on the one hand and
manufactured products on the other. Floyd's argument is that these
prices have changed through movements in the exchange rate rather
than in the domestic price levels. Clearly, such real shocks must be
taken into account in any further analysis of relative price movements
between two countries since monetary impulses and accompanying
rates of inflation do not seem to be an important part of the
explanation.

As noted above, practitioners of the monetary approach usually avoid the use of price index data.[4] The argument is that purchasing-power parity does hold using actual transactions prices. The data we obtain, however, are so poor that the law of one price appears to be violated. Monetarists continue on the assumption that this law holds in reality and then formulate exchange-rate determination models in which the price levels have been solved out.

This is a practice that this author generally supports. None the less, there is room for investigation of the construction of the price index series in order to see whether there are differences here that are creating problems with the empirical investigation of purchasing-power parity. For example, it is relevant to know how government services are entered into the calculation of the CPI and the GNP implicit price deflator. Given the size of the government sector in the United States and Canada, any difference in construction of these series due to this source could have a marked influence on their ratio. What is obvious in the Canadian context is that many price lists tend to be virtual reproductions of U.S. dollar ones, with a mark-up somewhat greater than the exchange-rate difference. Presumably, if Canadian prices get substantially out of line over this period, this can be compensated for by special discounts or other informal changes that would not be incorporated into price indices. Parkin and Bade (1979) capture this notion by arguing that Canadian prices appear to be equal to U.S. prices converted at a long-run exchange rate of parity.

The conclusion of this section is that these price data would apparently cause difficulty with any monetary approach analysis. The basic reason is that posted prices do not appear to respond with the speed that that theory postulates. Whether the explanation for this is that posted prices are accurate representations of transactions prices but adjust slowly, or that posted prices are not accurate, it seems to be difficult to do empirical work on price indices using a monetary model in structural form. As Freedman and Longworth (1980) and Huber (1980) point out, these timing problems are sufficiently serious that only a more elaborate model can hope to capture them.

4. The Canadian Current Account

Early models of the monetary variety did not distinguish between money and other assets. As a result, those models rely very much on the current account to bear the burden of adjustment to any shock to the economy. (See, for example, Dornbusch (1973) and Laidler and O'Shea (1980).) The argument is that the economy needs time in order to alter the size of its nominal wealth stock. Later models put the process of portfolio readjustment as the central feature of re-equilibration to any disturbance. The presence of the interest rate in models (A) and (B) above makes clear that they distinguish between money and other financial assets.

Figure 2 presents the balance on current-account transactions for Canada during most of the post-war era, expressed as a percentage of GNP. It is possible to pick out a number of features that stand out from these data. Notable is the impact of the investment boom in natural-resource industries in the period 1955–1957. In addition, the periods 1964–1965 in the trade account and 1965–1966 in the current account are unusual, presumably reflecting effects of the 1962 devaluation, direct investment in Canadian production as a result of the Auto Pact, and the Vietnam war effort in the United States. Finally, leads and lags seem to have affected the current-account data for 1969 and 1970. Both years are quite different from surrounding ones, but they fully offset each other since they are equal but of opposite sign.

Once these special cases are out of the way, the basic pattern of the current account can be discerned more clearly. It appears to be one of a debtor country that is moving towards a creditor position slowly but surely. Along the way, exogenous set-backs occur that impede this progress. The investment boom of the mid-1950s added further debt to the economy so that interest payments at that time reached their highest level as a percentage of GNP. This level was not reached again until 1977, during a period we shall deal with later in this section.

It is well known that the stages of the balance of payments are tautological if one assumes away the possibility of abrupt changes in the stock of claims on the economy owned by foreign residents. In such a view, a developing economy needs physical and financial capital and, therefore, immediately moves to a debtor position with capital inflows covering the needed plant and equipment that are reflected in a deficit in the trade account. As the productive capacity of the economy starts to grow, capability to export grows as well. Therefore, over this time the economy moves towards a stronger position on the trade account. Indeed, it can be shown that, of necessity, an economy moves to a surplus in the trade account before the capital account moves into deficit. The reason is that throughout this period the debt-service account remains in deficit.

Canada seemed to have moved to such a position by the early 1970s; that is, the surplus on the trade account was sufficient to cover interest and dividend payments, and to push the current account into surplus and the capital account therefore into deficit. The oil price shock and other exogenous changes threw the economy off its track and depressed the emerging surplus in the trade account, an argument we will make in the next section. But for the moment it is important to see how inflation alters the perspective with respect to the stages of the balance of payments.

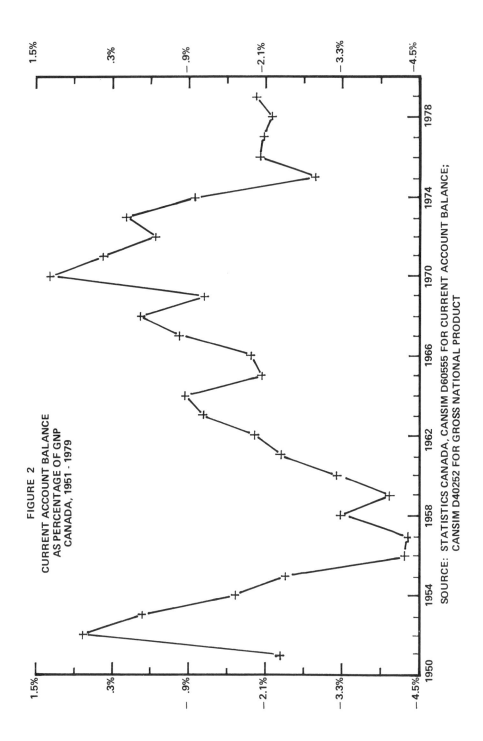

FIGURE 2
CURRENT ACCOUNT BALANCE
AS PERCENTAGE OF GNP
CANADA, 1951 - 1979

SOURCE: STATISTICS CANADA, CANSIM D60555 FOR CURRENT ACCOUNT BALANCE;
CANSIM D40252 FOR GROSS NATIONAL PRODUCT

With an ongoing inflation, clearly some of the interest and dividend payments reflect return of capital rather than true servicing of a capital stock whose real value is not changing over time. As a result we would expect a deficit on interest and dividends to be blown up during inflationary periods. This is precisely what has occurred in the 1970s in the current account and, therefore, the high level of debt service should not be viewed with great alarm. Indeed, some writers, notably Parkin and Bade (1979), go so far as to see a corrected debt-service account measure for Canada during the late 1970s as being in surplus rather than in deficit. Freedman (1979) also applies this line of argument, but he finds that the debt-service account, although reduced in size, remains in deficit. In particular, Freedman finds that the share of GNP represented by the deficit on interest and dividends did rise during this period, but not nearly so much as unadjusted figures portray.

It is clear from Freedman and independently from Barber and McCallum (1980) that the problem with the Parkin and Bade methodology is that their analysis is exclusively in terms of nominal financial-market instruments. Once one realizes that some of this debt service represents dividend payments on equity capital, the methodology is no longer appropriate. This is true for two reasons. First, inflation should have no impact on the real value of such market instruments precisely because equity represents the claim to ownership of physical capital. Thus, if companies are doing depreciation accounting appropriately, the values of shares on the stock markets should increase roughly in line with the rate of inflation. It is more likely, however, that such firms are making further investments in physical capital using retained earnings. This has a double effect on the connection between the interest and dividend account and the real value of underlying assets. On the one hand, looking exclusively at that account, one gets an unduly low value for the real value of foreign-owned claims outstanding. On the other hand, any retained earnings used for investment should increase the value in the future of such firms above and beyond the ongoing rate of inflation, thereby increasing those claims without any indication of this in the balance-of-payment accounting.

The distortion of these figures by the ongoing inflation is particularly important in the late 1970s. As a result, this author intends to use adjusted data, as do Barber and McCallum (1980), in future research.

5. Fiscal Policy, the Current Account, and Exchange Rates

The previous section argued that, except for exogenous shocks, the current account shows a continuing improvement throughout the post-war era. One of the shocks that we wish to emphasize here is public-sector borrowing. Not only did such borrowing have a strong effect on the current account, but, as we will show, it also had a strong influence over the exchange rate. The measure of public-sector borrowing that we will use is the surplus or deficit reported in Statistics Canada's *National Income and Expenditure Accounts* for all levels of government expenditures. (Because of its exclusion of borrowing by Crown corporations, this is a more appropriate measure than is the Net New Issues that has a central role in Dunn (1978).)

As noted above, the investment boom of 1955 through 1957 is an important episode in Canadian post-war economic experience. With the ending of that boom and the election of the Diefenbaker government, public-sector borrowing grew substantially as the au-thorities, in part, attempted to sustain the boom through running large deficits. This period of deficit financing ended only with the defeat of the Gordon budget in 1963, which headed the government towards a less stimulative fiscal policy. This more conservative stance lasted throughout the 1960s, and well into the 1970s. The budgets moved again into deficit in 1974 as the federal government indexed the personal income tax and as the oil subsidy for eastern Canada became more expensive after the oil price shock.

The discussion of inflation accounting, important to analysing the current account, is equally applicable to measurements of the govern-ment deficit, especially after the mid-1970s. Many authors have made the point, notably Barber and McCallum (1980), that allowing for inflation has the effect of making the deficit much smaller than its reported value during this period. None the less, any measure of the fiscal deficit finds that 1975 was a major turning point in the level of public-sector borrowing.

Figure 3 shows how the government deficits at all levels have varied throughout the post-war period. It is apparent from comparing Figures 2 and 3 that there is a very similar pattern to the current-account deficit and the government budget deficit. There is, therefore, a strong correlation between government-sector borrowing and the current-account deficit.

The extent of this relationship is measured by a simple linear regression the results of which are reported in Table 1. In running these regressions, we left out the years, mentioned in the previous section, that seemed to be particularly affected by the exogenous factors.[5] All variables were measured as proportions of GNP in order to offset the fact that there was a continuing level of inflation and, of course, of real growth over this period. The coefficient of government budget deficit as a percentage of GNP is 3 in most of these estimates, indicating that 30 per cent of any deficit spills over into the foreign sector and causes a deficit in the current account. This result is the same as that found by Dornbusch and Fischer (1980) for the United Kingdom's experience since the mid-1960s, and it roughly corresponds to the proportion of GNP that is traded with the rest of the world. The argument is that an increase in government expenditure increases income (if it is an endogenous variable) and, therefore, saving and imports as well. Crowding out causes these changes to be small in comparison with the usual multiplier results under fixed interest rates and exchange rates. If income is exogenous, as in model (A) above, fiscal policy has an influence by moving transactions from the private sector to the public sector and, in the process, reducing disposable income. To be consistent with the regression reported here, $\lambda \cdot \bar{w}$ should equal .3.

Because of the size of the Canadian financial market, it is not surprising that some of this deficit represents borrowing that was done abroad. It would appear to be sensible, therefore, to include the level of such surplus or deficit as one of the variables in any explanation of foreign borrowing. This author was surprised to see that the general level of borrowing did not play a more important role in Freedman and Longworth's (1980) regressions of foreign borrowing. Traditional explanations of capital flows have been expressed in terms of interest-rate differentials, but if this phenomenon that we have

Table 1

RELATIONSHIP BETWEEN THE CURRENT-ACCOUNT BALANCE AND THE GOVERNMENT BUDGETARY BALANCE, 1952–1978

Equation 1.   Ordinary Least Squares

$$\text{CASOY} = \begin{array}{cc} -.912 + & .628 \cdot \text{GBSOY} \\ [-3.80] & [4.54] \end{array}$$

$$\text{Log of Likelihood Function} = -27.4$$
$$R^2 = .5205$$
$$D.W. = .9394$$

Equation 2.   Cochrane-Orcutt Iterative Technique

$$\text{CASOY} = \begin{array}{cc} -1.45 + & .311 \cdot \text{GBSOY} \\ [-3.10] & [2.60] \end{array}$$

$$\text{Log of Likelihood Function} = -19.7$$
$$R^2 = .7154$$
$$D.W. = 1.44$$
$$\rho = .66$$

Equation 3.   Maximum Likelihood Technique

$$\text{CASOY} = \begin{array}{cc} -.947 + & .327 \cdot \text{GBSOY} \\ [-1.64] & [2.65] \end{array}$$

$$\text{Log of Likelihood Function} = -22.1$$
$$R^2 = .1868$$
$$D.W. = 1.62$$
$$\rho = .75$$

Numbers in brackets are t statistics.

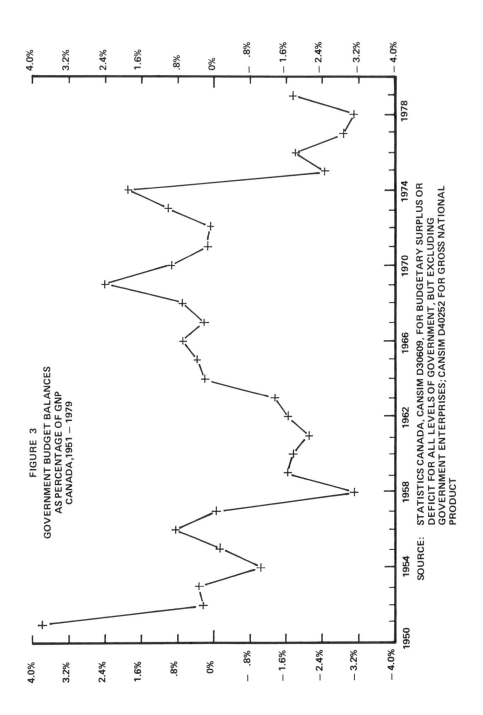

FIGURE 3
GOVERNMENT BUDGET BALANCES
AS PERCENTAGE OF GNP
CANADA,1951 – 1979

SOURCE: STATISTICS CANADA, CANSIM D30609, FOR BUDGETARY SURPLUS OR
DEFICIT FOR ALL LEVELS OF GOVERNMENT, BUT EXCLUDING
GOVERNMENT ENTERPRISES; CANSIM D40252 FOR GROSS NATIONAL
PRODUCT

outlined is of significance, it is clear that public-sector borrowing might have substantially more explanatory power than any interest-rate differential approach.

One of the important findings in Rhomberg (1964) is that fiscal policy in the Canadian context causes an increase in the value of the Canadian dollar. The reader will remember that the effect of fiscal policy on the exchange rate was ambiguous in the Mundell-Fleming model, being dependent on the relative slopes of the balance-of-payments (B.P.) locus and the money-market (L.M.) equilibrium locus. Rhomberg's finding is consistent with that model if the B.P. locus is flatter than the L.M. locus. In such a case, high interest rates should be associated with an appreciation of the Canadian dollar. This connection has been made in many popular discussions of the influence of financial markets upon the exchange rate, but there has been less emphasis on the fact that both interest rates and the exchange rate are endogenous in any sensible model and depend on other variables, such as fiscal policy. On this argument, fiscal policy causes interest rates and exchange rates to move in such a way as to cause some crowding out of private-sector expenditure.

The 1958–1960 experience was repeated in 1975–1977 when interest rates and the exchange rate were quite high. There were, however, substantial differences in the latter period as we will show in a subsequent section.

6. American and Canadian Interest Rates

Many observers of Canadian financial policy have noted the parallelism of the movements of interest rates in the United States and Canada during the post-war period. In most cases, this phenomenon has been attributed to behaviour of the Bank of Canada, which has been criticized for not doing more with the monetary freedom it has under flexible exchange rates.

It was this parallelism that Mundell (1964), for example, saw as the reason for the failure of the first flexible exchange-rate regime to insulate the domestic economy from the U.S. business cycle in the 1950s. Similarly, Wonnacott (1965) and Poole (1967) bemoan this situation persisting during the Coyne era of low inflation and high unemployment. In this way, modern critics of the high-interest-rate policy of the Bank of Canada currently are drawing upon a long tradition. (Such criticism has been strongest from the Canadian Institute for Economic Policy, and has been presented in monographs by Barber and McCallum (1980), Donner and Peters (1979), and Robinson (1980).)

This author's feeling is that the Bank of Canada has done a good job during the post-war period, except perhaps during the early 1970s, but was constrained by the degree to which it could move interest rates.

This idea is captured by the notion of currency substitution, a subject that we will discuss below. The present task is to get a more accurate measure of the degree of parallelism of these interest rates.

Table 2 reports the mean and standard deviation of a number of different interest rates and yield divergences over three periods: first float (October 1950–May 1962), fixed (June 1962–May 1970), and second float (June 1970–August 1980). The Canadian and U.S. long interest rates are reported separately, as are their uncovered differentials. It is remarkable that despite large standard deviations of the individual interest rates, their difference has a quite small degree of

Table 2
MEANS AND STANDARD DEVIATIONS OF VARIOUS
CANADIAN AND AMERICAN INTEREST RATES
REPORTED ON AN ANNUAL BASIS

	First Float		Fixed		Second Float		Fixed and Second Float	
	Mean	Stan. Dev.	Mean	Stan. Dev.	Mean	Stan. Dev.	Mean	Stan. Dev.
1. Short-term CAN	—	1.26	5.68	1.49	8.35	2.69	7.15	2.59
2. Short-term US	—	.85	5.16	1.81	7.65	2.79	6.52	2.68
3. COV DIFF	—	—	.229	.423	.377	.506	.310	.474
4. FOR DIFF	.510	.990	.292	.702	.329	1.70	.312	1.34
5. Long-term CAN	—	.45	6.85	1.22	9.62	1.29	8.55	1.25
6. Long-term US	—	.57	5.82	1.16	8.73	1.23	7.61	1.85
7. Uncovered Long-term DIFF	.43	.21	1.03	.13	.885	.344	.941	.290
8. Uncovered Short-term DIFF	.17	.68	.521	.686	.706	1.62	.623	1.29

Sources: **First Float:**

Canadian short-term interest rate: weighted average tender yield on treasury 3-month bills from Poole (1967), source International Monetary Fund, *International Financial Statistics*.

U.S. short-term interest rate: unweighted average tender rate on treasury 90-day bills from Poole (1967), source International Monetary Fund, *International Financial Statistics*.

Forward differential: average of noon rates over the monthly Bank of Canada, *Statistical Summary*, various issues.

Canadian long-term interest rate: yield on Canadian government 3 per cent perpetual bond on last trading day of the month from Poole (1967), source Bank of Canada (unpublished).

U.S. long-term interest rate: yield on long-term government bonds, "consolidated series" from January 1953, "old series" prior to January 1953 from Poole (1967), source *Federal Reserve Bulletin*.

Fixed and Second Float:

Canadian short-term interest rate: finance company paper, CANSIM B14017.

U.S. short-term interest rate: commercial paper, 90-day (adjusted), CANSIM B54412.

Forward differential: forward premium or discount, U.S. dollar in Canada, 90-day, CANSIM B14034.

Canadian long-term interest rate: 10 provincial bonds, CANSIM B14014.

U.S. long-term interest rate: corporate bonds industrial average, CANSIM B54413.

variability. The results reported for these interest rates for the first floating period are from Poole (1967), and they are different from the interest rates used for subsequent periods. For this reason, the means for these interest rates are not directly comparable, but the standard deviations probably are.

Canadian long interest rates can be characterized very succinctly. They have always been slightly higher than U.S. rates, with the differential never being greater than 2 per cent. During 90.5 per cent of this period, the differential was between 50 and 150 basis points. For 8 per cent of the time it was less than 50 basis points, so that for only 1.5 per cent of the time was it greater than 150 basis points. Apparently investors see Canadian bonds as very similar to, but riskier than, U.S. ones, so that a small, steady, positive differential between these yields persists.[6]

When considering covered short-term interest-rate differentials, one finds that interest-rate parity holds approximately much of the time. Frenkel and Levich (1977) found that transactions costs change substantially over time. With their measures of these costs, a large fraction of these observations satisfy interest-rate parity. McCormick (1979) has shown that the Frenkel-Levich results may overestimate transactions costs since they use data that reflect transactions undertaken at times that were probably as much as one hour, and perhaps as much as nine hours, apart. Clearly, with the current volatility of exchange rates, one would not expect interest-rate parity to hold for transactions occurring so far apart in time. McCormick's reservations about Frenkel and Levich's data sources should be repeated in the present context *a fortiori*.

The uncovered short-term differential has much greater variability than do others. This differential can be measured using the forward premium on the U.S. dollar. The observations of this premium on an annual basis are reported in Figure 4. It shows that the forward premium was between +2 per cent and −1 per cent during 86 per cent of the time of the first floating period and 79 per cent during the time of the fixed and second floating period. It should be noted that these measures probably give an exaggerated reading of the forward premium since the actual twelve-month value tends to be less than four times the 90-day one because of transactions costs. This discussion of the data in Figure 4 leads to the conclusion that the premium in the forward U.S. dollar−Canadian dollar market has tended to be quite small.

7. Empirical Regularities in Canadian Exchange-Rate Movements

The previous section demonstrated that the forward premium or discount on the Canadian dollar has been quite small.[7] There is little

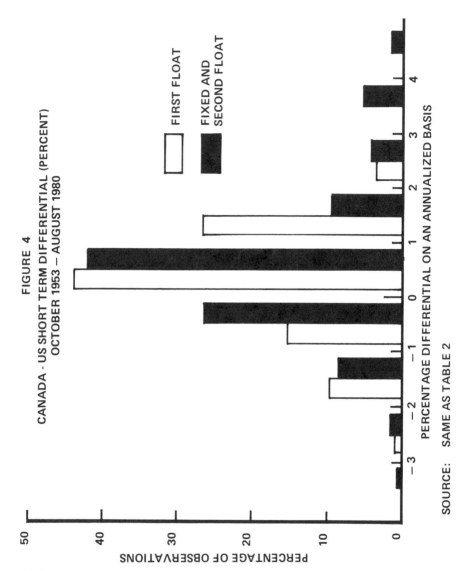

FIGURE 4

CANADA - US SHORT TERM DIFFERENTIAL (PERCENT)
OCTOBER 1953 – AUGUST 1980

difference between the first flexible exchange-rate period and the
second one in this regard, especially when the run from October 1975
to March 1977 is treated as a special case. During the fixed period, of
course, there are much smaller forward differentials than during these
flexible periods.

It is common to argue that the forward rate is an unbiased predictor
of the future spot rate. (See, for example, Frenkel (1977).) This is true
if the forward exchange market is efficient, and if speculators are risk
neutral. There is now evidence that this result does not hold for
Canada during the 1970s. Hansen and Hodrick (1980) show that

prediction errors are intertemporally correlated with each other, so that past errors could have been used in a decision rule to obtain extraordinary profits. The implication of this is that either the market was inefficient, or there were time-varying risk premia. Longworth (1981) finds that a regression of actual changes in the spot price of foreign exchange upon the forward differential yields a statistically significant coefficient of the wrong sign. This result holds for a sample period starting near the beginning of the current float and ending just before the election victory of the Parti québécois in Quebec. However, when subsequent monthly observations are added to the sample, the sign of the relevant regression coefficient changes sign and is insignificantly different from zero.[8]

Although the forward differential may be a biased estimate of the change in the spot, it has certainly provided an accurate gauge of the size of that change. Namely, during most of the post-war period, the exchange rate has moved very little, consistent with a forward differential that is usually less than 1 per cent per year. Thus, from 1952 to 1960 the exchange rate never moved by more than 4 per cent on a year-end basis. Similarly, for 1970−1975 there is no trend in the exchange rate and only small year-by-year movements. These are consistent with the return of the differential to within the plus or minus 1 per cent bounds after only a few months if it ever ventured outside them.

When the exchange rate has changed substantially, the movement has been quite abrupt. This occurred in 1962, 1970, and 1977. The 1970 episode is unique in this regard in that floating caused the exchange rate to appreciate immediately by approximately 5 per cent. In the 1962 case, no devaluation was necessary since the exchange rate was pegged at a level consistent with current market transactions.

One interesting characteristic of these periods of abrupt change is that they have occurred some time after a substantial change in the size of the budget deficit. Furthermore, during the interim between changes in the deficit and the movement of the exchange rate, the currency tended to move in the opposite direction from its eventual change. Thus, the large widening of the deficit in 1958 caused an appreciation of the exchange rate until 1960, when the large depreciation occurred. The budget situation was much improved in 1964, but in 1968 there was an exchange-rate crisis that put the economy in a position to have a revaluation in 1970. Finally, the deficit financing of 1974−1977 raised interest rates and appreciated the currency until October of 1976 when it started a large depreciation.

As noted above, the connection of appreciation with deficits and depreciation with surpluses is a plausible one for economists who use the Mundell-Fleming model. Indeed, it was pointed out that one of the widely cited conclusions from Rhomberg's (1964) study of the Canadian economy is that expansionary fiscal policy causes an appreciation of the domestic currency. The argument there is that the interest rate rises with such a policy change and this causes a capital inflow that puts the balance of payments into an incipient surplus, thus putting upward pressure on the value of the Canadian dollar.

Portfolio balance models also find such a connection between fiscal policy and the exchange rate, although the argument in this case is based upon the policy's effects upon the arguments in the demand function for money. But clearly this phenomenon is a short-run one because it puts the trade account into deficit. (In model (A) above, fiscal policy reduces y_d and thereby $\tilde{w}$.) Furthermore, the borrowing of the authorities raises the necessary level of interest payments to service the debt. These effects must eventually cause a depreciation even from the pre-policy-change level of the exchange rate. A term that may be used to characterize such a postulated exchange-rate movement is 'back shooting' to indicate that the short-term movement of the exchange rate is opposite from its eventual direction of motion.

In looking at these periods, one would have to give a very sympathetic reading of the data to discern any strong manifestation of 'back shooting'. For the year 1959, it is possible to see the Canadian dollar appreciating despite its long-term trend downwards over the subsequent two years. However, the appreciation from former levels was at most 3 per cent. Similarly, in 1974–1976 there is clear appreciation of the Canadian dollar by roughly 4 per cent despite a discount that widened to unprecedented proportions. The discount of the forward Canadian dollar reached a maximum of 466 basis points during this period. Consistent with this, U.S. and Canadian interest rates diverged to an extent that had never been witnessed before, that is, to as much as 4.5 to 5 per cent. This is the period that causes Longworth to find inefficiency in the foreign exchange market, so it may be worth devoting a little more time to it.

Clearly, during 1976, the exchange rate moved in a direction opposite from that indicated by the forward rate. Also, fiscal policy was clearly an important element in this episode, as is evidenced by the central place that unprecedented provincial borrowing plays in most discussions of this period. These provinces may be the key to dealing with the inefficiency problem, and simultaneously the 'back shooting' phenomenon. Dunn (1978) has demonstrated the lack of sophistication of some provincial and local borrowers, some of whom went to the bond market without any forward cover, perhaps because they were unaware of the potential for large exchange-rate changes. Since these provinces are major elements in the Canadian financial markets and probably important holders of Canadian dollar demand deposits, it would be surprising not to find that they had created apparent inefficiency in the foreign exchange market.

To attribute all the unusual aspects of that period to the functioning of fiscal policy would be to overestimate the effect that that policy can have. We should remember the changes in other programs that Ottawa was making at that time. The 'inflation fighters' were just being put into place. The Saskatoon manifesto, in which the governor of the Bank of Canada committed the Bank to following a monetary rule with gradually lowered targets, was enunciated on 5 September 1975. More dramatically, wage and price controls were introduced on Thanksgiving Day, in October 1975, in a televised speech by the Prime Minister. This author has no difficulty in imagining that individuals at that time were making radical readjustments in both their expectations and their portfolios. Such a view suggests that this period probably should be interpreted outside a model that explains the rest of post-war experience.

8. Elements of a New Model of Exchange-Rate Determination

It is now widely conceded that models of exchange-rate determination formulated during the 1960s and early 1970s do not do a good job in explaining exchange-rate movements after 1976.[9] Models that have been formulated more recently in order to explain current experience have tended to exhibit a priori inefficiency; that is, they explain the current value of the exchange rate in terms of its lag values. It would probably be useful to try to identify the characteristics of a model of exchange-rate determination that continued with market efficiency but took more account of the factors that have apparently had an influence on the exchange rate in the Canadian context.

In formulating a model of exchange-rate determination, it is necessary to remember some of the empirical regularities from our post-war experience. Particularly outstanding regularities are (1) the parallelism of the U.S. and Canadian interest rates, especially long-term ones; (2) the small forward differential against the U.S. dollar, except during the period October 1975–March 1977; (3) the close connection between the current-account deficit and the deficits of the public-sector budgets; (4) the delayed reaction of the exchange rate to changes in these budget stances; and (5) the abruptness with which the exchange rate makes its infrequent large movements.

It seems that although the general direction of Canadian monetary policy is important to the current value of the exchange rate, the fiscal stance of the authorities has had the dominant role in its determination. In so saying, one does not need to give up, at all, a monetary view of exchange-rate determination. Instead, what is needed is the forging of an extra link between the fiscal deficits and the extent to which they are expected to be financed in the future by monetary growth.

Rational expectations models have argued that the current value of the exchange rate depends upon all future expected changes in the money supply appropriately discounted, as in equation (8) above. Any such linkage must be made with the realization that current deficits are poor guides to future monetary growth. This is true for two reasons. First, in order to assess future monetary growth, one needs to know whether the current deficit is a temporary or permanent one (a distinction that Harris and Purvis (1981) emphasize in their work). A temporary deficit requires only a limited amount of financing and, consequently, should have a very small impact on future monetary growth. The second point is that it is essential to infer from the actions of the authorities what proportion of deficits will be financed in the future by taxes, since only the proportion that is left over needs to be financed by the inflation tax.

This distinction between temporary and permanent deficits may be a key element in explaining why there is a two- to three-year delay between the increase in fiscal deficits and the depreciation of the currency. Only if a deficit is repeated a few years in a row do people see it as more than a transitory phenomenon. In both 1961 and 1976 there were, in addition, shocks to expectations that made depreciation inevitable. In 1961 the authorities began to talk down the exchange rate and quickly found that a potential exchange crisis had developed. In November of 1976, the Parti québécois election victory caused people to readjust their expectations radically. None the less, it is important to see that these shocks came after a number of years of deficit finance so that people were more likely to see the deficits as remaining fairly permanent.

This distinction is important also in currency substitution models. Boyer and Kingston (1980) have cited the parallelism of U.S. and Canadian interest rates to support their conjecture that the two currencies are very close substitutes for each other. This is especially true of long-term bonds, probably reflecting the very similar inflation experiences that the two countries have had over more than a century.

In such a model, the distinction between temporary and permanent becomes even more crucial. The reason is that in the case of high substitution, there is no possibility of an anticipated divergence in the rates of inflation. Therefore, both long and short rates should have very small divergences, if any, and the forward differential should be small as well. This argues that the long-term rates of growth of currencies of various denominations cannot differ substantially, for if they did they would cause the higher inflating one to disappear entirely from circulation. None the less, permanent changes in the supplies of either currency have well-known monetarist influences upon the exchange rate, whereas temporary changes have no influence at all. To put this point in another way, currency substitution causes individuals to increase the weight they put on future policy actions relative to that on present ones. Finally, reassessment of the levels of future money supplies causes a jump in the exchange rate from one level to another, with no effects upon the size of the forward differential.

This model has not been extended to the case of bond-financed fiscal policy because of the complexities that that would entail. However, such a policy will have effects upon the exchange rate if it is assumed either that services provided by the public sector are valued at below their cost by the private sector that utilizes them, or that demands for certain assets, such as money, depend on disposable income as in model (A) above.

9. Conclusion

The conclusion of this paper can be summarized rather quickly. In spite of the attractiveness and simplicity of monetary models of the economy, they do not have much explanatory power for the Canadian experience since the Second World War when they are written out more fully in structural form. Such models have been successful in explaining the elements that go into exchange-market pressure: foreign exchange reserves and the exchange rate. However, they have not had much success in explaining other variables, such as price level and interest-rate movements. This cursory review of the data concludes that it is unlikely that monetary explanations will be particularly successful in the future.

This conclusion is not novel, and it is something that economists who have more experience with the data have known all along. In fact, there has been a great tendency on the part of macro-economists in Canada to explain developments in the economy in terms of special circumstances attaching to certain times in our experience. The positive contribution that this paper makes is to point out that there have been three factors which have been at work throughout the post-war period determining the basic movements of the interesting macro-economic variables. Of central importance to the Canadian economy has been the high substitutability between domestic-currency- and U.S.-dollar-denominated market instruments. This substitutability has been such that from demand conditions alone there has been a high degree of parallelism between Canadian and U.S. rates of interest. Such substitution lowers the impact of current money-supply changes upon the exchange rate and the interest rate, and therefore makes the Bank of Canada's attempt to use its monetary independence more difficult.

Others have argued that with perfect currency substitution the exchange rate is indeterminate. This arises from a model in which the past has no influence independent of conditioning our expectations of the future. Certainly, in the Canadian context, parity psychology has had a strong role in exchange-rate determination, and is a strong counter-argument to those who envisage the possibility of exchange-rate indeterminacy here. Indeed, it should be noted that a fuller statement of the exchange-rate indeterminacy result is that with perfect currency substitution, although the exchange rate is indeterminate, it is anticipated to stay constant throughout the indefinite future. In light of the indeterminacy of the initial condition only, an exchange rate near unity seems like a natural one for the U.S.-Canadian situation.

This author's belief is that currency substitution in North America is high but far from perfect. As a result of this high substitution, all current and future actions of the Bank of Canada have important influences upon the exchange rate. In order to make clear its intention, therefore, the Bank should probably indicate bounds within which it is willing to let the exchange rate fluctuate. It has done this informally in the market-place, but a clearer explicit statement of its exchange-rate policy may now be appropriate. The Bank may also want to jettison the now untenable position that current monetary policy is the all-important influence upon the exchange rate. In pointing out the important influence of fiscal actions, it can pass along some of the burden of defending the exchange rate to Parliament and the Minister of Finance.

The second element of great importance in the economy's development since the Second World War has been its movement from a debtor position towards a creditor one. Canada came out of the war with a substantial debt that was being paid off during the late 1940s and early 1950s. The investment boom in natural resource industries in 1955 to 1957, taken to be exogenous here, substantially increased our debtor position. None the less, the post-war period can be seen as one of constantly improving trade and current accounts on the part of the private sector due to endogenous factors alone. This general tendency has been thwarted also by the authorities' deficit financing that rose to substantial proportions in the periods between 1958 and 1962, and since 1974.

Since the private sector is moving towards balance on the current account, those of us who see the deficit there as a substantial problem would clearly like to give the private sector more time in a framework of relatively free trade. Indeed, a strong argument can be made that much of this deficit would be eliminated were the authorities to take a more sensible stand on energy pricing in Canada. Certainly proposals like that of Robinson (1980) do not seem particularly sensible since they lose for the Canadian economy the benefits that free trade can provide, and provide no greater price incentives than are inherent in the substantial devaluation since 1976.

The final point of this paper has been to argue that fiscal policy seems to have had a central role in macro-economic developments in the external sector during the whole post-war period. The current account and the government budget deficits match each other very closely. Similarly, the exchange-rate depreciations of 1961–1962 and of 1977–1978 can be linked with the substantial deficit financing that began a few years before. In noting the importance of fiscal policy, we are reiterating a conclusion at which Laidler and O'Shea (1980) arrived in their monetarist model of the United Kingdom. However, it is possible to incorporate fiscal elements and still stay within a strictly monetarist framework by considering individuals' expectations of the extent to which this deficit financing will be paid in the future through monetary growth and the consequent inflation tax. On such a view, fiscal policy has a strong impact because it affects people's expectations about future money growth. The argument, therefore, is about the size of the government's deficit, rather than about the size of the government sector as a whole, which Barber and McCallum (1980) take to be the chief point of contention. There are many reasons for having a smaller government sector in Canada, but they are motivated by considerations of resource allocation rather than by macro-economic reasoning.

In highlighting the importance of fiscal policy during this period, this paper is in the spirit of some work that economists in the United States are doing at the present time.[10] Their analysis suggests that Friedman (1948) put forward a sensible policy for macro-economic stabilization. He suggested that the money supply should be altered only in order to finance surpluses or deficits in the federal budget, and then the financing should be 100 per cent in monetary form. In this way, the 1948 policy prescription is diametrically opposed to his popular k-per cent rule that was presented first in 1959.

Presumably what convinced Friedman of the preferability of his second rule was the empirical work that he was doing with Anna Schwartz on business cycles in the United States during the decade of the 1950s. It was therefore on empirical grounds that Friedman adopted his monetary rule rather than the theoretical reasons that recent monetarists have been using. Furthermore, this empirical work was done on the closed U.S. economy rather than on an open economy such as that of Canada. It is noteworthy as well that the late 1940s was the time when "The Case for Flexible Exchange Rates" was being written (Friedman, 1953). One wonders whether Friedman's policy prescriptions for monetary and exchange-rate policy for a small open economy would be the same if he had done empirical work for such a situation.

Notes

* The author is grateful to Robert J. Hodrick, Geoffrey Kingston, Allan Meltzer, and Michael Parkin for helpful discussions on the topic of this paper. This research was started during the author's year of sabbatical leave at Carnegie-Mellon University. Financial support was generously provided by the Social Sciences and Humanities Research Council through a research fellowship. Subsequent summer support from Carnegie-Mellon is also gratefully acknowledged.

[1] Theoretical work on the monetary approach is reported at length in Frenkel and Johnson (1978). In addition there are accompanying empirical pieces in that volume. The best known empirical work on the monetary approach is that by Connolly and da Silveira (1979), Girton and Roper (1977), and Laidler and O'Shea (1980).

[2] The main variables that are left out of most monetary approaches to exchange-rate determination are the price levels. Notable examples of this methodology include Bilson (1979) and Frenkel (1979).

[3] Hansen and Hodrick (1980) and Stockman (1978) are examples of research in which the Canadian economy was the outlier.

[4] Laidler and O'Shea (1980) are unique in that they include price terms in their model of the U.K. open economy, but it should be remembered that their model is applicable only to the fixed exchange-rate period. Hodrick (1978) provides justification for the exclusion of price variables in empirical testing of the monetary approach. The resulting models are repeated often in empirical work associated with the monetary approach, especially work originating from the University of Chicago.

[5] Specifically, the following years were excluded: 1956–1957, 1965–1966, and 1969.

[6] The expectation of future parallelism of Canadian and U.S. long-term rates and rates of inflation can be exemplified by the following quotation taken from Freedman and Longworth (1980). "For example, the implication of a one percentage point differential between Canadian and U.S. rates of inflation over twenty years is a 22 per cent depreciation of the Canadian dollar over that period. Even if the former seemed possible, the latter may not have seemed plausible to Canadians" (p. 38).

[7] This seems especially true in comparison with other countries. Using data from *International Financial Statistics* (August 1980), this author finds that for the years 1973–1979 the closing quotations of the forward differentials against the U.S. dollar for three countries were as follows:

	mean	standard deviation
Canada	− .5220	1.7504
Germany	3.032	2.9556
United Kingdom	−4.059	4.4664

This shows the greater size and volatility of the forward differential for countries other than Canada.

[8] Longworth (1981) notes that "with the exception of 1977, the current spot rate . . . [provided] . . . a better forecast of the future spot rate . . . than [did] . . . the current forward rate. The Canadian–U.S. exchange market remains a puzzle."

[9] Freedman and Longworth (1980) note the fact that exchange-rate equations that appeared to work for the 1970–1976 period do not seem to work so well for the subsequent period. This can be remedied in part by adding dummy variables for the subsequent periods. However, models for which this updating works tend to be ones in which the foreign exchange market is not efficient, as, for example, is true of the Haas-Alexander (1979) model.

[10] Much of this discussion is taking place at an informal level, but the name that is usually associated with the view that monetary policy's influence may have been over-emphasized is the University of Minnesota, and especially Professor Neil Wallace. For a more conventional model representing the profession's doubts on this score, see McCallum (1981).

References

Barber, Clarence L. and McCallum, John C.P. (1980) *Unemployment and Inflation: The Canadian Experience*. Ottawa: Canadian Institute for Economic Policy.

Bilson, John F.O. (1979) "The Deutsche Mark/Dollar Rate: A Monetary Analysis." *Carnegie-Rochester Conference Series on Public Policy* (a supplementary series to the *Journal of Monetary Economics*) 11: 59–101.

Bordo, M. and Choudri, E. (1977) "The Behaviour of the Prices of Traded and Non-traded Goods: The Canadian Case 1962–74." Mimeo. Ottawa: Carleton University.

Boyer, R.S. and Kingston, Geoffrey H. (1980) "Currency Substitution: A Perfect Foresight Optimizing Analysis." Centre for the Study of International Economic Relations, Working Paper No. 8019. London: University of Western Ontario.

Caves, Richard E. and Reuber, Grant L. (1971) *Capital Transfers and Economic Policy: Canada, 1951–1962*. Cambridge, Mass.: Harvard University Press.

Connolly, Michael and da Silveira, José Dantas. (1979) "Exchange Market Pressure in Postwar Brazil: An Application of the Girton-Roper Monetary Model." *American Economic Review* 69 (June): 448–54.

Connolly, Michael and Taylor, Dean. (1976) "Adjustment to Devaluation with Money and Nontraded Goods." *Journal of International Economics* 6 (August): 289–98.

Courchene, Thomas J. (1976) *Money, Inflation, and the Bank of Canada*. Montreal: C.D. Howe Research Institute.

Donner, Arthur W. and Peters, Douglas D. (1979) *The Monetarist Counter-Revolution: A Critique of Canadian Monetary Policy 1975–1979*. Ottawa: Canadian Institute for Economic Policy.

Dornbusch, Rudiger. (1973) "Devaluation, Money, and Nontraded Goods." *American Economic Review* 63 (December): 871–80.

Dornbusch, Rudiger and Fischer, Stanley. (1980) "Sterling and the External Balance." In *Britain's Economic Performance*, edited by Richard E. Caves and Lawrence B. Krause, pp. 21–80. Washington, D.C.: The Brookings Institution.

Dornbusch, Rudiger and Krugman, Paul. (1976) "Flexible Exchange Rates in the Short Run." *Brookings Papers on Economic Activity* 3:537–84.

Dunn, Robert M., Jr. (1978) *The Canada–U.S. Capital Markets: Intermediation, Integration, and Policy Independence*. Montreal: C.D. Howe Research Institute.

Floyd, John E. (1977) "Perspectives on Recent Monetary Policy." Toronto: University of Toronto, Institute for Policy Analysis.

Frankel, Jeffrey A. (1979) "On the Mark: A Theory of Floating Exchange Rates Based on Real Interest Differentials." *American Economic Review* 69 (September): 610–22.

Freedman, Charles. (1979) "A Note on Net Interest Payments to Foreigners Under Inflationary Conditions." *Canadian Journal of Economics* 12 (May): 291–99.

Freedman, Charles and Longworth, David. (1980) "Some Aspects of the Canadian Experience with Flexible Exchange Rates in the 1970s." Bank of Canada Technical Report No. 20. Ottawa: Bank of Canada.

Frenkel, Jacob A. (1977) "The Forward Exchange Rate, Expectations, and the Demand for Money: The German Hyperinflation." *American Economic Review* 67 (September): 653–70.

Frenkel, Jacob A. and Johnson, Harry G., eds. (1978) *The Economics of Exchange Rates: Selected Studies*. Reading, Mass.: Addison-Wesley.

Frenkel, Jacob A. and Levich, Richard M. (1975) "Covered Interest Arbitrage: Unexploited Profits?" *Journal of Political Economy* 83 (April): 325–38.

Frenkel, Jacob A. and Levich, Richard M. (1977) "Transaction Costs and Interest Arbitrage: Tranquil Versus Turbulent Periods." *Journal of Political Economy* 85 (December): 1209–26.

Friedman, Milton. (1948) "A Monetary and Fiscal Framework for Economic Stability." *American Economic Review* 38 (June): 245–64.

Friedman, Milton. (1953) "The Case for Flexible Exchange Rates." In *Essays in Positive Economics*, pp. 157–203. Chicago: University of Chicago Press.

Girton, Lance and Roper, Don. (1977) "A Monetary Model of Exchange Market Pressure Applied to the Postwar Canadian Experience." *American Economic Review* 67 (September): 537–48.

Haas, Richard D. and Alexander, William E. (1979) "A Model of Exchange Rates and Capital Flows: The Canadian Floating Rate Experience." *Journal of Money, Credit and Banking* 11 (November): 467–82.

Hansen, Lars Peter and Hodrick, Robert J. (1980) "Forward Exchange Rates as Optimal Predictors of Future Spot Rates: An Econometric Analysis." *Journal of Political Economy* 88 (October): 829–53.

Harris, Richard G. and Purvis, Douglas D. (1981) "Diverse Information and Market Efficiency in a Monetary Model of the Exchange Rate." *Economic Journal* 91 (December): 829–47.

Hodrick, Robert J. (1978) "An Empirical Analysis of the Monetary Approach to the Determination of the Exchange Rate." In *The Economics of Exchange Rates: Selected Studies*, edited by Jacob A. Frenkel and Harry G. Johnson, pp. 97–116. Reading, Mass.: Addison-Wesley.

Huber, Paul A. (1980) "The Canadian Current Account: Lagged Reactions to Exchange Rate Disequilibrium." Mimeo. Halifax: Dalhousie University.

Laidler, David and O'Shea, Patrick. (1980) "An Empirical Macro-model of an Open Economy Under Fixed Exchange Rates: The United Kingdom 1954–1970."*Economica* 47 (May): 141–58.

Longworth, David. (1981) "Testing the Efficiency of the Canadian-U.S. Exchange Market Under the Assumption of No Risk Premium." *The Journal of Finance* 36 (March): 43–49.

McCallum, Bennett T. (1981) "Monetarist Principles and the Money Stock Growth Rule."*American Economic Review* 71 (May): 134–38.

McCormick, Frank. (1979) "Covered Interest Arbitrage: Unexploited Profits? Comment." *Journal of Political Economy* 87 (April): 411–17.

Mundell, Robert A. (1964) "Problems of Monetary and Exchange Rate Management in Canada." In *Canadian Banking and Monetary Policy*, 2d ed., edited by James P. Cairns, H.H. Binhammer, and Robin W. Boadway, pp. 101–11. Toronto: McGraw-Hill Ryerson, 1972.

Parkin, Michael and Bade, Robin. (1979) "The Canadian Balance of Payments: 1948–1978." In *Issues in Canadian Public Policy (II)*, edited by Ronald G. Wirick and Douglas D. Purvis, pp. 105–41. Proceedings of a Conference at Queen's University, Institute for Economic Research, 1979. Kingston: Queen's University.

Poole, William. (1967) "The Stability of the Canadian Flexible Exchange Rate, 1950–1962." *Canadian Journal of Economics and Political Science* 33 (May): 205–17.

Rhomberg, Rudolf R. (1964) "A Model of the Canadian Economy Under Fixed and Fluctuating Exchange Rates." *Journal of Political Economy* 72 (February): 1–31.

Robinson, H. Lukin. (1980) *Canada's Crippled Dollar: An Analysis of International Trade and Our Troubled Balance of Payments*. Ottawa: Canadian Institute for Economic Policy.

Selody, Jack. (1979) "A Monetary Model of Canadian Price and Output Fluctuations." Ph.D. dissertation, University of Western Ontario.

Stockman, Alan C. (1978) "Risk, Information, and Forward Exchange Rates." In *The Economics of Exchange Rates: Selected Studies*, edited by Jacob A. Frenkel and Harry G. Johnson, pp. 159–78. Reading, Mass.: Addison-Wesley.

Wonnacott, Paul. (1965) *The Canadian Dollar: 1948–1962*. Toronto: University of Toronto Press.

Comment

by
Brian L. Scarfe

Russ Boyer's interesting paper surveys some of the theoretical and empirical literature on the determinants of the Canadian balance of payments and the U.S. dollar exchange rate, and provides some useful insights into our actual historical experience in the post-war period. Although he appears to have strong sympathies for the monetary approach to exchange rates and the balance of payments, Boyer does suggest that a number of important qualifications may be required if this approach is to explain successfully the stylized facts of our recent balance-of-payments and exchange-rate experiences. In particular, the law of one-price notions of purchasing-power parity and real interest-rate parity do not appear to hold, at least from a short-run point of view. There are a number of reasons for this, which must include the existence of non-traded goods as well as imperfections in the substitutability of both domestically produced and foreign-produced goods and services and domestic and foreign securities.

It is fairly well known that in the short run the Canadian selling prices of many tradable commodities do not respond to small-scale changes in the foreign exchange rate. One possible reason for this is that published selling prices do not accurately reflect the true prices at which transactions are actually occurring; rather, they reflect list prices that respond to the average prices at which transactions are occurring only after some short time lag. On this view, the failure of Canadian selling prices to respond in the short run to small-scale changes in the foreign exchange rate is a statistical illusion rather than a real phenomenon. Another reason, however, is that in normal circumstances, firms have inelastic exchange-rate expectations, pricing their products in Canada in relation to similar products available in the United States on the basis of their view of the 'normal' exchange rate. The main consequence of this phenomenon, where it occurs, is that small-scale changes in the foreign exchange rate will *not* serve to create deviations between foreign price movements and domestic price movements unless these changes are expected to be permanent and firms change their view of the 'normal' exchange rate. On the further assumption that observations on the actual exchange rate lead firms to adapt their view of the 'normal' exchange rate, perhaps fairly quickly but not instantaneously, a time lag is introduced into the response of the economy to changes in the actual exchange rate. In econometric studies of the short-run behaviour of sectoral prices in the Canadian economy, for example, this time lag often shows up in the fact that statistical estimates of the elasticities attached to U.S. price variables are significantly larger than statistical estimates of the elasticities attached to the price of U.S. dollars. If the time profile of the lagged response of particular Canadian prices to movements in U.S. prices differs from the time profile of their lagged response to the price of U.S. dollars, no inference may of course be drawn about long-run elasticities simply from the observation that short-run elasticities differ.

There are, one suspects, good reasons for dissimilarities between these two lag patterns. Individual firms are likely to be very familiar with monitoring and interpreting the movements of the narrow range of micro-economic prices with which they are crucially concerned. Through trade associations and other institutional linkages, they are quickly able to take a view about the direction in which these prices, whether they are domestic or foreign, are likely to move. This is less so with the exchange rate, which is determined by macro-economic interactions that are only remotely connected with the discretionary pricing decisions that an individual firm has to make in the short run. Thus, variations in Canadian prices may reflect variations in U.S. prices without regard to the possibility that the exchange rate may also be changing. (This is also likely to be true for asset prices, particularly stock market prices, though more for psychological than for institutional reasons.) A similar argument can be applied to the short-run discretionary behaviour of individual trade unions, who may bargain for approximate wage parity with their American counterparts without regard to the possibility of exchange-rate movements. These linkages all depend upon the expectation that the U.S. dollar exchange rate will remain roughly constant over time, or at least upon exchange-rate expectations that are generally inelastic in the short run.

The expectation that the U.S. dollar exchange rate will remain roughly constant through time may well be deeply rooted in Canadian traditions. It is associated with the fact that the Canadian economy has experienced and is expected to continue experiencing common overall movements with the U.S. economy. Although this expectation of a roughly constant exchange rate may make it difficult to insulate the economy from *external* shocks, it may well be an important element in the stability of the economy in response to *internal* shocks. This point is well illustrated by the monetary instabilities created in 1961–1962, when the all too successful attempt by the government to 'talk' down the exchange rate undermined this firmly entrenched expectation.

If the behaviour of private speculators is normally governed by exchange-rate expectations that are inelastic in the short run, that is, they behave as if there exists a normal or customary level of the exchange rate that responds or adapts only with some fairly short lag to underlying economic conditions including the actual level of the exchange rate, then speculative activity will normally help to stabilize the foreign exchange market. On the other hand, the possibility of short-run overshooting or volatility of exchange-rate movements whenever expectations do occasionally lead to a switching of regimes from stabilizing to destabilizing speculation may force the authorities to manage the floating exchange rate by 'leaning against the wind' in both directions. But the fact that the authorities are known to lean against the wind is one important reason why under normal circumstances exchange-rate expectations are inelastic (and why they may appear to be inefficient in the econometric evidence) and, therefore, why speculative activity is normally stabilizing.

There can be little doubt that the existence of stabilizing speculation must itself depend upon the existence of a previous history of roughly constant exchange rates. Moreover, its continuity may depend upon the imposition of monetary policies that are not very different from those of one's trading partners. Thus, the need to maintain exchange-rate expectations that are normally inelastic, and thereby encourage stabilizing rather than destabilizing speculation, may reduce the flexibility of the monetary authorities to pursue an independent monetary policy under floating exchange rates. In consequence, the floating exchange-rate regime may exhibit some of the characteristics of a fixed exchange-rate regime, since the authorities must have *and be perceived to have* some view as to the appropriate level of the exchange rate, at least in the short run.

Moreover, even if fundamentally different monetary policies were temporarily pursued, the short-run inelasticity of exchange-rate expectations would reduce the impact of these policies on both the actual exchange rate and other related economic variables. Thus, from the point of view of stabilization policy, the inelasticity of exchange-rate expectations (just like the maintenance of a fixed exchange rate) is highly beneficial if the external environment remains stable and if disturbances are domestic in origin. However, when large-scale disturbances are occurring in the world economy, these expectations (like the maintenance of a fixed exchange rate) make it more difficult to stabilize the economy through the use of the exchange rate as an insulating device.

My comments so far give a clear rationale for the existence of managed flexible exchange rates in which the authorities lean against the wind, rather than freely floating exchange rates. They also explain short-run departures from both purchasing-power parity and real interest-rate parity by invoking the notion that exchange-rate expectations are normally inelastic. These short-run departures from the law of one price were the first of three themes in Boyer's paper. I turn now to the second theme, namely the impact of fiscal policy on the balance of payments and the exchange rate.

Although money and monetary policy have important interactions with the overall balance of payments and the exchange rate, both nominal variables, Canada's longer-term balance-of-payments problem (if it has one) is a problem of composition. To change this composition in favour of smaller capital inflows and a smaller current-account deficit must entail some restructuring of real economic magnitudes. In particular, if we wish to reduce the current-account deficit by monetary expansion and currency depreciation, it is essential also to use fiscal policy to reduce the size of the overall government-sector deficit, and thereby lower the real rate of interest in Canada while simultaneously allowing the current account to expand. We cannot, however, move permanently towards lower real interest rates or change the balance-of-payments composition by using monetary policy alone.

Except in so far as government deficits and surpluses lead directly to changes in the nominal stock of money, their main long-run impact is simply to alter the equilibrium real rate of interest. In so doing, government deficits and surpluses have important and often crucial longer-run effects on the structure of the economy. But as far as changes in the overall level of employment are concerned, over the longer term, fiscal policy is rendered ineffective by the complete 'crowding out' of its impact. That is to say, an expansion in government expenditure relative to taxation tends to generate changes in the real rate of interest, which imply both lower exports of goods and services relative to imports and lower real investment relative to domestic savings. Fiscal policy therefore has an important effect on the equilibrium composition of the balance of payments, with higher government-sector deficits (or smaller surpluses) always implying larger current-account deficits (or smaller surpluses). Since private domestic investment and private savings will be affected by the stance of fiscal policy, particularly through its effect on the real rate of interest, this correlation between deficits and surpluses is a positive one, but should not be thought to be a 'dollar for dollar' relationship. The crowding-out effects of fiscal deficits are simply spread between the investment-savings balance and the current account of the balance of payments. Boyer's calculations suggest that about 30 per cent of the impact of fiscal deficits comes out on the current-account deficit and 70 per cent on the investment-savings shortfall.

Not only does fiscal policy have a strong influence on the composition of the balance of payments, it also affects the overall payments balance and the exchange rate. The increased real interest rates generated by larger government-sector deficits lead to larger capital inflows and appreciation of the Canadian dollar in the short run as investors adjust their asset portfolios. These inflows outweigh the current-account effects in the short run, thereby implying that the balance-of-payments equilibrium locus is flatter than the money-market-equilibrium locus in the standard income and interest-rate (Hicks-Hansen-Mundell) diagram. The closeness of ties between Canadian and U.S. money markets makes Canada perhaps peculiar in these relative slopes; nevertheless, Canadian real interest rates are neither constant nor entirely determined in New York.

The appreciation of the Canadian dollar is, however, only a short-run phenomenon (or back-shooting phenomenon, as Boyer calls it). Once asset portfolios have been adjusted to the new higher interest-rate differential, and both the increased longer-term debt service costs and the crowding-out effects on the trade balance of the larger fiscal deficit begin to weigh on the balance of payments, the currency will begin to depreciate. These latter effects may take two to three years to materialize, but they show up very clearly in the post-war data. Although the short-run effect of a larger fiscal deficit may be to appreciate the Canadian dollar, the long-run effect of a sustained deficit is Canadian dollar depreciation. Thus, in the long run, the balance-of-payments-equilibrium locus is definitely steeper than the money-market-equilibrium locus.

The third theme in Boyer's paper concerns the important impacts of real shocks of the terms-of-trade variety on the Canadian economy and its balance of payments. In particular, the ratio of the world price of the economy's exportable goods to the world price of the economy's imports increased markedly in the 1972–1974 period, and declined again in 1976–1978. This external shock ought to have been taken into account by Boyer before he reached the conclusion that the size of the current-account deficit has been falling in relationship to Canadian gross national product. Once one removes the effects of the improvement in the terms of trade in 1972–1974 and the deterioration in 1976–1978, it is somewhat less clear that there remains a trend towards reduction in the relative size of the current-account deficit over the post-war period, though there have obviously been cyclical movements in the deficit-to-gross-national-product ratio.

Although nominal or monetary shocks have real repercussions in the short-run transitional period of adjustment to these shocks, in longer-run equilibrium only nominal variables (like the rate of inflation or the exchange rate) will be affected. Real shocks, such as rising world energy prices, are a different matter. In an open economy, the most important form of real shock is a change in the terms of trade. Since these shocks cannot be fully offset by exchange-rate changes, there is no easy way of insulating the domestic economy from their impact. Indeed, for an adverse terms-of-trade shock, the temporary consequences will be to raise both the inflation rate and the unemployment rate. Any attempt at monetary accommodation to ease temporarily the burden on the unemployment rate will worsen the inflationary situation and, in the process, only postpone the inevitable unemployment consequences to a future period. Nevertheless, depending upon the policy choices made by the authorities in the face of this intertemporal trade-off, adverse shocks to the real side of the economy may still be accommodated, in part, by variations in monetary policy. However, as we have suggested, monetary expansion to ease the output deflationary effects of these shocks, and thereby temporarily maintain employment, inevitably leads to a worsening of the price inflationary effects. There is, therefore, no escape from the stagflationary consequences that such adverse terms of trade or relative price shocks generate. The distributional problem of sharing the real burden of adjustment to these shocks cannot be avoided by the use of monetary policy; indeed, the real burden of adjustment provides additional fuel to the inflationary fires that can only be kept in check if the rate of resource utilization is allowed to fall and the unemployment rate to rise, at least temporarily. By exacerbating the price inflationary consequences of adverse real shocks, monetary accommodation simply postpones the inevitable real adjustment problem; but on the political as opposed to the economic front, there may always be something to be gained in the short run by postponing the agony. Finally, indexation of money wage rates to the consumer price index is clearly an undesirable policy option in the face of an adverse terms-of-trade shock, although indexation to an index of domestic output prices need not have the same destabilizing (and inflation-accelerating) effects in this context. Real shocks and indexation of money wage rates to the consumer price index are incompatible; in this sense, real shocks cannot be indexed.

In an economy like Canada's with considerable regional diversity, relative price shocks can clearly have differential impacts across the country. Indeed, a positive terms-of-trade shock for one region may be a negative one for another region. This, of course, creates serious problems for the management of monetary and exchange-rate policies. Nevertheless, some currency depreciation may be allowed to offset a terms-of-trade shock that on the whole is adverse, even if it is of benefit to one region, provided also that some appreciation is also allowed to offset a terms-of-trade shock that on the whole is positive. Although the Canadian dollar was eventually allowed to depreciate after the adverse terms-of-trade movement in the 1976–1978 period, it was most unfortunate for the acceleration of inflation in Canada that appreciation was not attempted in the 1972–1974 period. Indeed, a perverse depreciation was instead permitted. Among many others, I have written extensively about this inflationary episode.[1]

The particular experience of the 1975–1980 period is of considerable interest, given the inability of econometric models that explained earlier experience also to explain exchange-rate and balance-of-payments changes in this period. What is clear in retrospect is that in reaction to its excessively easy monetary policies of 1971–1974, a looseness that permitted our relative costs and prices to get out of line with those in the United States, the Bank of Canada initiated, in the fall of 1975, a tight monetary policy that continued to be so at least until the spring of 1977. The impact of this policy was to create an historically large interest-rate differential *vis-à-vis* the United States, to generate large-scale capital inflows, and to postpone the necessary downward adjustment of the Canadian dollar that our previous inflationary excesses had made inevitable. The unemployment cost of this policy has been substantial, both because of its negative impact on the trade balance, and because it reduced the volume of investment in Canada — directly through higher interest rates and indirectly via the capacity-utilization effects of an over-valued exchange rate. This is not at all to say that the Bank's policies were in the wrong direction, as suggested by Barber and McCallum,[2] and Donner and Peters.[3] Indeed, the looseness of our federal fiscal policy has placed an additional burden on monetary policy in our anti-inflationary fight, and has led to tighter monetary policies than otherwise would have been necessary, since the Bank of Canada seems to have been determined not to monetize the growing fiscal deficit and thereby exacerbate our inflationary situation. The fault, therefore, lies mostly with our federal fiscal policies.

One of the most important requirements of policy today is to get both Canadian savings and foreign borrowing into productive investment rather than into the financing of current government-sector deficits, since our real problem in Canada is an investment rate (and therefore a labour productivity growth rate) that has been too low, especially over the 1975–1980 period. We must get our fiscal-monetary balance back on course, by which I mean making real progress towards reducing the federal government deficit and the associated substantial absorption of funds from the money market so that we can afford to reduce our real interest rates and perhaps thereby permit a slightly more expansionary monetary policy, which would be good for both the level of productive investment and, via keeping the exchange rate in the $0.84 U.S. range, exports as well. The capacity-utilization effects of maintaining the Canadian dollar in this range are clearly an important ingredient in an investment and productivity-orientated policy package.

Notes

[1] Brian L. Scarfe, (1977) *Cycles, Growth, and Inflation: A Survey of Contemporary Macrodynamics* (Toronto: McGraw-Hill), Chapter 13.

[2] Clarence L. Barber and John C.P. McCallum, (1980) *Unemployment and Inflation: The Canadian Experience* (Ottawa: Canadian Institute for Economic Policy).

[3] Arthur W. Donner and Douglas D. Peters, (1979) *The Monetarist Counter-Revolution: A Critique of Canadian Monetary Policy 1975–1979* (Ottawa: Canadian Institute for Economic Policy).

Comment

by
Dale W. Henderson*

Introduction

This comment is divided into four sections. Section 1 is a description of a version of the Mundell-Fleming model of a single open economy. In Section 2 that model is employed to highlight one important reason for undertaking direct analyses of the behavioural relations of the current and capital accounts of the balance of payments such as those performed in some of the round table papers. In Section 3 the model is used to analyse different methods of financing an increase in government spending in an effort to follow up on Boyer's suggestive remarks on the relationship between fiscal policy and the exchange rate. Section 4 contains comments on two specific aspects of Boyer's paper.

1. The Model

Consider the following period model of a single open economy that is called the home country:[1]

$$- S + D + C = 0, \tag{1}$$

$$L^d - L_{-1} - \delta D = 0, \tag{2}$$

$$B^d - B_{-1} + \overset{*}{B}{}^d - \overset{*}{B}{}_{-1} - (1 - \delta)D = 0, \tag{3}$$

$$S + L_{-1} - L^d + B_{-1} - B^d + E(F_{-1} - F^d) \equiv 0, \tag{4}$$

$$C + \overset{*}{B}{}^d - \overset{*}{B}{}_{-1} - E(F^d - F_{-1}) = 0. \tag{5}$$

This model is referred to as the general Mundell-Fleming model. Equation (1) is the condition for goods market equilibrium; nominal saving (S) must equal the sum of the nominal government deficit (D) and the nominal current-account surplus (C).[2] Equation (2) is the condition for home money-market equilibrium; home residents' nominal money demand (L^d) must equal their holdings of money last period (L_{-1}) plus that part of the government deficit financed by the issue of money (δD). Equation (3) is the condition for equilibrium in the home currency securities market; the sum of the nominal demands for home currency securities by home residents (B^d) and foreign residents $(\overset{*}{B}{}^{d})$ must equal the sum of the holdings last period of home residents (B_{-1}) and foreign residents $(\overset{*}{B}_{-1})$ plus that part of the government deficit financed by the sale of home currency securities $[(1 - \delta)D]$. Equation (4) is the wealth accumulation identity for home residents; home residents' nominal saving must equal the sum of their acquisitions of home money and home currency securities and the home currency value of their acquisition of foreign currency securities, which is given by the home currency price of foreign currency (E) times the difference between home residents' nominal demand for foreign currency securities (F^{d}) and their holdings of these securities last period (F_{-1}), both measured in foreign currency. Adding (1), (2), and (3) and taking account of (4) yields equation (5), which is the condition for equilibrium in the balance of payments under freely floating exchange rates; the current-account surplus must equal the negative of the capital-account surplus, which, in turn, equals foreign residents' acquisitions of home currency securities minus the home currency value of home residents' acquisitions of foreign currency securities.[3] Since (5) is identically equal to the sum of (1), (2), and (3), only three of these four equilibrium conditions are independent. The equilibrium conditions for the goods market, the home money market, and the balance of payments are used in the analysis below.

Now the behavioural relations are described. Home real saving $(s = S/P)$ is given by

$$\overset{+\quad +\quad\quad +\quad\quad -\ +}{S/P = s(y^{D}, i - \gamma, \overset{*}{i} + \epsilon - \gamma, A_{-1}/P, \sigma).} \tag{6}$$

P is the home currency price of home goods. y^{D} is home real disposable income:

$$y^{D} = y + i_{-1}B_{-1}/P + \overset{*}{i}_{-1}EF_{-1}/P - t. \tag{7}$$

y is home real output:

$$y = y(W/P), y' < 0, \tag{8}$$

where W is the fixed home currency home nominal wage. The nominal interest rates on home (foreign) currency securities this period and last period are i and i_{-1} $(\overset{*}{i}$ and $\overset{*}{i}_{-1})$ respectively.[4] t is real taxes. ϵ is the anticipated rate of depreciation of the home currency. γ is the anticipated rate of increase in the home price index:

$$\gamma = \omega\pi + (1 - \omega)\epsilon. \tag{9}$$

ω is the fraction of home expenditure devoted to home goods. π is the anticipated rate of increase in the price of the home good, and the anticipated rate of increase in the foreign currency price of the foreign good is assumed to be zero. Expectations are assumed to be either static or regressive:

$$\epsilon = \theta(\bar{E}/E - 1), \quad \theta \geqslant 0, \tag{10}$$

$$\pi = \phi(\bar{P}/P - 1), \quad \phi \geqslant 0, \tag{11}$$

where $\bar{E}$ and $\bar{P}$ are the constant long-run equilibrium values of E and P. A_{-1} is home residents' beginning of period nominal wealth:

$$A_{-1} = L_{-1} + B_{-1} + EF_{-1}. \tag{12}$$

σ is a shift variable.

The real government deficit is given by

$$D/P = g + i_{-1}\bar{B}_{-1}/P - t, \tag{13}$$

where g is real government spending, and $\bar{B}_{-1} = B_{-1} + \overset{*}{B}_{-1}$.

The real current-account surplus is given by

$$C/P = \overset{+}{x(E/P)} - \overset{+}{(E/P)m}(\overset{-}{y^D - s}, \overset{-}{E/P}, \mu) + \overset{*}{i}_{-1}EF_{-1}/P - i_{-1}\overset{*}{B}_{-1}/P. \tag{14}$$

$x(\cdot)\,[m(\cdot)]$ is the quantity of exports [imports].[5] μ is a shift variable.

Home residents' real asset demands are given by

$$L^d/P = l(\overset{+}{y}, \overset{+}{E/P}, \overset{-}{i}, \overset{-}{\overset{*}{i} + \epsilon}, \overset{+}{A_{-1}/P + s}, \overset{+}{\lambda}), \tag{15}$$

$$B^d/P = b(\overset{-}{y}, \overset{-}{E/P}, \overset{+}{i}, \overset{-}{\overset{*}{i} + \epsilon}, \overset{+}{A_{-1}/P + s}, \overset{-}{\lambda}, \overset{+}{\beta}), \tag{16}$$

$$EF^d/P = f(\overset{-}{y}, \overset{-}{E/P}, \overset{-}{i}, \overset{+}{\overset{*}{i} + \epsilon}, \overset{+}{A_{-1}/P + s}, \overset{-}{\beta}). \tag{17}$$

The relative price of the foreign good enters asset demands in the way shown because purchases of foreign goods are among the transactions that give rise to the demand for real money balances. λ and β are shift variables.

Foreign residents' real demand for home currency securities is given by

$$\overset{*}{B}^d/P = (E/P)\overset{*}{b}(\overset{+}{i - \epsilon}, \overset{-}{\overset{*}{i}}). \tag{18}$$

Under plausible assumptions, the conditions that excess demand in the goods market $[Y(\cdot)]$, excess demand in the money market $[L(\cdot)]$, and the balance of payments $[BOP(\cdot)]$ equal zero can be rewritten as[6]

$$Y(\overset{-}{P}, \overset{-}{i}, \overset{+}{E}, \overset{+}{g}, \overset{-}{t}, \overset{-}{\sigma}, \overset{+}{\mu}) = 0, \tag{19}$$

$$L(\overset{+}{P}, \overset{-}{i}, \overset{+}{E}, \overset{-}{g}, \overset{?}{t}, \overset{+}{\sigma}, \overset{+}{\lambda}) = 0, \tag{20}$$

$$BOP(\overset{-}{P}, \overset{+}{i}, \overset{+}{E}, \overset{+}{t}, \overset{?}{\sigma}, \overset{+}{\mu}, \overset{+}{\beta}) = 0. \tag{21}$$

These three equations determine the three endogenous variables P, i, and E. In Figure 1, the Y schedule is derived using (19); the L schedule is derived using (20), and the BOP schedule is derived using (21). The L schedule may be steeper, as in Figure 1, or flatter than the BOP schedule. Appreciation of the home currency shifts the Y schedule southwest, the L schedule southeast, and the BOP schedule northwest. The BOP_{PS} schedule is the BOP schedule when foreigners regard home and foreign currency securities as perfect substitutes $(\overset{*}{b}_1 \rightarrow \infty)$ so that $i = \overset{*}{i} + \epsilon$. Appreciation of the home currency shifts BOP_{PS} up (has no effect on BOP_{PS}) when expectations are regressive (static).

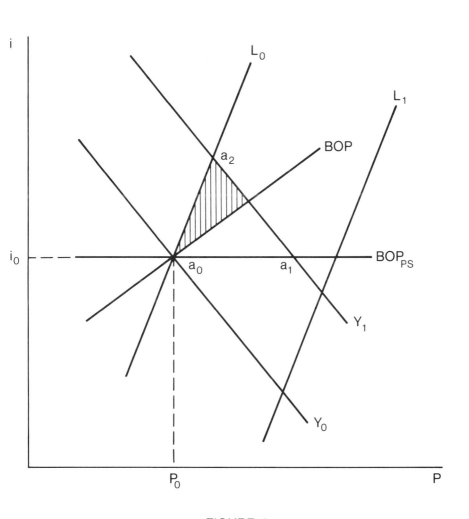

FIGURE 1

2. Analysing the Balance-of-Payments Accounts

In constructing explanations for outcomes for the balance-of-payments accounts and making projections of developments in these accounts, it is appropriate to rely heavily on two basic relationships: (1) the condition that the current-account surplus must be equal to national saving, private saving minus private investment plus the government surplus, and (2) the condition that under freely fluctuating exchange rates the current-account surplus and the private capital-account surplus must sum to zero. At a minimum these relationships can be used as consistency checks for explanations and projections of movements in the balance-of-payments accounts. However, at times during the round table discussions, there was a tendency to claim more for simple analyses based on these relationships than they can deliver.

Some contributors seemed to be arguing that attention can be focused entirely on the proximate determinants of national saving when explaining or projecting the current and capital accounts. Unfortunately the hard work of isolating the proximate determinants of the current and capital accounts cannot, in general, be avoided. It is well known, but not always remembered, that many of the proximate determinants of national saving are endogenous variables. Changes in the exogenous variables that directly enter only the behavioural relations of the current and capital accounts usually affect the values of the endogenous variables that are among the proximate determinants of national saving. This is one important reason for undertaking direct analyses of the behavioural relations of the current and capital accounts such as those performed in some of the round table papers.

There is one extreme set of circumstances in which the proximate determinants of some parts of the current and capital accounts can be ignored in explanations and projections of these accounts. Suppose that foreigners regard the home good and home currency securities of a small open economy as perfect substitutes for the foreign good and foreign currency securities; that is, suppose x', $\overset{*}{b}_1 \to \infty$. Assume further that the foreign currency price of the foreign good is fixed at unity and that $\overset{*}{i}$ is unchanging. Then P, i, and E depend only on the exogenous variables that directly enter home savings and the market for home money (g, t, σ, λ) and not on the exogenous variables that directly enter only home residents' demands for foreign goods and foreign securities (μ, β).[7] Given g, t, σ, and λ and the condition for home money-market equilibrium, P, i, and E are determined since $P = E$ and $i = \overset{*}{i} + \epsilon$. Given these variables, national saving is determined. The current-account surplus and capital-account surplus can be determined recursively, and changes in μ and β can be ignored.

In more general circumstances in which foreigners regard either home and foreign goods or home and foreign currency securities or both the two goods and the two securities as imperfect substitutes, the situation is different. Suppose that foreigners regard the two securities as perfect substitutes $(\overset{*}{b}_1 \rightarrow \infty)$ but that they regard the two goods as imperfect substitutes. Then, P, i, and E depend on μ as well as on g, t, σ, and λ. Given g, t, σ, λ, and μ, the condition for money-market equilibrium, and the condition that national saving must equal the current-account surplus, P, i, and E are determined since $i = \overset{*}{i} + \epsilon$. A shift in domestic residents' consumption preferences towards domestic goods and away from foreign goods $(d\mu > 0)$ leads to a rise in P, a rise in i (unless expectations are static), and a fall in E.[8] Y_1 in Figure 1 is the shifted goods-market-equilibrium schedule, and the new equilibrium lies in the triangle $a_0 a_1 a_2$. The capital-account surplus can be determined recursively, and changes in β can be ignored.

Alternatively, suppose that foreigners regard the two goods as perfect substitutes $(x' \rightarrow \infty)$ but that they regard the two securities as imperfect substitutes. Then, P, i, and E depend on β as well as on g, t, σ, and λ. Given g, t, σ, λ, and β, the condition for home money-market equilibrium, and the condition that national saving must equal the negative of the capital-account surplus, P, i, and E are determined since $P = E$. A shift in domestic residents' asset preferences away from foreign currency securities and towards home currency securities $(d\beta > 0)$ leads to a decrease in P, a fall in i, and a fall in E.[9] The current-account surplus can be determined recursively, and changes in μ can be ignored.

Of course when foreigners regard both the two goods and the two securities as imperfect substitutes, both β and μ matter for the determination of P, i, and E and, therefore, of national saving. One purpose of studies such as those of some of the round table papers that focus directly on the current and capital accounts is to isolate the effects of exogenous variables such as β and μ that directly enter only those accounts. In any case such exogenous variables must be taken into account in explanations and projections of the current and capital accounts even if the analysis focuses primarily on the proximate determinants of national saving.

3. Fiscal Policy and the Exchange Rate

In this section attention is focused on the relationship between fiscal policy and the exchange rate that has been emphasized by Boyer. The use of a period model makes it possible to conduct a relatively straightforward analysis of the implications of different methods of financing an increase in government spending.[10]

Mundell (1963) considers the effects of bond-financed $(dg > 0, \delta = 0)$ or balanced-budget $(dg = dt > 0)$ increases in government spending under the assumption that foreigners (at least) regard home and foreign securities as perfect substitutes ($\overset{*}{b}_1 \to \infty$ so that $i = \overset{*}{i} + \epsilon$). He also assumes that expectations are static ($\theta = \phi = 0$ so that $\pi = \epsilon = 0$) and that money demand is independent of the relative price of the home good and wealth ($l_2 = l_5 = 0$).[11] He concludes that either kind of increase in g leads to an appreciation of the home currency (fall in E) and leaves output unchanged. Given Mundell's assumptions, changes in the exchange rate affect neither the home interest rate ($i = \overset{*}{i}$) nor the excess demand for money ($L_E = 0$). With the supply of money fixed, P and, therefore, y must remain unchanged. The excess demand for goods created by either kind of increase in government spending must be completely offset by a deterioration in the current account induced by a fall in E. Y_1 in Figure 1 is the shifted goods market equilibrium schedule. Declines in E affect neither L nor BOP_{PS}, so the new equilibrium is at a_0.

If the perfect-substitutes assumption is retained, but θ or l_2 or l_5 is positive, a bond-financed increase in g must still lead to a fall in E, but P and y rise.[12] If $\theta > 0$, a fall in E raises $\overset{*}{i} + \epsilon$, thereby raising i and creating an excess supply of money ($L_i < 0$). Similarly, if l_2 or l_5 is positive, a fall in E creates an excess supply of money ($L_E > 0$). In all of these cases, decreases in E make room in the money market for rises in P and y, and the new equilibrium lies in the triangle $a_0 a_1 a_2$ in Figure 1. The results for a balanced-budget increase in g are a little more complicated. If $l_5 = 0$ but θ or l_2 is positive, then E falls and P and y rise for the same reasons they do with bond financing. However, if $l_5 > 0$, then the home currency may depreciate even though P and y must rise. The rise in taxes cuts saving thereby creating an excess supply of money. If the rise in P required to clear the goods market at a constant E (and, therefore, constant i) does not remove this excess supply of money (that is, if L_1 lies to the right of a_1 as in Figure 1), the home currency must depreciate (E must rise). This is the first case in which an increase in g may lead to a rise in E.

Fleming (1962) considers the effects of a bond-financed increase in g under the assumption that home and foreign currency securities are imperfect substitutes. E falls if the L schedule is steeper than the BOP schedule, as in Figure 1, where the new equilibrium lies in the shaded triangle. E rises if the L schedule is flatter than the BOP schedule. In both cases P and y rise even if $\theta = l_2 = l_5 = 0$. These are the familiar results alluded to by Boyer. The results for a balanced-budget increase in g are a little more complicated since in the general Mundell-Fleming model both import demand and asset demands depend on taxes. E is more likely to rise, and the tendency for P to rise is reinforced because the reduction in saving cuts money demand.[13] E is more likely to fall, and the tendency for P to rise may be partially offset or even reversed because a balance-of-payments surplus is created. The reduction in home spending cuts imports, and the reduction in saving cuts home residents' demand for foreign-currency securities.

That an increase in g may lead to a rise in E is most clear in the case of a money-financed increase in g. This possibility exists even under the Mundell assumptions. If the rise in P required to clear the goods market at a constant E (and, therefore, constant i) does not raise nominal money demand by enough to absorb the increase in the money supply (that is, if L_1 lies to the right of a_1 as in Figure 1), E must rise. The possibility that E may rise continues to exist if the perfect-substitutes assumption is retained but the assumption that $l_2 = l_5 = \theta = 0$ is dropped, and also if the perfect-substitutes assumption is dropped. In general, E rises if Y_1 and L_1 intersect below the BOP schedule in Figure 1.

So far attention has been focused on the first-period effects of different methods of financing an increase in g, and it has been shown that E may either fall or rise. Now it is argued that even if E falls in the first period, it may rise in succeeding periods; that is, there is a possibility that what Boyer calls 'backshooting' may occur. Two cases are considered as examples. For simplicity, it is assumed that effects operating through interest payments are small enough that they can be neglected.[14]

Consider first the case of money financing under the Mundell assumptions, one of which is that real money demand is independent of real wealth ($l_5 = 0$), and under the additional assumption that real saving is independent of real wealth ($s_4 = 0$). In the second period there are no additional exogenous changes in the goods market since real government spending is simply maintained at its new higher level. However, since the real government deficit is maintained at its new higher level, there is an additional increase in the money supply. E, P, and y rise above their first-period levels. It can be shown that even if E falls in the first period, it may end up higher than its pre-shock level in the second.[15]

Now consider the case of bond financing in the general Mundell-Fleming model under the assumptions that $s_4 = l_5 = 0$. Since first-period nominal saving increases, beginning-of-period nominal wealth in the second period increases, and beginning-of-period real wealth in the second period tends to increase. Thus, second-period demand for foreign currency securities tends to rise. E and i rise above their first-period levels, but the effect on P is ambiguous.[16] As before, it can be shown that even if E falls in the first period, it may end up higher than its pre-shock level in the second.[17]

4. Comments on Two Aspects of Boyer's Paper

One of the many interesting results reported in Boyer's paper is a linear regression of the current-account deficit as a proportion of GNP on the government budget deficit as a proportion of GNP. Boyer finds a significant coefficient that is roughly equal to the ratio of imports to GNP in Canada and emphasizes the importance of his result. It is important to understand the relationship between fiscal policy and the current account, but it is not clear what to make of Boyer's regression. The statistical problems with the regression are obvious: both variables are almost certainly endogenous variables, and even if the government deficit were exogenous, it is almost certainly not orthogonal to other exogenous variables that should enter a reduced-form equation for the current account. More importantly, Boyer never really tells us why we should expect to find a stable relationship of the type he reports. His regression covers periods of both fixed and managed floating exchange rates. Under the Mundell assumptions, for example, increases in the government deficit resulting from, say, increases in government spending cause increases in the current-account deficit of equal size under floating exchange rates but increases of a much smaller size under fixed rates. The Mundell assumptions are extreme, but the point remains that, according to theory, changes in exchange regime should alter the fiscal-policy–current-account relationship. It would have been useful if Boyer had tested for changes by dividing his sample. The analysis of the last section suggests that the relationship should be different under different methods of deficit financing. In many models the effects of an increase in the government deficit depend on whether government spending is increased or taxes are reduced. One way for Boyer to have cross-checked his finding would have been to compare it with the results of fiscal-policy simulations of some of the econometric models of the Canadian economy. In short, the discovery of this apparent empirical regularity raises at least as many questions as it answers.

Boyer presents a thought-provoking and controversial asset-demand-based hypothesis to explain relatively small and relatively stable forward premia on the Canadian dollar *vis-à-vis* the U.S. dollar and relatively small and relatively stable Canadian-U.S. nominal interest differentials. According to Boyer, Canadian money (currency and demand deposits) is a very good substitute for U.S. money; that is, so-called currency substitution is high, presumably because the two moneys can be used for many of the same purposes and because agents are not very risk averse. If both moneys are to be held, the expected rate of appreciation cannot be very large. Then, given low risk aversion, uncovered interest arbitrage forces U.S. and Canadian interest rates to near equality, and covered interest arbitrage leads to a small forward premium. The controversial aspect of this logically complete hypothesis is the crucial role played by high currency substitution. It would have been useful if Boyer had summarized some of the empirical evidence on U.S.-Canadian currency substitution. Of course, there are competing hypotheses to explain the empirical regularities addressed by Boyer. It has often been argued that Canadian interest rates have been managed so that they closely track U.S. interest rates. If this is so, then only covered interest arbitrage is needed to explain small forward premia. One very rough test of the explanatory power of this hypothesis would be to compare the experience of the post-Saskatoon-manifesto period with that of the early 1970s and the earlier floating period. The problem is that, apparently for good reason, Boyer thinks that the data for the period October 1975–March 1977 "should be interpreted outside a model that explains the rest of post-war experience." However, there are still some data points left. Empirical evidence that Canadian intervention policy is one of leaning against the wind, the long history of quite similar U.S. and Canadian inflation rates that are at least partly the result of economic policy, and the accompanying parity psychology further complicate attempts to evaluate Boyer's provocative hypothesis based on currency substitution.

Appendix

This appendix contains algebraic derivations of some of the results presented in the text. Units are chosen so that in the initial equilibrium $E = P = 1$. The total differentials of the three equilibrium conditions represented by equations (19), (20), and (21) can be arranged in matrix form as

$$\begin{bmatrix} Y_P & Y_i & Y_E \\ L_P & L_i & L_E \\ BOP_P & BOP_i & BOP_E \end{bmatrix} \begin{bmatrix} dP \\ di \\ dE \end{bmatrix} = \begin{bmatrix} -\underline{Y}'_z \; \underline{dz} \\ -\underline{L}'_z \; \underline{dz} \\ -\underline{BOP}'_z \; \underline{dz} \end{bmatrix}. \tag{A1}$$

Explicit expressions for the partial derivatives of the excess demand functions with respect to the endogenous variables are given by

$$Y_P = (\alpha - 1)y_P - \alpha(i_{-1}B_{-1} + \overset{*}{i}_{-1}F_{-1}) \\ + (1 - m_1)[s_4 A_{-1} - (s_2 + s_3)\omega\phi] - \eta < 0, \tag{A2}$$

$$Y_i = -(1 - m_1)s_2 < 0, \tag{A3}$$

$$Y_E = \alpha \overset{*}{i}_{-1} F_{-1} - (1 - m_1)\{s_4 F_{-1} + [s_2(1 - \omega) - s_3\omega]\theta\} + \eta > 0, \tag{A4}$$

$$L_P = l_1 y_P + (L_{-1} - l_2 - l_5 A_{-1}) + l_5 s_P + \delta i_{-1}\bar{B}_{-1} > 0, \tag{A5}$$

$$L_i = l_3 + l_5 s_2 < 0, \tag{A6}$$

$$L_E = l_2 - l_4\theta + l_5 F_{-1} + l_5\{(1 + s_4 + s_1 \overset{*}{i}_{-1})F_{-1}$$
$$+ [s_2(1 - \omega) - s_3\omega]\theta\} > 0, \tag{A7}$$

$$BOP_P = Y_P - f_1 y_P - (F_{-1} - f_2 - f_5 A_{-1}) + (1 - f_5) s_P$$
$$+ (\overset{*}{b} - \overset{*}{B}_{-1}) + i_{-1}\bar{B}_{-1} < 0, \tag{A8}$$

$$BOP_i = Y_i - f_3 + \overset{*}{b}_1 + (1 - f_5) s_2 > 0, \tag{A9}$$

$$BOP_E = Y_E - f_2 + (f_4 + \overset{*}{b}_1)\theta + (1 - f_5)\{(1 + s_4 + s_1 \overset{*}{i}_{-1})F_{-1}$$
$$+ [s_2(1 - \omega) - s_3\omega]\theta\} + \overset{*}{b} > 0, \tag{A10}$$

where

$$0 < s_1 < 1, 0 < m_1 < 1, 0 < \alpha = (1 - m_1)(1 - s_1) < 1, \tag{A11}$$

$$y_P = -y' > 0, \tag{A12}$$

$$\eta = m[\eta_x(x/m) - \eta_m - 1] > 0, \eta_x = x'/x > 0, \eta_m = m'/m < 0, \tag{A13}$$

$$-1 < s_4 < 0, \tag{A14}$$

$$L_1 - l_2 - l_5 A_{-1} \geqslant 0, \tag{A15}$$

$$F_{-1} - f_2 - f_5 A_{-1} \leqslant 0, 1 - f_5 > 0, \tag{A16}$$

$$\overset{*}{b} - \overset{*}{B}_{-1} = 0, \tag{A17}$$

$$s_P = s_1 y_P - s_1(i_{-1}B_{-1} + \overset{*}{i}_{-1}F_{-1}) + (s_2 + s_3)\omega\phi - s_4 A_{-1} > 0. \tag{A18}$$

The assumptions stated in the text regarding the signs of the partial derivatives of the basic behavioural relations plus some additional plausible assumptions imply the indicated signs for the partial derivatives of the excess demand functions. Most of the additional assumptions are summarized in (A11) through (A18). (A11) through (A13) are conventional assumptions. According to (A14), a unit increase in real wealth lowers real saving by less than a unit. (A15) states that the sum of the relative price and wealth elasticities of the real demand for money are less than one. The two conditions stated in (A16) are (1) that the wealth elasticity of the real demand for foreign currency securities exceeds one plus the relative price elasticity, and (2) that a unit increase in real wealth raises the real demand for foreign currency securities by less than a unit. (A17) holds if derivatives are evaluated at an initial equilibrium with a zero budget deficit $(D = 0)$. According to (A18), an increase in the price of the home good raises real saving even though it reduces real interest income. Under static expectations $(\phi = \theta = 0)$, (A11) through (A18) plus the additional assumption that initial home holdings of foreign currency securities are positive $(F_{-1} > 0)$ imply the indicated signs for $Y_P, Y_i, Y_E,$ $L_P, L_E,$ and BOP_E. Under regressive expectations $(\phi, \theta > 0)$, these signs are implied if θ is small enough. Under either assumption about expectations the conventional signs for L_i, BOP_P, and BOP_i must be assumed.

Changes in the exogenous variables included in the vector dz are considered, and dz' is given by

$$dz' = (dg \; dt \; d\sigma \; d\mu \; d\lambda \; d\beta). \tag{A19}$$

Explicit expressions for the vectors of the partial derivatives of the excess demand functions with respect to the exogenous variables for which changes are considered are given by

$$\underline{Y}_z' = (\quad 1 \qquad\qquad\qquad -\alpha \quad -(1-m_1)s_5 \quad -m_3 \quad 0 \quad\quad 0), \tag{A20}$$

$$\underline{L}_z' = (-\delta \qquad\qquad -l_5 s_1 + \delta \qquad\quad b_5 s_5 \quad 0 \quad l_6 \quad 0), \tag{A21}$$

$$\underline{BOP}_z' = (\quad 0 \;\; m_1(1-s_1)+f_5 s_1 \quad (m_1-f_5)s_5 \;\; -m_3 \;\; 0 \;\; -f_6), \tag{A22}$$

where $m_3, f_6 < 0$. The exogenous variables $W, \bar{E}, \bar{P}, \overset{*}{i}, i_{-1}, \overset{*}{i}_{-1}, \bar{B}_{-1}, B_{-1},$ $\overset{*}{B}_{-1},$ and F_{-1} are held constant throughout the analysis.

Let H represent the matrix of the partial derivatives of the excess demand functions with respect to the endogenous variables and let $\Delta = det \, H$. Then

$$\Delta = -L_P(Y_i BOP_E - BOP_i Y_E) + L_i(Y_P BOP_E - BOP_P Y_E)$$
$$- L_E(Y_P BOP_i - BOP_P Y_i). \tag{A23}$$

Sensible comparative static results are obtained if, and only if, $\Delta > 0$. Given the assumptions made above, Δ is definitely positive if $Y_P BOP_E - BOP_P Y_E < 0$. It is shown below that this condition is definitely met under static expectations; it can be met under regressive expectations if θ is small enough. Of course, Δ can still be positive even if this condition is not met.

Now an illustration of the argument in Section 2 is provided. For simplicity, attention is restricted to the case of static expectations. Consider the effects of endogenous shifts down in the demand for imports $(d\mu)$ and the demand for foreign currency securities $(d\beta)$ on the price of the home good. If home and foreign residents regard home and foreign goods and home and foreign currency securities as imperfect substitutes, these effects are given by

$$dP = (m_3/\Delta)[L_i(BOP_E - Y_E) + L_E(Y_i - BOP_i)]d\mu$$
$$+ (f_6/\Delta)(L_E Y_i - L_i Y_E)d\beta. \tag{A24}$$

Note that

$$BOP_E - Y_E = Q > 0, \tag{A25}$$

$$BOP_P - Y_P = R > 0, \tag{A26}$$

$$Y_P BOP_E - BOP_P Y_E = Y_P Q - Y_E R < 0, \tag{A27}$$

where Q and R are independent of η and $\overset{*}{b}_1$. Now if, on the one hand, $\overset{*}{b}_1 \to \infty$, then BOP_i approaches infinity, and $dP/d\beta$ approaches zero, but $dP/d\mu$ remains finite:

$$dP/d\mu \to -m_3 L_E/(L_P Y_E - L_E Y_P) > 0. \tag{A28}$$

If, on the other hand, $x' \to \infty$, then η and, therefore, $-Y_P$, Y_E, $-BOP_P$, and BOP_E approach infinity, and $dP/d\mu$ approaches zero, but $dP/d\beta$ remains finite:

$$dP/d\beta \to -f_6 L_i/[(L_P + L_E)(BOP_i - Y_i) - L_i(Q + R)] < 0. \tag{A29}$$

Of course, if both x' and $\overset{*}{b}_1$ approach infinity, then exogenous shifts in neither the demand for imports nor the demand for foreign currency securities affect the price of the home good or, for that matter, any of the endogenous variables.

Now the results discussed in Section 3 are derived. Let the ijth minor of the matrix H be represented by Δ_{ij}. Given the assumptions made above, $\Delta_{11}, \Delta_{21}, \Delta_{23}, \Delta_{32} < 0$; $\Delta_{12}, \Delta_{33} > 0$; $\Delta_{13}, \Delta_{22}, \Delta_{31} \gtrless 0$; $\Delta_{22} < 0$ when $\theta = 0$ as shown in (A27). The effects on the endogenous variables of a bond-financed increase in government spending ($\delta = 0$) are given by

$$dP = -(1/\Delta)\Delta_{11} dg > 0, \tag{A30}$$

$$di = (1/\Delta)\Delta_{12} dg > 0, \tag{A31}$$

$$dE = -(1/\Delta)\Delta_{13} dg \gtrless 0. \tag{A32}$$

$dE < 0$ when the L schedule is steeper than the BOP schedule ($\Delta_{13} > 0$). The Mundell assumptions are the assumptions that $\overset{*}{b}_1 \to \infty$ and that $l_2 = l_5 = \theta = 0$. Under these assumptions $dP = di = 0$ and $dE < 0$. If $\overset{*}{b}_1 \to \infty$ but l_2 or l_5 or θ is positive, then $dP > 0$, $di \gtrless 0$ as $\theta \gtrless 0$, and $dE < 0$.

The effects on the endogenous variables of a money-financed increase in government spending ($\delta = 1$) are given by

$$dP = -(1/\Delta)(\Delta_{11} + \Delta_{21}) dg > 0, \tag{A33}$$

$$di = (1/\Delta)(\Delta_{12} + \Delta_{22}) dg \gtrless 0, \tag{A34}$$

$$dE = -(1/\Delta)(\Delta_{13} + \Delta_{23}) dg \gtrless 0. \tag{A35}$$

Under the Mundell assumptions $dP > 0$, $di = 0$, and $dE \gtrless 0$.

The effects on the endogenous variables of a balanced-budget increase in government spending ($dg = dt$) are given by

$$dP = -(1/\Delta)\{(1 - \alpha)\Delta_{11} + l_5 s_1 \Delta_{21} \\ + [m_1(1 - s_1) + f_5 s_1]\Delta_{31}\} dg \gtrless 0, \tag{A36}$$

$$di = (1/\Delta)\{(1 - \alpha)\Delta_{12} + l_5 s_1 \Delta_{22}$$
$$+ [m_1(1 - s_1) + f_5 s_1]\Delta_{32}\} dg \gtrless 0, \tag{A37}$$

$$dE = - (1/\Delta)\{(1 - \alpha)\Delta_{13} + l_5 s_1 \Delta_{23}$$
$$+ [m_1(1 - s_1) + f_5 s_1]\Delta_{33}\} dg \gtrless 0. \tag{A38}$$

If $\theta = f_5 = 0$, then $dP > 0$ since $1 - \alpha > m_1(1 - s_1)$ and $BOP_E > Y_E$. If, in addition, $\Delta_{13} > 0$ and $l_5 = 0$, then $dE < 0$. If, furthermore, $l_2 = 0$ so that $L_E = 0$, then $di > 0$. Under the Mundell assumptions $dP = di = 0$ and $dE < 0$. If $\overset{*}{b}_i \to \infty$ and $\theta = l_5 = 0$ but $l_2 > 0$ so that $L_E > 0$ then $dP > 0$, $di = 0$, $dE < 0$.

Notes

* Discussions with Guy Stevens and Richard Haas led to improvements in the comment. This comment represents the views of the author and should not be interpreted as reflecting the views of the Board of Governors of the Federal Reserve System or other members of its staff.

[1] Patinkin (1965) systematically developed a period model of a closed economy. Silber (1970), Brunner and Meltzer (1972), and Meyer (1975) use variants of this model. Stevens (1976) and Tobin and de Macedo (1981) set up explicit period models of a single open economy. For a continuous time model that includes the same kinds of goods and assets, see Henderson (1977).

[2] For simplicity it is assumed that investment, the capital stock, and, therefore, equity claims on the capital stock are zero. It is assumed below that home and foreign currency securities are imperfect substitutes because wealth holders are risk averse. If wealth holders are risk averse, equity claims on home capital and home currency securities of the type considered here are not perfect substitutes. Thus, extending the model to allow for investment, a capital stock, and equity claims on that stock, would necessitate adding a market for equity claims as in Tobin and de Macedo (1981). Making this extension would complicate the model and would not affect the central arguments of this comment.

[3] This result is also derived in Stevens (1976) and Tobin and de Macedo (1981).

[4] $\overset{*}{i}$ is taken to be exogenous. It may be assumed either that the home country is small in the market for foreign currency securities or that the foreign authorities peg $\overset{*}{i}$.

[5] The foreign currency price of the foreign good is taken to be exogenous, and units are chosen so that it is equal to one unit of foreign currency. It may be assumed either that the home country is small in the market for the foreign good or that the foreign authorities peg the foreign currency price of the foreign good.

[6] These assumptions are spelled out in the Appendix.

[7] The exogenous variables, W, $\bar{E}$, $\bar{P}$, $\overset{*}{i}$, i_{-1}, $\overset{*}{i}_{-1}$, $\bar{B}_{-1}$, B_{-1}, $\overset{*}{B}_{-1}$, and F_{-1} are held constant throughout the analysis.

[8] For proof that P rises, see the Appendix.

[9] For proof that P falls, see the Appendix.

[10] Silber (1970), Brunner and Meltzer (1972), and Meyer (1975) use period models to analyse the implications of different methods of financing an increase in government spending in closed economies. Suggestive comments on the use of period models to analyse fiscal policy in open economies are contained in Isard (1978) and Henderson (1978). Tobin and de Macedo (1981) use a fully developed period model to analyse the effects of fiscal policy in open economies.

[11] Mundell (1963) further assumes that the price of the home good is fixed, but, given his other assumptions, his results follow even when P is variable.

[12] Argy and Porter (1972) point out that Mundell's strong output result disappears if $\theta > 0$. Don Roper emphasized to me in 1972 that this result does not hold if $l_2 > 0$. Tobin and de Macedo (1981) recognize that it is no longer true if $l_5 > 0$.

[13] For proof of the assertions in this and the next paragraph, see the Appendix.

[14] Interest payments do not enter the analysis under a system of taxes and transfers suggested by Allen and Kenen (1980). Each government taxes away the interest receipts of its country's residents and transfers that part of its revenues arising from its country's residents' interest receipts from the other country back to the government of the other country. Given this set of taxes and transfers, the goods market-equilibrium condition is $P(-s + g - t_0 + x) - Em = 0$; the balance-of-payments-equilibrium condition is $Px - Em + \overset{*}{B}{}^d - B_{-1} - E(F^d - F_{-1}) = 0$, and real disposable income is $y^D = y - t_0$, where t_0 is autonomous taxes.

[15] If s_4 and l_5 are positive, there are additional effects to be considered. Since first-period nominal saving increases, beginning-of-period nominal wealth in the second period increases. (First-period nominal saving definitely increases if, as is being assumed, E falls in the first period and if $F_{-1} > 0$; it may decrease if E falls but $F_{-1} < 0$ or if E rises and $F_{-1} > 0$.) Second-period saving tends to fall, but end-of-period real wealth in the second period tends to rise because $0 < s_4 < 1$. The excess demand for goods tends to rise, and the demand for money tends to increase. A complete analysis would have to take account of these additional, second-period 'impact' effects that lead to pressure on E to fall. It can be shown that if $0 < l_5 < 1$ but $s_4 = 0$, then E definitely rises in the second period.

[16] The result that the effect on P is ambiguous is implied by $dP/d\beta$ in (A24) in the Appendix.

[17] As before, if s_4 and l_5 are positive, there are additional effects to be considered. An argument analogous to the one in note 15 leads to the conclusions that second-period saving tends to fall but that end-of-period real wealth in the second period tends to rise. The excess demand for goods tends to rise; the demand for money tends to rise, and the demand for foreign currency securities tends to rise by less than it would if $s_4 = 0$. A complete analysis would have to take account of these additional second-period 'impact' effects that lead to pressure on E to fall, since by assumption the L schedule is steeper than the BOP schedule.

References

Allen, Polly R. and Kenen, Peter B. (1980) *Asset Markets, Exchange Rates, and Economic Integration*. Cambridge: Cambridge University Press.

Argy, Victor and Porter, Michael G. (1972) "The Forward Exchange Market and the Effects of Domestic and External Disturbances Under Alternative Exchange Rate Systems." *International Monetary Fund Staff Papers* 19 (November): 503–32.

Brunner, Karl and Meltzer, Allan H. (1972) "Money, Debt, and Economic Activity." *Journal of Political Economy* 80 (September/October): 951–77.

Fleming, J. Marcus. (1962) "Domestic Financial Policies Under Fixed and Under Floating Exchange Rates." *International Monetary Fund Staff Papers* 9 (November): 369–80.

Henderson, Dale W. (1977) "Modeling the Interdependence of National Money and Capital Markets." *American Economic Review* 67 (February): 190–99.

Henderson, Dale W. (1978) "Fiscal Policy in Closed and Open Economies: A Comment." In *Public Policies in Open Economies*, edited by Karl Brunner and Allan H. Meltzer, pp. 181–202. Carnegie-Rochester Conference Series on Public Policy, Vol. 9. Amsterdam: North-Holland.

Isard, Peter. (1978) *Exchange Rate Determination: A Survey of Popular Views and Recent Models*. Princeton Studies in International Finance No. 42. Princeton, N.J.: Princeton University, Dept. of Economics, International Finance Section.

Meyer, Laurence H. (1975) "The Balance Sheet Identity, the Government Financing Constraint, and the Crowding-Out Effect." *Journal of Monetary Economics* 1 (January): 65–78.

Mundell, R.A. (1963) "Capital Mobility and Stabilization Policy Under Fixed and Flexible Exchange Rates." *Canadian Journal of Economics and Political Science* 29 (November): 475–85.

Patinkin, Don. (1965) *Money, Interest, and Prices*, 2d ed. New York: Harper and Row.

Silber, William L. (1970) "Fiscal Policy in IS-LM Analysis: A Correction." *Journal of Money, Credit and Banking* 2 (November): 461–72.

Stevens, Guy V.G. (1976) "Balance of Payments Equations and Exchange Rate Determination." International Finance Discussion Papers No. 95. Washington, D.C.: Board of Governors of the Federal Reserve System.

Tobin, James, and de Macedo, Jorge Braga. (1981) "The Short-Run Macroeconomics of Floating Exchange Rates: An Exposition." In *Flexible Exchange Rates and the Balance of Payments: Essays in Memory of Egon Sohmen*, edited by John S. Chipman and Charles P. Kindleberger, pp. 5–28. Amsterdam: North-Holland.

Summary
of
Discussion

The general discussion centred largely on two of the empirical regularities noted by Boyer: the apparent relationship between the current-account deficit and the government balance, and the parallelism of U.S. and Canadian nominal interest rates, especially long-term rates. Regarding the current account–government deficit linkage, *John Floyd* pointed out that, in principle, a high government deficit might induce no capital-account or current-account change if the private sector responds to the government deficit by increasing its own savings in order to meet higher future tax liabilities. The regression coefficient on the government deficit could be viewed as indicating the extent to which the private sector regarded the deficit as increasing its wealth, that is, the extent to which its behaviour did not recognize the associated future tax liabilities. To the extent that higher government deficits were not matched by higher private savings, there would be a capital inflow that would induce current-account adjustment. The role of the capital account in the linkage should be recognized.

Other participants explored the extent to which the observed association could be explained within the framework of a conventional income-expenditure model. A relatively low fiscal multiplier coupled with a high import propensity would suggest a coefficient on the government deficit in the estimated range in response to discretionary fiscal action. The automatic cyclical response of the deficit would also provide an explanation of the directional relation between government deficit and current-account deficit in response to variations in export demand.

The apparent strength of expectations of rough constancy in the exchange rate, as reflected in the parallelism of Canadian and U.S. long interest rates, was stressed by *Charles Freedman*, *Paul Krugman*, and *Pierre Fortin*. Freedman noted the implications of this strongly held expectation for the interim response of the Canadian economy to any systematic divergence in Canadian and U.S. monetary policy. Several panelists questioned whether it was useful to follow Boyer in terming the situation one of high substitutability between the

Canadian and U.S. currencies. Expectations as to Canadian central bank behaviour in response to U.S. monetary conditions might be more important than potential formal substitutability of currencies in the explanation.

John Grant drew attention to data issues in analysing the extent of parallelism in the behaviour of long-term interest rates. Comparison of yields on similar maturity Government of Ontario, U.S. and Canadian pay bond issues provided an attractive basis for such an analysis as no adjustment for changing differential risk was required. Among other things, the historical record on this basis did contain one period (1971) in which there was a negative spread between Canadian — and U.S. — pay issues, a result not found in Boyer's historical summary. In explaining interest-rate spreads, Grant argued that it was preferable to look at the total gap between domestic investment and savings as likely to be reflected in pressure on the bond market, rather than just at the government deficit.

On a separate issue, *Robert Dunn* suggested that the experience immediately following 1962 constituted a counter-example to the assertion by Laffer and others that changes in the exchange rate are not effective in changing the current-account balance. However, the move to less expansionary fiscal policy at the time was important in allowing the depreciation to improve the current account rather than be washed out by inflation.

Imperfect Hindsight: A Summary of the Issues

6

by
John F. Helliwell

Every summarizer needs an organizing principle, a matrix of cells in which to jam unyielding authors so as to leave a final impression that key policy issues have been dealt with in an organized and comprehensive manner. I shall pretend to have identified two broad policy problems and three vantage points, providing a total of six commodious cells. The first two papers, by Freedman and by Longworth, dealt with the strategy and tactics of setting and implementing monetary and exchange-rate targets. I shall treat this as one broad policy problem. The other three papers, those by Dunn, Bruce, and Boyer, all deal with the causes and structure of Canada's long-standing habit of having a trade deficit financed by long-term capital inflows. The policy issue at stake is presumably to decide whether it is a good habit or a bad one to have a trade deficit of this size, and, if it is a bad habit, to find out where and how to join Debtors Anonymous.

If, as Smith earnestly hoped in his introductory remarks, we are all high thinkers in full flight, then it is reasonable to hope that we have an airplane, if not the fuel for it, and to identify the three policy viewpoints of where we choose to sit on the plane. Being mostly rather cautious and moderate Canadians, few of the speakers were very far out on the right or left wings (which would, in any event, be an insecure and windy place to perch), although Boyer, Wirick, and Courchene were quick to choose right-hand window seats, with a perfect-sidesight rational expectations view as far as Western Ontario. A very large number of the other participants tried to find seats on the centre aisle, perhaps for fast exit or perhaps for faster service from the bar trolley. Their general view, you see, is that markets work, but do so rather inefficiently and imperfectly, so that it is prudent to stick close to a reliable source of supply. Some of the speakers on the aisle noticed several vacant seats by the left-hand windows (although it was alleged that there were copies of the *Toronto Star* waiting for them), and tried to present, for Cripps' and Godley's sake, the generally unpresented Cambridge (U.K.) viewpoints that markets do not work, that prices do not reflect opportunity costs, and that balance-of-payments deficits ought to be removed by some combination of devaluation, import restrictions, and some means of finding and supporting potential winners in the manufacturing industry.

Let me turn now to the policy issues posed or suggested by the first two papers. In the first paper, Freedman, famous as the Bank of Canada's verbal machine gun with the high $\bar{R}^2$, presented a series of models focused on the tactical question of how, under various assumptions about uncertainty and lags, a central bank could face the tactical problem of hitting a target rate of growth of a broad monetary aggregate. In the context of his models, and in his analysis of U.S. experience, he tended to support the Bank of Canada's use of interest-rate management as a tactic with M1 as the target. Within the target range, the Bank acts so as to smooth interest rates or exchange rates, depending on which seems most erratic at the moment. The commentators, Floyd and Courchene, both advocated base control as both tactic and strategy. Let me try to spell out the fundamental policy issues, as I see them, on which Freedman and his discussants disagreed.

As I understand the proposals of both Floyd and Courchene, the Bank of Canada's strategy should be to adopt a rule for the future growth of base money, and its operating tactic should be to deviate from that announced target only through the discount window, and preferably at a penalty rate. This policy leaves the minimum amount of policy discretion to the Bank of Canada, especially if the targets are set to follow a steady growth path laid out several years in advance. This type of policy quite naturally reflects a view from the right-side window seats with the perfect view, as it is a strategy that works best if bankers and participants in private financial markets need know only the path of base money in order to set a stable pattern of interest rates and money-supply growth.

Those in the centre and left of the plane respond that individual banks operating under a system of lagged reserve requirements will not know how much of the known reserves would be theirs and, hence, will not know how to set their interest rates and to determine their desired size. This need not, of course, raise any problems for the base controllers, providing they accept that without collusion between the banks about market share (or instant communication, to provide an electronic *tâtonnement* to allocate next period's reserves), the system, as a whole, will always either have excess reserves or will be short and will have to obtain recourse from the discount window of the Bank. This means that the target for base money will never be hit exactly, and that the inter-bank market will have very low interest rates when there are excess reserves, and interest rates equal to the rediscount rate when reserves are shy.

What is behind all this rather arcane discussion? On the one hand, the discussants want a monetary policy with little or no strategy or tactics left in the hands of the central bank, and with interest-rate smoothing being done by the far-seeing bankers and other private market participants. From the floor, Grant noted the demoralized state of the bond market when interest rates flop around. Quite predictably, the response from the right side was that the bond market was uncertain only because the Bank of Canada had not been firm enough in announcing and sticking to a monetary growth target, while from the centre it was treated as one of the costs of the highly variable U.S. interest rates, themselves due primarily to excessive U.S. adherence to base control.

The analytical and empirical question that did not come out very clearly in the discussion, but which is fundamental to any decision, is whether the shift to hands-off setting of base money by the Bank of Canada would lead to highly variable interest rates forever, or whether the private sector merely needs a little time to learn the ropes and to acquire confidence in the central bank's resolve to stick to its policy.

Precisely the same issue arises in the case of the foreign exchange market. Here, too, policy makers and high thinkers in full flight must first decide whether the high variability of exchange rates since 1973 imposes a cost. If it does, then they must decide whether the variability will grow less as market participants form more stable and powerful expectations as time passes, or whether there is a case for active official exchange-rate stabilization. Such stabilization might take the form of direct purchases or sales of foreign exchange, the use of short-term monetary policy flexibility (when the aggregate is safely within the target range) to smooth the exchange rate, or the abandonment of monetary growth targets in favour of a stable exchange rate. As you might guess, those by the starboard windows would tend to favour the cleanest of floats, those in the middle would favour the first two kinds of intervention on occasion, while those with a view as far as the New Cambridge Macroeconomics would favour a managed value for the currency, at a level low enough to assure a competitive manufacturing sector.

Longworth's paper was clearly relevant to these policy issues, although they were not posed very directly in the paper. He first presented more evidence about the failure of purchasing-power parity to apply to Canada over most of the 1970s. He then went on to show that interest-rate parity seemed to be a fairly stable and well-maintained relationship, but that the lagged forward rate generally added nothing (see his equation 3.4) to the lagged spot rate in explaining the current spot rate. He concluded that the interest-rate parity relationship may safely be assumed to be part of a model of exchange-rate determination. Unfortunately, his other results and other evidence suggest that the relationship is true, but not useful, because it holds mainly by moving the forward rate rather than the spot rate, and does not provide any new information (beyond that already in the interest differential itself) about the future movement of the spot rate.

In the latter part of his paper, Longworth makes a two-pronged case that the foreign exchange market is inefficient, and that false signals provided by the rate lead to international misallocation of resources. If his evidence were accepted, it would provide a case for one or more of the three types of exchange-rate stabilization that I have mentioned. The discussants made two key points about his two-pronged attack. First, they noted that his standards of efficiency were overly strict, requiring the existence of a leisure class of far-sighted foreign exchange traders with no transactions costs. If the market is to be shown to be economically inefficient, it must be true that some trading rule, whether based on an economic forecasting model or a ouija-board, must be able to make profits in excess of transactions costs on a continuing basis, using only information available at the time the bets are made. Tests of this sort, which are being done by Paul Boothe at the University of British Columbia, also allow the comparable testing of alternative foreign exchange models, in terms of their ability to forecast the future spot rate and also the current forward rate. If a sensible model explains the future spot rate well, but is not popular with the market (in the sense that it does not explain the forward rate equally well), then it gives rise to the possibility of profitable betting, and hence of a more convincing demonstration of exchange-market inefficiency.

We should recognize, however, that even if one did not find convincing evidence of economic inefficiency in the sense I have just described it, it might, nevertheless, be desirable to smooth out random fluctuations in the exchange rate if it were relatively cheap to do so, and if the stabilized value increased the accuracy or the certainty of private-sector expectations.

In the final main section of his paper, Longworth presented equations showing the apparent impact of variations in the exchange rate on the distribution of output between the tradable and non-tradable sectors. This, he suggests, shows that exchange-rate variability imposes real resource costs on the economy. Longworth says that small exchange-rate changes lead to substantial shifts of production from the tradable to the non-tradable sectors, but Bruce reported in his paper that the imports and exports themselves do not respond very much to relative prices. We are invited to envisage the Canadian dollar dropping a penny, leading a barber in Brantford to produce hair-pieces for the overseas market only to find they cannot be sold.

The final three papers dealt directly or indirectly with the question of the causes, structure, and implication of Canada's continuing current-account deficit financed by long-term capital inflows. Several references were made to the need for treating the inflationary component of foreign interest payments as a capital outflow rather than an import of services, and, following the Australians and, more recently, the Americans in treating retained earnings on foreign-owned capital as an import of services financed by a capital-account inflow of equal size. After these offsetting adjustments, it was generally agreed that the resulting deficit should be measured as a share of GNP, and the stock of debt measured relative to either total domestic assets or to the domestic capital stock.

What are the policy issues? I think there are three. First, is the size of the deficit a matter for policy concern? Secondly, are there policy implications if the government sector and the national economy are both in deficit? Thirdly, are there, or should there be, policy concerns relating to the structure of either the current account or the capital account?

On the first question, Sparks presented the issue in the clearest light by describing the international capital market as providing the means for Canadians to absorb more now and less later on. If, at the margin, the real rate of return on spending now is equal to the international cost of capital, then we can be grateful for the existence and availability of international capital and unconcerned about the size or persistence of the current-account deficit. Seen in this context, the links hypothesized by Dunn between Canadian demography and the deficit, and by both Dunn and Boyer between the government deficit and the current-account deficit, may be usefully descriptive or even of some help in forecasting, but they have no policy implications.

But what if, as several speakers suggested, Canadian spenders are not all far-sighted optimizers with infinite horizons? This leads to the second issue, the apparent link between government deficits and national deficits. From the starboard side, the likely villains live in Ottawa and the provincial capitals. In their analysis, the high-absorbing governments are securing their own re-election by the pork-barrel, and financing it all on a giant American Express card with the repayments to be made by subsequent governments and taxpayers. There is a similar starboard-side analysis of debt-financed government absorption in the closed economy. The policy relevance of the international capital market is that it provides the access to world goods and capital on a scale that permits great scope for converting millions of nagging little financial worries into one staggering debt that even Household Finance would balk at.

The view from the left-hand windows also starts with the proposition that a marginal increase in the government deficit, in a world of high capital mobility, will lead to a large increase in the current-account deficit. But the policy analysis then starts to diverge rather markedly, for the problem is not seen by them as wasteful governments building up debts for future taxpayers, but as governments trying valiantly to increase domestic demand and output, and being frustrated by high import propensities and international capital flows. Thus, in the New Cambridge view, the trade deficit is bad because it stops the expansionary fiscal policy from achieving its desired impact on domestic output and employment. The implied policy remedies include various restrictions on the imports of goods or capital, perhaps including pegging the exchange rate at a low level to encourage the manufacturing sector. Those in the middle aisle are generally unconvinced by the quality and nature of the evidence offered on either side, although they tend to shift a couple of seats to the right every time there is an increase in the (inflation-adjusted) government deficit.

This brings me to the third policy question, that of the structure of the trade-account deficit and of the matching capital-account surplus. Bruce illustrated fairly constant long-term shares of staples and manufactures in Canada's trade, and hence concluded that the de-industrialization so widely discussed, in relation to the natural gas revenues of the Netherlands and the increasing oil revenues of the United Kingdom, is of little relevance to Canada. The facts of the Canadian case are that its staples base is so varied that there are relatively moderate changes at the aggregate level in the division of total output between the staple and manufacturing sectors. However, when we look on a regional basis rather than a broad sectoral basis, that is, when we look at Alberta in relation to the rest of the country, then one has every right to expect resource-allocation effects of a size that merit a separate conference focused on the problems of regional reallocation of income and output within a country.

As for the structure of the capital account, the perceived policy issue, or non-issue, depending on where you sit, is the relative costs and benefits of direct and portfolio investment, and of equity versus debt.

In dealing with the policy issues relating to the size and structure of the current-account deficit/capital-account surplus, I have not referred directly to the econometric results presented. In my view, those results were too partial and too preliminary to invite attempts to use them as a basis for policy conclusions. In general, I would echo Henderson's advice that it is likely to be misleading, or worse, to look at either the current or capital account, or, equally, the difference between domestic savings and investment, as exogenous when one is analysing either the size or the structure of either the current or capital account. In empirical and theoretical models alike, one needs the complete system, in however rudimentary a form, in order to be convincing.

The Members of the Institute

Board of Directors

The Honourable John B. Aird, O.C., Q.C.
(Honorary Chairman),
Lieutenant Governor of Ontario, Toronto
The Honourable Robert L. Stanfield, P.C.,
Q.C. (Chairman), Ottawa
Louis Desrochers, Q.C. (Vice-Chairman),
McCuaig, Desrochers, Edmonton
James T. Black
President, The Molson Companies Limited,
Toronto
Richard Cashin
President, Newfoundland Fishermen, Food
and Allied Workers' Union, St. John's
Claude Castonguay, C.C.
President, The Laurentian Fund Inc.,
Quebec
Guy Chabot, C.A.
Raymond, Chabot, Martin & Paré,
Montreal
Roger Charbonneau
President, Banque nationale de Paris
(Canada), Montreal
Dr. Henry E. Duckworth, O.C.
President Emeritus, University of
Winnipeg
Dr. Regis Duffy
President, Diagnostic Chemicals Ltd.,
Charlottetown
Dr. James D. Fleck
Faculty of Management Studies, University
of Toronto
Peter C. Godsoe
Executive Vice-President, The Bank of
Nova Scotia, Toronto
The Honourable William M. Hamilton, O.C.,
P.C., President & Chief Executive Officer,
Employers' Council of British Columbia,
Vancouver
David Hennigar
Atlantic Regional Director, Burns Fry Ltd.,
Halifax
Tom Kierans
President, McLeod, Young, Weir Ltd.,
Toronto
Roland J. Lutes, C.A.
Clarkson, Gordon & Co., Saint John
E.M. Mills
Director, Calgary Chamber of Commerce
Dr. Tom Pepper
Executive Director, Saskatchewan
Research Council, Saskatoon
Guy Roberge, Q.C.
Ottawa
Gordon Robertson, C.C.
President, The Institute for Research on
Public Policy, Ottawa

Mrs. Claudine Sotiau
President & Director General, Régie de
l'assurance automobile du Québec, Quebec
Bryan Vaughan, C.M.
Toronto

Secretary
Peter C. Dobell
Director, Parliamentary Centre, Ottawa

Treasurer
Dr. Louis G. Vagianos
Executive Director, The Institute for
Research on Public Policy, Halifax

Executive Committee
The Honourable Robert L. Stanfield
(Chairman)
Louis Desrochers (Vice-Chairman)
Claude Castonguay
E.M. Mills
Gordon Robertson

Investment Committee
Tom Kierans (Chairman)
Peter C. Dobell
Peter C. Godsoe
Paul Little

Council of Trustees

Government Representatives
Michael Decter, Manitoba
Fred Dickson, Nova Scotia
Greg Fyffe, Saskatchewan
Colin Heartwell, Yukon
Harry Hobbs, Alberta
Michael J.L. Kirby, Canada
Mark Krasnick, British Columbia
Robert A. Nutbrown, Prince Edward Island
John H. Parker, Northwest Territories
Jean-K. Samson, Quebec
Gordon Smith, Canada
Barry Toole, New Brunswick
John Tory, Ontario
David Vardy, Newfoundland

Members at Large
Dr. Stefan Dupré (Chairman)
Department of Political Economy,
University of Toronto
Doris Anderson, O.C.
Toronto
Professor Kell Antoft
Institute of Public Affairs, Dalhousie
University, Halifax
Dr. Marie-Andrée Bertrand
School of Criminology, University of
Montreal
Dr. Roger Blais, P.Eng.
Director, Centre d'innovation industrielle
(Montréal)

Institute Management

Gordon Robertson	President
Louis Vagianos	Executive Director
John M. Curtis	Director, International Economics Program
Gérald d'Amboise	Director, Small and Medium-sized Business Program
Barbara L. Hodgins	Director, Western Resources Program
Barry Lesser	Director, Regional Employment Opportunities Program
Zavis P. Zeman	Director, Technology and Society Program
W.T. Stanbury	Senior Program Adviser
Donald Wilson	Director, Conferences and Seminars Program
Gail Grant	Associate Director, Conferences and Seminars Program
Dana Phillip Doiron	Director, Communications Services
Ann C. McCoomb	Associate Director, Communications Services
Tom Kent	Editor, *Policy Options Politiques*

The Institute for Research on Public Policy

Publications Available*
June 1983

Books

Leroy O. Stone & Claude Marceau	*Canadian Population Trends and Public Policy Through the 1980s*. 1977 $4.00
Raymond Breton	*The Canadian Condition: A Guide to Research in Public Policy*. 1977 $2.95
Raymond Breton	*Une orientation de la recherche politique dans le contexte canadien*. 1977 $2.95
J.W. Rowley & W.T. Stanbury, eds.	*Competition Policy in Canada: Stage II, Bill C-13*. 1978 $12.95
C.F. Smart & W.T. Stanbury, eds.	*Studies on Crisis Management*. 1978 $9.95
W.T. Stanbury, ed.	*Studies on Regulation in Canada*. 1978 $9.95
Michael Hudson	*Canada in the New Monetary Order: Borrow? Devalue? Restructure!* 1978 $6.95
David K. Foot, ed.	*Public Employment and Compensation in Canada: Myths and Realities*. 1978 $10.95
W.E. Cundiff & Mado Reid, eds.	*Issues in Canadian/U.S. Transborder Computer Data Flows*. 1979 $6.50
David K. Foot, ed.	*Public Employment in Canada: Statistical Series*. 1979 $15.00
Meyer W. Bucovetsky, ed.	*Studies in Public Employment and Compensation in Canada*. 1979 $14.95
Richard French & André Béliveau	*The RCMP and the Management of National Security*. 1979 $6.95
Richard French & André Béliveau	*La GRC et la gestion de la sécurité nationale*. 1979 $6.95

---

* Order Address: The Institute for Research on Public Policy
P.O. Box 9300, Station A
TORONTO, Ontario
M5W 2C7

Leroy O. Stone &   *Future Income Prospects for Canada's Senior*
Michael J. MacLean   *Citizens.* 1979 $7.95

Richard M. Bird   *The Growth of Public Employment in Canada.* 1979
                             $12.95

G. Bruce Doern &   *The Public Evaluation of Government Spending.*
Allan M. Maslove, eds.   1979 $10.95

Richard Price, ed.   *The Spirit of the Alberta Indian Treaties.* 1979
                             $8.95

Richard J. Schultz   *Federalism and the Regulatory Process.* 1979
                             $1.50

Richard J. Schultz   *Le fédéralisme et le processus de réglementation.*
                             1979 $1.50

Lionel D. Feldman &   *Bargaining for Cities. Municipalities and*
Katherine A. Graham   *Intergovernmental Relations: An Assessment.* 1979
                             $10.95

Elliot J. Feldman &   *The Future of North America: Canada, the United*
Neil Nevitte, eds.   *States, and Quebec Nationalism.* 1979 $7.95

Maximo Halty-Carrere   *Technological Development Strategies for*
                             Developing Countries: A Review for Policy Makers.
                             1979 $12.95

G.B. Reschenthaler   *Occupational Health and Safety in Canada: The*
                             Economics and Three Case Studies. 1979 $5.00

David R. Protheroe   *Imports and Politics: Trade Decision Making in*
                             Canada, 1968–1979. 1980 $8.95

G. Bruce Doern   *Government Intervention in the Canadian Nuclear*
                             Industry. 1980 $8.95

G. Bruce Doern &   *Canadian Nuclear Policies.* 1980 $14.95
Robert W. Morrison, eds.

Allan M. Maslove &   *Wage Controls in Canada, 1975–78: A Study of*
Gene Swimmer   *Public Decision Making.* 1980 $11.95

T. Gregory Kane   *Consumers and the Regulators: Intervention in the*
                             Federal Regulatory Process. 1980 $10.95

Albert Breton &   *The Design of Federations.* 1980 $6.95
Anthony Scott

A.R. Bailey & D.G. Hull	*The Way Out: A More Revenue-Dependent Public Sector and How It Might Revitalize the Process of Governing.* 1980 $6.95
Réjean Lachapelle & Jacques Henripin	*La situation démolinguistique au Canada : évolution passée et prospective.* 1980 $24.95
Raymond Breton, Jeffrey G. Reitz & Victor F. Valentine	*Cultural Boundaries and the Cohesion of Canada.* 1980 $18.95
David R. Harvey	*Christmas Turkey or Prairie Vulture? An Economic Analysis of the Crow's Nest Pass Grain Rates.* 1980 $10.95
Richard M. Bird	*Taxing Corporations.* 1980 $6.95
Albert Breton & Raymond Breton	*Why Disunity? An Analysis of Linguistic and Regional Cleavages in Canada.* 1980 $6.95
Leroy O. Stone & Susan Fletcher	*A Profile of Canada's Older Population.* 1980 $7.95
Peter N. Nemetz, ed.	*Resource Policy: International Perspectives.* 1980 $18.95
Keith A.J. Hay, ed.	*Canadian Perspectives on Economic Relations With Japan.* 1980 $18.95
Raymond Breton & Gail Grant	*La langue de travail au Québec : synthèse de la recherche sur la rencontre de deux langues.* 1981 $10.95
Diane Vanasse	*L'évolution de la population scolaire du Québec.* 1981 $12.95
Raymond Breton, Jeffrey G. Reitz & Victor F. Valentine	*Les frontières culturelles et la cohésion du Canada.* 1981 $18.95
H.V. Kroeker, ed.	*Sovereign People or Sovereign Governments.* 1981 $12.95
Peter Aucoin, ed.	*The Politics and Management of Restraint in Government.* 1981 $17.95
David M. Cameron, ed.	*Regionalism and Supranationalism: Challenges and Alternatives to the Nation-State in Canada and Europe.* 1981 $9.95

Heather Menzies

Women and the Chip: Case Studies of the Effects of Informatics on Employment in Canada.
1981 $6.95

Nicole S. Morgan

Nowhere to Go? Possible Consequences of the Demographic Imbalance in Decision-Making Groups of the Federal Public Service. 1981 $8.95

Nicole S. Morgan

Où aller? Les conséquences prévisibles des déséquilibres démographiques chez les groupes de décision de la fonction publique fédérale.
1981 $8.95

Peter N. Nemetz, ed.

Energy Crisis: Policy Response. 1981 $10.95

Allan Tupper &
G. Bruce Doern, eds.

Public Corporations and Public Policy in Canada.
1981 $16.95

James Gillies

Where Business Fails. 1981 $9.95

Réjean Lachapelle &
Jacques Henripin

The Demolinguistic Situation in Canada: Past Trends and Future Prospects. 1982 $24.95

Ian McAllister

Regional Development and the European Community: A Canadian Perspective. 1982 $13.95

Robert J. Buchan,
C. Christopher Johnston,
T. Gregory Kane,
Barry Lesser,
Richard J. Schultz &
W.T. Stanbury

Telecommunications Regulation and the Constitution. 1982 $18.95

W.T. Stanbury &
Fred Thompson

Regulatory Reform in Canada. 1982 $7.95

Rodney de C. Grey

United States Trade Policy Legislation: A Canadian View. 1982 $7.95

John Quinn &
Philip Slayton, eds.

Non-Tariff Barriers After the Tokyo Round.
1982 $17.95

R. Brian Woodrow &
Kenneth B. Woodside, eds.

The Introduction of Pay-TV in Canada: Issues and Implications. 1982 $14.95

Stanley M. Beck &
Ivan Bernier, eds.

Canada and the New Constitution: The Unfinished Agenda. 2 vols. 1983 $10.95

Douglas D. Purvis, ed.,
assisted by Frances Chambers

The Canadian Balance of Payments: Perspectives and Policy Issues. 1983 $24.95

Roy A. Matthews   *Canada and the "Little Dragons."* 1983 $11.95

Charles Pearson &   *Trade, Employment, and Adjustment.* 1983 $5.00
Gerry Salembier

Charles F. Doran   *Economic Interdependence, Autonomy, and
                                   Canadian/American Relations.* 1983 $5.00

F.R. Flatters &   *Common Ground for the Canadian Common
R.G. Lipsey   Market.* 1983 $5.00

E.P. Weeks &   *The Future of the Atlantic Fisheries.*
L. Mazany   1983 $5.00

Occasional Papers

W.E. Cundiff   *Nodule Shock? Seabed Mining and the Future of the
(No. 1)   Canadian Nickel Industry.* 1978 $3.00

Robert A. Russel   *The Electronic Briefcase: The Office of the Future.*
(No. 3)   1978 $3.00

C.C. Gotlieb   *Computers in the Home: What They Can Do for
(No. 4)   Us—And to Us.* 1978 $3.00

Raymond Breton &   *Urban Institutions and People of Indian Ancestry:
Gail Grant Akian   Suggestions for Research.* 1979 $3.00
(No. 5)

K.A.J. Hay   *Friends or Acquaintances? Canada and Japan's
(No. 6)   Other Trading Partners in the Early 1980s.*
                                   1979 $3.00

Thomas H. Atkinson   *Trends in Life Satisfaction Among Canadians,
(No. 7)   1968–1977.* 1979 $3.00

Fred Thompson &   *The Political Economy of Interest Groups in the
W.T. Stanbury   Legislative Process in Canada.* 1979 $3.00
(No. 9)

Pierre Sormany   *Les micro-esclaves : vers une bio-industrie
(No. 11)   canadienne.* 1979 $3.00

Zavis P. Zeman &   *The Dynamics of the Technological Leadership of
David Hoffman, eds.   the World.* 1980 $3.00
(No. 13)

Russell Wilkins   *Health Status in Canada, 1926–1976.* 1980 $3.00
(No. 13a)

Russell Wilkins   *L'état de santé au Canada, 1926–1976.*
(No. 13*b*)   1980 $3.00

P. Pergler   *The Automated Citizen: Social and Political Impact*
(No. 14)   *of Interactive Broadcasting.* 1980 $4.95

Donald G. Cartwright   *Official Language Populations in Canada:*
(No. 16)   *Patterns and Contacts.* 1980 $4.95

Reports

Dhiru Patel   *Dealing With Interracial Conflict: Policy*
                         Alternatives. 1980 $5.95

Robert A. Russel   *Office Automation: Key to the Information Society.*
                         1981 $3.00

Irving Brecher   *Canada's Competition Policy Revisited: Some New*
                         Thoughts on an Old Story. 1982 $3.00

Donald J. Daly   *Canada in an Uncertain World Economic*
                         Environment. 1982 $3.00